JUST ADD DUST
Overland from Cape to Cairo

Justin Fox • Mike Copeland
Cameron Ewart-Smith • Don Pinnock

Edited by Justin Fox

KWELA BOOKS

© Copyright of the images rests with the following individuals:
Robyn Daly (pp.25, 32, 34, 37, 41, 43, 45, 50 52, 54 and 55),
Justin Fox (pp.36, 42 and 47),
Marek Patzer (p.57) and Don Pinnock (pp.27, 29 and 38).
The images of Uys Krige (p.127) appear courtesy of Eulalia Krige.

Copyright © 2004 Justin Fox, Mike Copeland,
Cameron Ewart-Smith and Don Pinnock
c/o Kwela Books
40 Heerengracht, Cape Town 8001;
P.O. Box 6525, Roggebaai 8012
kwela@kwela.com

All rights reserved.
No part of this book may be reproduced or transmitted in any form or by any electronic or mechanical means, including photocopying and recording, or by any other information storage or retrieval system, without written permission from the publisher.

Cover design by Alexander Kononov
Typography by Nazli Jacobs
Set in Cheltenham
Printed and bound by Paarl Print, Oosterland Street, Paarl, South Africa

First edition, first printing 2004
ISBN 0-7957-0191-8

http://www.kwela.com

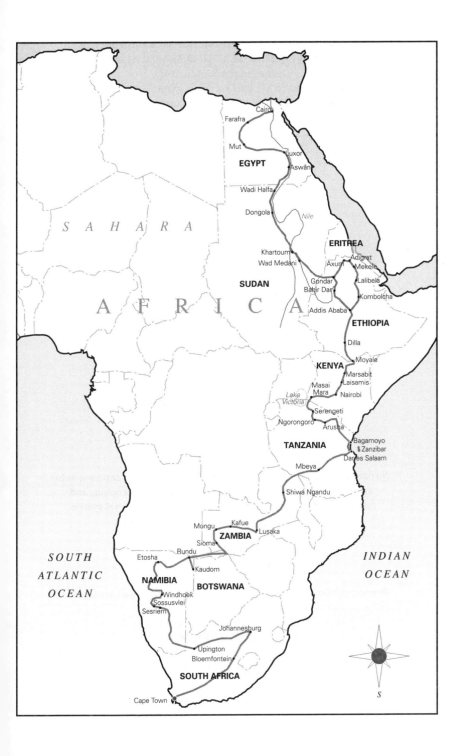

Contents

GETTING SET: The exquisite corpse drinks the old continent   3
Justin Fox

CAPE TOWN TO LUSAKA: The road is the mode   11
Mike Copeland

LUSAKA TO NAIROBI: Shooting the East African breeze   28
Cameron Ewart-Smith

NAIROBI TO ADDIS ABABA: Rummaging through Africa's attic   58
Justin Fox

ADDIS ABABA TO CAIRO: The desert road north   98
Don Pinnock

GETTING SET

The exquisite corpse drinks the old continent

Justin Fox

GETTING SET

Africa's southwestern tip has a curious relationship with the rest of the continent. The citizens of Cape Town have traditionally seen themselves as separate, aloof, cerebral. They view the continent upside down, with the southern end as its head. Living on a paradisaical peninsula of vineyards and dazzling beaches, many feel the Cape has more in common with the Côte d'Azur than with the dry heartland. Some would even welcome a rise in sea level that flooded the Cape Flats and returned the peninsula to its prehistoric island state. But in the past decade things have been shaken up. New immigrants from across southern Africa, and indeed the continent, have begun to settle in the shadow of Table Mountain. That's not to say they've been welcomed. Often quite the contrary.

Under apartheid South Africa's northern borders were closed: beyond the Limpopo lurked Marxist warmongers, genocide and endemic anarchy – a colonial vision that hadn't altered much in centuries. The furthest you could get from Africa's darkness, or so the theory went, was the sun-kissed Cape of Good Hope, the Tavern of the Seas; in reality sanctions, bush wars and a loathing of the racist white tribe sealed the country off from the rest of the continent.

Growing up in an ostracised South Africa all the members of our Cape to Cairo team had nursed dreams of exploring the con-

Africa's southwestern tip has a curious relationship with the rest of the continent. The citizens of Cape Town have traditionally seen themselves as separate, aloof, cerebral. They view the continent upside down, with the southern end as its head. Living on a paradisaical peninsula of vineyards and dazzling beaches, many feel the Cape has more in common with the Côte d'Azur than with the dry heartland. Some would even welcome a rise in sea level that flooded the Cape Flats and returned the peninsula to its prehistoric island state. But in the past decade things have been shaken up. New immigrants from across southern Africa, and indeed the continent, have begun to settle in the shadow of Table Mountain. That's not to say they've been welcomed. Often quite the contrary.

Under apartheid South Africa's northern borders were closed: beyond the Limpopo lurked Marxist warmongers, genocide and endemic anarchy – a colonial vision that hadn't altered much in centuries. The furthest you could get from Africa's darkness, or so the theory went, was the sun-kissed Cape of Good Hope, the Tavern of the Seas. In reality sanctions, bush wars and a loathing of the racist white tribe sealed the country off from the rest of the continent.

Growing up in an ostracised South Africa all the members of our Cape to Cairo team had nursed dreams of exploring the continent. But our northern neighbours reached the South before we got to them. Long before diplomatic relations with other African countries were re-established, they started arriving. Rwandans walking south to avoid the bloodshed, Zimbabweans looking for jobs, Angolans 'learning English', Nigerians smuggling drugs, Congolese working as car guards. Africa arrived at the foot of the Table and demanded to be fed, clothed, employed.

These new arrivals were, and still are, often despised, particularly in poorer black communities where it is felt jobs are being lost to foreigners. They call them 'kwerekwere', a xenophobic term meaning African from outside South Africa. These interlopers are very dark-skinned, dangerously good-looking and over-ambitious. They're better at selling things, they steal jobs and women. The kwerekwere are beaten, thrown off trains, verbally abused, harassed by police and have their documents torn up. But in most cases they're just law-abiding visitors here for short stints, trying to make an honest buck to send home to desperate families . . . and they often employ South Africans to sell their exotic wares.

On Greenmarket Square and in the Pan-African Market on Long Street you hear French, Portuguese, Swahili, Amharic. The art and craft of the continent is there, to add a little ethnic spice to the suburban home: Dogon doors, Axumite crosses, Tuareg swords, Maasai blankets, Malawian chairs.

Our band of overlanders had all come into contact with 'kwerekwere'. The car guards outside Cameron Ewart-Smith's home were from the Congo, while Mike Copeland had befriended Ethiopians and Somalis at Paarl station and had taken to dining with them. I'd met a Senegalese man who was prepared to sell me his prized metre-high statue of Tintin brought on a plane from the Ivory Coast. Don Pinnock moonlights as a criminologist and through his research on gangs had got to know diamond-studded, Mercedes-driving Nigerian drug lords. So, 'darker-skinned' Africa had reached the southern tip, and Cape Town was the richer for it.

South Africans, on the other hand, are less inclined to venture much beyond their neighbouring states. Out there be dragons and Bob Mugabes.

As white men on an expedition through the continent's heart, we were aware of the ironies. We weren't in good company. In recent history South African forays northward generally involved R1 rifles and air support. Earlier sorties were hardly more encouraging. Our colonial forebears had failed to distinguish themselves in the diplomacy stakes. Of course there were the illustrious and benign explorer types – Livingstone, Burton, Speke, Grogan – whose paths we would repeatedly cross. But even their legacies – imperial arrogance and dubious treatment of local people – couldn't exactly be considered inspirational.

And then there was Cecil John Rhodes. Any journey from Cape to Cairo must travel in his shadow. Like all imperialists he had a dream, but his was more ambitious than most. Rhodes wanted to paint the continent pink from base to tip, creating a vast British protectorate. What's more, he envisaged a railway line running the length of its spine. These were grand plans indeed: still today, more than a century later, his railway dream is no closer to realisation. It's possible to reach Nairobi by train, but thereafter the Kenyan deserts, Ethiopian highlands and Saharan wastes put paid to further rail travel.

'Your hinterland is there' reads the inscription under the imperialist's bronze bust at Rhodes Memorial beneath the crags of Devil's Peak. Before our departure I walked up there at first light to pay reluctant homage, snaking through the pines of Table Mountain's eastern slopes. Designed by Herbert Baker, the building is a shrine to patriotism and the cult of the imperial hero. Before he died, Rhodes had discussed with his young architect the construction of a 'lion house' on a site close to his favourite viewpoint on the mountain. The Egyptian inspiration and lion motif are symbolic of Rhodes's pan-African dream. It was chilly among the temple's columns and I found a seat on the granite steps and waited for the sun to rise. The place felt creepy, depressing even.

I sat surrounded by four pairs of bronze, sphinx-like lions, all gazing with pregnant expectation. The century that separated me from them had seen the disintegration of all the imperial ideals Rhodes had striven for. It had been an empty exercise bringing misery to so many. After the colonial withdrawal, almost every country had been left in a shambles.

Suddenly a rind of sun lifted above the Hottentots Holland Mountains and rinsed the temple in soft light. The place was transformed. The statue of 'Energy', a prancing stallion ridden by a naked man shielding his face from the sun, seemed about to leap from its plinth and gallop north. Invigorated, the memorial breathed with Rhodes's ambition. The tainted imperial dream was still there, hanging in the pine-scented air. The whole African continent stretched at my feet, there for the taking. It was both sinister and compelling. 'Just a hop, skip and jump and you'll be in Cairo,' the pines whispered in my ear. I felt somehow beholden to the old boy. He'd paid for part of my education and endowed my university, just out of view in the trees to my right. I supposed it couldn't hurt to take him along in the Land Rover.

Hopefully our party of post-colonial wanderers would leave a light, almost imperceptible footprint. Throughout the journey we would meet nostalgic colonialists who hankered after a bygone hegemony, as well as a new breed of white Africans trying to do things differently. They were often South African farmers or displaced Zimbabweans, sometimes adventure-seeking Europeans. Many of them made the right sounds about sustainable development, ecotourism, putting money and energy back into their communities. Time will reveal whether these are vestiges of the old patterns or seeds of a new relationship where whites see themselves and are seen by the locals as intrinsically part of the continent and its future.

In Rhodes's day the journey from Cape to Cairo was still an unattained grail, a magical rite of passage through Africa's heart. Conrad, Stanley, Kipling and Haggard added fuel to the stereotypical view of an interior full of hostile tribes, unspeakable rituals and missionary-size cooking pots. Ewart Grogan, an unhailed Cambridge undergraduate, was the first European to go the distance. Dubbed 'the boldest and baddest of a bold, bad gang' of pioneering Kenyan settlers, Grogan did the transcontinental epic to win the hand of a woman. At the age of 22 he fell in love with a young heiress and was required to prove his mettle to her stepfather before they could marry. It took him three years to complete the south-to-north traverse, arriving in Cairo in 1900. He became an instant celebrity and returned to London to marry his intended.

Since Grogan's time there has been a flood of Cape to Cairo travellers and there was certainly nothing pioneering about our trip. In the past 18 months alone, four books have appeared chronicling such a trek. So why bother with yet another description? Because it remains one of the world's great journeys, a symbol in its own right. Just the words 'Cape to Cairo' still conjure visions of wide open spaces, plains brimming with game, desert nomads, forest pygmies and Pharaonic mysteries. Even in the 21st century, it's an unpredictable journey that quickens the pulse.

Each transcontinental tale is unique, and each brings wider understanding to the subject, like the critical mass that gathers beneath a great book, elevating it the way a mole does soil. Ours would be different in another way. We'd be singing the story in four-part (dis)harmony. This manner of telling has its drawbacks. Any extended literary themes or narrative development dissolves with each new storyteller. But there are benefits too. What is lost in cohesion can be gained in variety (the spice of a travelling life) and in the postmodern device – unusual outside fiction – of four different voices being brought to bear on the same journey. Each new arrival ushers in a rash of fresh impressions, always most glaring at the start of a trip but liable to get lost or taken for granted over long distances and discourses.

Our cross-Africa trek was to be divided into equal parts, a new writer flying in for each leg and one person, Mike Copeland, going the whole distance from Cape to Cairo. Thus the team consisted of four photojournalists and one principle driver, Mike, a veteran overlander who'd spent years crisscrossing the continent. He'd recently returned from a journey to Cairo using only public transport. Robyn Daly, Cameron Ewart-Smith, Don Pinnock and myself flew in and/or out in relays.

Our primary task would be to write, photograph and video each leg for *Getaway* travel magazine. Each of us would also pen a piece of the tale for a book, but photojournalist Robyn Daly, co-driver of the first leg to Lusaka, opted out of the writing. She shook her mane of recalcitrant blonde hair. 'You Camel boys do it on your own. I couldn't think of anything worse. I'd rather write for Mills and Boon.' So it would have to be a boys-only affair.

Robyn did, however, come up with the esoteric notion of this journey as an 'exquisite corpse'. The idea derives from the Surrealists who were fascinated by the 'mysteries of chance' and devised techniques for creating 'accidental' collages of words or images. They called it the *cadavre exquis*. It was based on an old parlour game in which each participant wrote a phrase on a sheet of paper, folded it to conceal the words, then passed it on for others to add their contributions. The technique got its name from the initial result of playing the game: '*Le cadavre exquis boira le vin nouveau*' (the exquisite corpse will drink the young wine).

An exquisite corpse, a three-month parlour *divertissement*, a children's game of broken telephone, pass the parcel or even – if the going and writing got tough – pin the tail on the donkey; whichever way we looked at it this travel-writing experiment was going to be an adventure.

So, our journey would be a four-legged animal. All four tales would develop themes corresponding to our own interests. Mike was producing an overlanding guidebook and was responsible for the vehicle and its equipment. He was consumed with gear tests and final adjustments before putting the Land Rover through its first bit of rough and tumble in southern Zambia. The route from Cape Town to Lusaka is familiar territory, close to home in a region where backup and technical support are near at hand. Any vehicle niggles and we could simply pop into a local Land Rover dealer and they'd be on the phone to their colleagues in Jo'burg.

Cameron is a marine biologist and he's wild about wildlife. His part of the journey took in East Africa's great game parks with the prospect of very close encounters with the Big Five in Ngorongoro Crater, the Serengeti and the Masai Mara. Appropriately too for a man who loves the sea, his leg was the only one that included some coastline, where he grabbed the opportunity to hitch a ride on a spice dhow to Zanzibar.

I'm a sucker for history and architecture and saw the third leg as a chance to rummage through Africa's archaic attic: Ethiopia's highland culture and Old Testament brand of Christianity. A tableland circuit would take us to sunken churches carved from stone, the Queen of Sheba's home and Gondar's fairytale castles.

Don has a passion for deserts. In the tradition of Thesiger and Chatwin he's ineluctably drawn to nomadic life. The final run through the desert to Cairo seemed tailor-made for him. Making the crossing during Ramadan – arriving in camps at sundown and being invited to break the fast with Nubian wanderers – only heightened the fascination. In addition, we feared the Egyptian border was going to be a potential hurdle and, as Don has a loathing for petty bureaucracy, we figured he'd be just the man to deal with Kafkaesque Egyptian officials. He was.

The originator of the idea and driving force behind the expedition was David Bristow, the editor of *Getaway*. He wouldn't be joining us, but would be pulling the strings from 'base camp' in Cape Town. In the weeks leading up to our September 2002 departure David kept the ship on course, making sure we were up to speed on all our tasks: organising sponsors, buying guidebooks and maps, booking flights, arranging for the Land Rover to be shipped back to South Africa from Cairo. David was particular about our recovery equipment, inoculations and choosing a safe route. He didn't want us mucking this up . . . getting ourselves hijacked, mislaying the vehicle somewhere in the desert or wrapping it around a pyramid.

Working for a travel magazine made preparations far simpler than they would normally be. Many companies, not least Land Rover South Africa, were keen to sponsor equipment. The vehicle, a Defender 110 Td5, seemed rugged enough and Landy spares are seldom a problem. Mike and Cameron were tasked with assembling all the goodies that encrusted the vehicle like barnacles. There were spare tyres, a dual battery system, exhaust snorkel and recovery gear, as well as an on-board safe and lock-up roller drawers for medical kits, carnets and passports. Most cherished was a gallant little fridge which kept our beers icy. Oh, and we ordered a customised number plate, 2CAIRO-WP, because – as Cameron said – some things you just gotta have.

As it was essential that the team keep in regular contact with home and update the magazine's website, the vehicle bristled with communications equipment. We installed a radio-based e-mail server (Bushmail) and carried a satellite phone, as well as a satellite-tracking device so our real-time movements could be followed on a website map. In the middle of our dashboard sat the GPS, allowing us to monitor our *own* position. This often provided some light relief, and incredulity, when we were lost in the darkness in the middle of nowhere. 'But Mike, we can't *possibly* be *there*!'

The route we chose had to avoid some countries and tread gingerly through others. Many regions along the way were in a mess. Zimbabwe's chronic fuel shortages meant we'd be skirting the more obvious route north. Angola and the DRC were out of the question. Famine gripped Malawi and Zambia, which we couldn't bypass. Tanzanian roads were likely to rattle us to pieces and the exorbitant park fees might squeeze the finances out of the trip. In Kenya President Moi was in the dying throws of a villainous dictatorship and vast tracts of northern Kenya were ungovernable, home to bands of lawless *shiftas* (bandits). Somalia was hell on earth and we wouldn't dream of going there. In peaceful Ethiopia a South African overlander had been murdered at a roadblock and that country's northern border with Eritrea – where the ceasefire was reputedly a thing of patches – was probably closed. This meant a trip through Sudan, where a full-scale civil war was on the go. As for Egypt, we didn't know whether the authorities would even allow a vehicle emerging from the war-torn Saharan sands to enter their country. Given the horror stories, you could be forgiven for thinking Africa was being engorged by its own stereotype. But this was more scaremongering than legitimate deterrent. In truth the route we picked held no more risk than driving through downtown Johannesburg at night.

Looking back, there were hardly any moments of danger but highs aplenty. For each of us the best bits were provided by the characters who crossed our path. The gauge of whether we were having a rewarding time or not correlated to whom we met. The continent is thick with road dwellers: African arteries are sociable places. It's hard to stop anywhere, even in the remotest parts, without someone appearing from behind a boulder or materialising out of the heat haze. Each of us has favourites.

For now, meet Ed, a man who symbolises the exploits of so many whites on the continent and provided the introduction to my leg.

I met him hot off the plane from Cape Town and trying to acclimatise to Nairobi's tropical highlands with their unfamiliar sights, smells and insidiously sticky heat. Mike drove me straight to Ed's house past billboards for Castle Lager and through suburbs thronged with rush-hour traffic. Fat-cat whites and Indians powered along in big 4x4s. *Matatus* (minibus taxis) emerged from muddy streets threading between shacks. Mike swung the Land Rover through a grand stone entrance and up a gravel drive. 'This is Ed's place. He's an old buddy. Well, actually the boss of a good friend who works in Addis and has now become a pal of mine. Just check out this house. God, the parties he used to throw here...'

Two staff members carried our bags past a half-Olympic swimming pool to the guest rooms. Ed, it turned out, was a Hollander, self-made millionaire, entrepreneur, party-animal, womaniser and adventurer. He was a big man in his fifties, well dressed with a cravat tucked into the top of his shirt.

'I have businesses in Uganda, in Ghana, in Tanzania,' said Ed over a drink that evening. 'Had to work my way around the blacks, the scams, the corruption, but I've done okay for myself. I'm into construction, engineering, security systems, you know, that sort of thing, ja?'

I didn't, but nodded. Despite the tropical heat, a fire crackled in the hearth of a cavernous room. The fireplace was plated in metal like the side of a ship. Ed saw me observing the details and said, 'I designed and built this place myself back in the '70s.' There were Maasai spears, grotesque wooden carvings and cacti for decoration. Servants moved silently in the shadows.

'I was in New Guinea in the army in '58, then Australia where I was involved in trade unions and women. But things got a bit hot and I had to leave in a hurry, ja? I took passage on a Norwegian ship as deckhand. To Cape Town. Then I came to Tanzania, looking to find my feet again in Africa, to make a buck. I started a shipping company and it did very well. But I was young, stupid. I fired the boyfriend of the daughter of the minister of labour. Next thing I'm kicked out the country. Just like that. Lost everything. That's Africa for you. You must watch the toes, ja?

'I started from scratch with nothing, penniless – just a simple workshop manager in Mombasa. I built it all up from there and now I have all this.' The sweep of his hand seemed to take in much more than the stone house, swimming pool, overgrown tennis court and vague lands beyond.

It was almost completely dark now and the three of us had worked our way through two cobwebbed bottles of Kanonkop Cabernet Sauvignon. We took the staircase down to Ed's basement dining room, where Africa and Gothic Europe had stumbled into one another: colonial baronial with dark wooden beams and

Dutch tiles on the wall. A servant in bow tie watched us eat and never allowed the levels in our glasses to drop below half.

'A few years ago I bought a 19-metre ketch in Holland and sailed her here. To Mombasa. She's a beautiful thing. We came through the Med, no problem. Down the Red Sea, no problem. Then the fucking Eritrean Navy comes out in an unmarked boat. It had two big engines and came screaming at us. Pirates, we thought. I started the engine and headed out to sea full throttle. I told my chaps lie down. Next thing, they're peppering our sails with machine-guns. Bang! Bang! Bang! Nailed the GPS.'

A butler interrupted, bearing aperitif cubes of Dutch cheddar impaled on miniature plastic forks, followed almost immediately by cottage pie. Mike and I were slumped in our high-backed chairs, struggling to find our mouths with our forks. Music filtered from another room: the unsettling combination of German lyrics with Hadgidakis's tunes.

'Then they boarded us, ramming the stern and leaping across, shouting, "Hands up!", pointing guns like fucking Rambo. They arrested us and made us sail to a shitty little port. I had to go ashore for "interrogation".' He rolled his eyes. 'I grab my logbook and chart with our route marked on it. Then up onto this rickety jetty with no planks, my heart going doof doof. This admiral is standing at the end of the jetty in his bloody ice-cream suit with a chest full of medals. I mean please, the *Eritrean* Navy! I decide attack is the best defence. I storm up to him and start ranting, "How dare you fire on one of her majesty's ships?"

'So he says to me, no, his agents told him we're going ashore along the coast, sneaking in and out at night. That we're spies. "Bullshit!" I shout, "Check my log."

'After an hour I'm free to go. But we weren't safe yet. We still had to run the gauntlet of the Somali pirates. We headed far offshore, 800 miles out to sea. Flat out with sails and motor. No lights, no radio contact. Shat ourselves. Those Somalis come out at 50 knots, trash and steal everything, rape your wife, shoot you. Just like that.'

Long silence.

'I used to do business in Somalia. Lovely people. Friendly people. You could fall down blind drunk in the streets and no one would pick your pocket. Then there was an incident where an Indian lady was sitting in her car, arm full of gold bangles dangling out the window, minding her own business. This guy with a machete comes along, lops off her arm. That was it. Then it all went tits up. I had to pull my security business out. No bloody security possible!

'Now my firm is in Kenya, Ethiopia and Uganda. Great place Uganda. We've become top dog since the brother of the president's security firm went bust. Stuff comes through in sealed boxes in our trucks from the Congo. We don't ask questions. Not our job to ask questions. Sometimes we're just told "stones". Ha, they want our ex-Koevoet South African white guy with a semi-automatic rifle to sit on the box . . . in an armoured car . . . all the way. The box goes to this little man in a flat in Dar. All the time he's sitting, waiting, sorting, buying. Stones.'

Ed wore the look of a man who'd go on talking all night, but Mike and I had a road to catch in the morning and I was exhausted from the flight. We stumbled to our rooms in a shower of tropical rain, past three security guards, two Staffordshire bull-terriers and one amorous Rottweiler.

That was my introduction to the Cape to Cairo circus. My tired eyes were out on stalks but Mike was taking it all in his stride. He'd been seven weeks on the road already. If it carries on like this, I thought as I drew a mosquito net over me, there'll be some stories to tell when we're done. And there were.

CAPE TOWN TO LUSAKA

The road is the mode

Mike Copeland

Robyn Daly and I left Cape Town on an inauspicious 9/11, a year to the day after the attack on New York's World Trade Center, heading for lands said to offer shelter to its perpetrators. First World tourists were cancelling their travel plans and here we were, tackling Africa. But our spirits were high as the sun crept over the Drakenstein Mountains and we took a last look back at the Fairest Cape. Spring buds stained the Paarl valley a pale green, and beyond the frown of Gordon Rock, Table Mountain was a faint mirage. The Land Rover was scheduled to arrive in Cairo three months and 22 500 kilometres later, a distant beacon at the nether end of the continent.

I've travelled widely in Africa and a few years ago undertook a similar trip, travelling from Cape to Cairo using only public transport. Apartheid had ended, Mandela was the popular new leader and a South African passport was carried with pride and accepted everywhere. What a pleasure it had been to be heading north into *terra incognita*. Riding on buses, trains, boats, trucks and anything else that was going my way, I meandered through Africa for three months.

This transcontinental journey was, however, a very different affair. Fully prepared with a vehicle straight out the box and equipment to make NASA edgy, I had the worrying responsibility of getting five of us through Africa. My companion to Lusaka, Robyn, was also anxious. Would I be a decent travelling companion and would she get the story she wanted? At the start of any long journey the stresses of planning and packing weigh heavily. Later, the trip becomes part of the rhythm of life and you can mould it to suit you. But now, it was the sorting out, settling in and finding-a-groove stage. Start badly and it could take a long time, maybe the entire journey, to make things right.

One thing that I couldn't make right was leaving my wife again for three months. I had to do it but couldn't really explain why, not even to myself. Except that the kids were grown up, the business was running itself and the urge to go and lose myself in Africa was too strong to resist.

It was in the autumn of 1655 that the first group of European adventurers struck north from the Dutch East India Company's fort on the shore of Table Bay. Eight soldiers under the leadership of Jan Wintervogel set out to make contact and trade with Khoisan clans and search for precious metals. They were away 19 days and lost only one man (he overdosed on bitter almonds) – a relatively successful expedition that proved such trips could be safely undertaken. I hoped ours would prove the same.

Chugging through Worcester we could afford to throw a friendly wave to the traffic cops manning a speed trap. Further on there was late snow on the Hex River Mountains as we sped up the N2, passing on our left row upon row of well-tended table-grape vines. Folk-tales tell of a beautiful young woman, Eliza Meiring, who challenged a young man to prove his love by bringing her a flower from the highest peak of the surrounding mountains. On his way down he fell to his death, still clutching the flower. Eliza, demented with grief, was confined to a small room, where she eventually took her own life. She is said to still haunt the valley as a *heks* (witch).

We had been given the added burden of making a video of the trip, and started off like pros. Robyn filmed out the window, inside the cab and took shots of the Land Rover zooming past with wind pumps and sheep in the background. It was still fun at this stage.

Later, as the travelling hardened, the video work would become a pain in the arse. But we persevered and ended up with over ten hours of footage which was cut into a one-hour film of the trip.

A skip-search of the radio stations offered the choice of popcorn music or the disheartening speech of President Bush's 9/11 commemorative service. Robyn slipped an Eric Clapton CD into the player. With my fingers tapping on the steering wheel we grooved on a short detour past the historic Lord Milner Hotel at Matjiesfontein. Built more than a hundred years ago by a Scot, James Logan, it served meals and offered accommodation to passengers on the newly-opened railway line north. The Anglo-Boer War brought prosperity with high-ranking army officials, war correspondents and recuperating soldiers enjoying Matjiesfontein's healthy Karoo air. Cecil John Rhodes, Olive Schreiner and Winston Churchill all visited this luxurious hostelry; many others came to rest here, some finally, as the nearby Boer War graveyard attests. It was a reminder that in Africa men have always fought for the land or its resources and seldom won.

The road was good and we were eating up the k's, stopping only to refuel ourselves and the Landy. Laingsburg, Prince Albert Road and Leeu Gamka. Passing through the Karoo's semi-deserted towns, I couldn't help feeling nostalgic for a time when these platteland dorps flourished. The garage with local mechanic who could fix any vehicle, a general dealer where you could buy everything from a roll of tobacco to a Joseph Rogers knife, the café which offered a mixed grill and milkshake at any hour of the day . . . They've largely vanished, forced out by Ultra Cities, Petroports and One Stops which are often owned by multinationals as part of some large investment portfolio. These garish centres of transient commerce taunt the unique local architecture and siphon off profitable business.

Robyn was at the wheel, strands of her long blond hair flying out the window. The vast, dry Karoo stretched to the horizon. This region was once home to millions of springbok, wildebeest, blesbok, quagga and eland. Early accounts of the migrations of huge herds seem barely credible. One describes the antelope invasion of Beaufort West in 1849. For three full days trekbokke filled the streets and gardens of this Karoo town on their way to greener pastures. Townsfolk hunted from their front stoeps and there was so much biltong to be cured that the town soon ran out of salt.

Nowadays sheep rule the vlakte in a cycle of boom and bust. When the world economy or fashion industry takes a dip and the wool market slumps, farmers are bankrupted and the auctioneers move in. But it's another story when demand is high. During the boom of 1950 an eccentric farmer who had an aversion to writing cheques paid for his new car with the wool picked off the barbed-wire fences around his property.

On a journey like ours, large towns such as Bloemfontein aren't the ideal place to overnight. I guess we should rather have stopped earlier at one of the villages that offer the kind of hospitality for which the Free State is renowned. But Tom's Place with its vinyl headboards and pine furniture with more cigarette burns than knots was just fine.

In the frost of the next dawn, with the Eagles singing of a tequila sunrise, we were off again. As we slid out of town my mind drifted back to childhood days. My dad had an old puddle-jumping Anglia that we used to load to window level. My sister and I would lie on top of the piles of luggage, wrapped up warmly as we always seemed to be travelling during the cold winter months. Mom would keep us happy with colouring-in books, sweets and games of I-spy-with-my-little-eye. People would stare in wide-eyed disbelief at some of the places we got to in that little car.

At the Shell Ultra City in Kroonstad Ruth Hollinger – tanned the colour of caramel with rosy cheeks and her accent giving away her origins – was pumping her tyres. She was from Ballyclare in County Antrim and had thighs that could squeeze the life out of a python. Cycling from Ireland on a bike that weighed more than she did, Ruth had made it to the World Summit on Sustainable Development earlier that month in Johannesburg, and was now nearing Cape Town, her final destination.

'I was flashed at yesterday,' said the angelic-looking lass in a lilting Irish brogue. "Twas only a wee problem . . .' She had calmly pedalled past a randy truck driver on a lonely stretch of Free State highway, his wedding tackle shrivelling in the icy wind.

Our first port of call was Johannesburg, more a duty stop than a destination. The Land Rover was to be exhibited at *Getaway*'s outdoor-travel show, so we spent the next few days like caged animals, waiting to be set free on the road again. Jo'burg was not the kind of place we wanted to linger in, but attending the travel show did give us the chance to meet plenty of people who also dreamed of driving to Cairo, and their enthusiasm was contagious. Many said we were lucky, but, I tried to argue, where's the luck? A trip like this is all about planning, sacrifices and reorganising your life. I knew I'd left an unhappy family behind.

Another benefit of staying over in Jo'burg was installing Bushmail in our vehicle. Relaying e-mails over short-wave radio took us a while to sort out, but proved an invaluable link later in the trip. Entrenched behind a large desk in suburban Gauteng, Jim Drummond, who organised it for us, was surrounded by computers, cables, modems and radios, all connecting him to the world. From lodge managers to lonely prospectors on the mountains and plains of wildest Africa, Jim was their link to the outside world. Medical emergencies would be seen to with a twiddling of knobs and a connecting of wires. For others out in the bush, Jim satisfied a yearning to talk to someone. I doubt he ever slept, except maybe at his desk.

We sorted and repacked the equipment and checked the accessories attached to our vehicle: bull bar, protective side step and spotlights, aluminium roof-rack with tent, jerry-can holders, fridge, a high-lift jack and a spade on brackets. The Landy was also fitted with an extra fuel tank, a water tank and an onboard air compressor. We were weighed down with so much stuff that sometimes I worried whether it would compromise the smooth running of the trip.

I broke a tooth on the morning we were due to leave. An omen? Perhaps. I'd been munching on a cheese-and-mushroom omelette at the hotel and crack!, I bit into something hard. Well, it would have to wait until we got to Windhoek, I figured. Nothing was going to make us postpone now. As it happened, Windhoek came and went, then Nairobi, then Cairo. It wasn't until I got back to Cape Town that I had the tooth seen to.

A special ramp had been constructed for the Land Rover at

the show, so we could drive off ceremoniously and out onto the road to Cairo. Speeches were made, cameras clicked; then the ramp creaked, swaying dangerously under the weight of the vehicle and all its gear before we edged safely down and away.

There's an odd anomaly among 4x4 owners in South Africa: city folks, who do little more adventurous than drive to the office or shopping mall, own the most outrageous off-road vehicles, while their poor rural cousins do the real bundu-bashing in simple 2x4 bakkies. I swear I could hear the desperate chorus of thousands of Jo'burg's 4x4s pleading 'Take us with you!' as we abandoned them to their fate of lifting the kids to school and visits to the parking area of the local gym.

Our progress through the maizelands around Sannieshof and Delareyville was swift and uneventful. Then came the oasis town of Upington on the mighty Orange. The river flows through an arid, desert-like countryside, channelling water from the rain-soaked Maluti highlands to the sea. For long stretches its waters are diverted to irrigate fields of lucerne, neat vineyards and orchards of sweet peaches. It was already dark when we drove down the avenue of palm trees that leads to the island camp on Die Eiland.

This paradise opposite Upington was first discovered in 1778 by Wikar, a deserter from the Dutch East India Company in Cape Town. He sowed watermelon- and pumpkin-seeds and, after some months of roaming up and down the river, returned to enjoy a bounty of fruit and vegetables. He also cultivated a healthy crop of marijuana. I needed no such help in relaxing when my head hit the pillow in my rooftop tent, Robyn below in her dome tent. We both slept like babies.

Heading for the Namibian border the next morning, we followed the never-ending rows of telephone poles, seemingly laid on by Telkom for the sole purpose of providing homes for sociable weaver birds. Huge chatter-filled nests engulfed the top-heavy poles.

The border is at a lonely outpost called Nakop, between Langklip and Ariamsvlei. Crossing was a painless affair. A burly soldier at the gate greeted us with a 'welkom meneer', and one of the cleaners waved us through customs with his feather duster. If only border crossings further north could be this simple – but that, I knew, was far too much to ask for.

For the benefit of travellers, a weather indicator has been erected outside the immigration office. It's a large rock hanging on a chain with the information: 'If the rock is hot, it's sunny; if it's wet, it's raining; if it's moving, it's windy; if it's white, it's snowing; and if you can't see it, it's misty.' Foolproof.

We'd crossed our first border successfully and were into the desert. Jimmy Dludlu provided musical company and even the dull throbbing of my tooth was forgotten. Keetmanshoop was just a quick pit stop to buy good game biltong and droëwors to sustain us on our long push into the Namib-Naukluft Park.

Driving in Namibia is pure pleasure. Tarred roads are pothole free and largely deserted, while gravel roads are pretty well maintained (I'm convinced Namibia has more graders than the rest of Africa put together). The only problem was that the roads had recently been 'reprioritised', a euphemism for 'they've changed all the damn numbers'. The C36 had become the C19, the D826 was now the C27. I was making notes and doing research for my Cape to Cairo guidebook, so all this was relevant and duly recorded.

The artist Adolf Jentsch captured the sense of endless space so well in his evocative paintings of arid plains and thorn trees.

During his early career in Dresden, Germany, a critic scathingly suggested Jentsch should ride horses rather than paint them. Fortunately, when he came to Namibia there weren't too many horses around and he concentrated on landscapes, for which he became rightly famous. With a web of dots and lines he depicted the sparse vegetation, open vlaktes, big skies and subdued colours of the land, washed out by the brilliant light. He was so accomplished that his paintings became the yardstick by which you measure the landscape, instead of the other way round.

We'd occasionally pass a farm gate and then it would seem an eternity before the next one slid past. This is a country where farms have to be huge, almost the size of a small European country, to sustain the hardy Persian sheep, also known as karakul. The pelts of day-old lambs are sought after around the world and karakul fleece, or astrakhan (once the private monopoly of the Russian tsars), has saved many a local farmer from bankruptcy.

We came to the border of the Namib-Naukluft National Park – at 50 000 square kilometres it's larger than Switzerland and one of the biggest parks in Africa. Originally proclaimed in 1907 as Game Reserve Number Three, it has grown as new areas have been added. The most recent addition was a diamond-prospecting region, which advanced its boundary south to Lüderitz. The park is to be an important component of the hotly debated and eagerly awaited transfrontier park that will stretch from the Augrabies National Park and Richtersveld in South Africa's Northern Cape all the way up the Namibian coast into southern Angola. In Namibia it will include the Namib-Naukluft, Skeleton Coast and Etosha national parks, and in Angola the Iona and Namibe reserves.

One of the places we wanted to visit in the park was Sesriem, a narrow canyon that earned its name because early pioneers needed *ses rieme* (six leather ropes) to lower a bucket down to draw water. The canyon is still a watering spot, but now only for birds and small game. The narrow gorge leads one to a waterhole whose shade is most welcome in the heat of the day.

For our first night in the area I'd wangled a booking at the ultra-luxurious Sossusvlei Mountain Lodge. Hidden discreetly behind a ridge, above a wide plain and floodlit waterhole, the stone buildings blend perfectly into the surroundings. Jennifer Tooley, our hostess, was gracious enough to overlook our dusty Mad Max attire as she showed us around the well-stocked wine cellar. A fine choice was made to accompany our meal on the patio. We dined under a blanket of stars. Down on the plain, jackals pounced and dug for rodents under the floodlights while bats hunted overhead. Later we climbed to the observatory on a hill behind the lodge to take a closer look at those stars. With a large computer-linked telescope and perfect night-time conditions, it was, in astronomical terms, just about as good as it gets.

Our next destination was the campsite at Sesriem. We hadn't made prior bookings. Of course it was full, so we had to forego the lovely shaded sites with their taps and tables and were banished to the camp that caters for overflow. There were no ablution blocks or other facilities and, given the smell of human effluent and noise from generators powering nearby petrol pumps, it was no place to linger. To compensate for our dreary surroundings, we hitched a ride in a hot-air balloon to float over the dunes the next day.

Before dawn we were striding across the veld to where our pilot, Eric, was directing the offloading of a large wicker basket and the brightly coloured envelope that would carry us aloft. While Robyn schmoozed the pilot, a suave Frenchman with impressive leather work-gloves and oh-so-casually-draped scarf, I studied the system of propane tanks, pipes and burners that he was operating in short blasts to fill the balloon. Large fans ran off a portable generator and funnelled hot air into the 6 000-square-metre ball. Slowly it took shape. The heat and bright light of the burners crackled and roared in the dark while a gang of assistants steadied the basket. Eric instructed us to scramble aboard and, with a couple more blasts from the burners, we scraped along the ground for a short distance before lifting gently into the sky.

Only a few centimetres clearance from the ground seemed to put us in a different realm. Our progress took us up into a sky whose stars were just fading to make way for the sun. The flat, dry Tsauchab Valley stretched towards Sossusvlei in the distance. Eric pointed out the different dunes flanking the valley: huge, crescent-shaped barchans that crept slowly forward as the winds shaped and re-shaped them and the smaller, star-shaped stellar dunes formed by variable winds blowing from all directions. Beyond them lay the mighty Uri Uchab Mountains and directly below us were scattered what Eric called fairy circles. No one has yet come up with a conclusive explanation for what causes these bare patches in the veld where nothing but the finest grass grows – maybe the fairies did have something to do with it ...

As our shadow floated across the bright red dunes, Eric did his tour guide thing: 'The iron oxide in the sand is responsible for the colour.' And: 'The bloody off-road drivers, they are *so* thoughtless. Look at all the damage they cause. *Merde*! Just look at the tracks across the valley floor. It will take years before they are gone.'

When the time came for our pilot to bring us down, he was careful to aim for a landing spot close to an established track. Eric warned that the touchdown was going to be more exciting than the take-off: 'The landing might be a bit, ah, *sportif*. Get down, hold on and flex your legs.'

The recovery team had followed us in a truck and was waiting to hold us down once we hit the ground. With much shouting and a fair bit of scraping, we eventually came to a halt. Eric pulled a cord which opened the envelope, releasing the hot air, and the balloon collapsed beside us.

The admirable tradition of cracking open a bottle of champagne on landing was started by the first balloonists, the Montgolfier brothers, to prove to astonished French farmers that they were not aliens. Now it is often used as a peace offering to irate farmers whose land is invaded when the balloon is blown off course. But we had the bubbly to ourselves, and it went down well with a breakfast feast of cold meats and croissants.

From Sesriem we headed deeper into the Namib to watch the sun setting behind Sossusvlei's dunes. The Tsauchab River flows once every few decades and when it does, the water runs up against a sand barrier to form a lake that attracts a fabulous variety of birds and animals. Most of the time, though, Sossusvlei is a flat, dusty pan where the occasional gemsbok hangs about looking disconsolate. In this parched spot one can feel the anticipation and longing for rain as animals and plants cling to life until the next short period of plenty.

We hiked to Dead Vlei, where the skeletons of old thorn trees

attest to wetter times. Robyn loved the abstract shapes formed by the branches and began photographing madly. The sun painted the dunes an even deeper red as it sank into the sand and the air began to cool. I just sat on a crest, mesmerised.

All roads hereabouts lead to Solitaire. What a great name: so apt for a one-donkey outpost of petrol pump and trading store. Moose is 'the man' here. People come from around the world to sample his home bakes. His speciality is apple crumble and, with good filter coffee, it's well worth an international flight. Moose, with his bushy beard and Tusker T-shirt, keeps plying his customers with overflowing plates, while still finding time to organise water supplies to be dropped off for the occasional crazy Japanese cyclist who tackles the rough and lonely road to Swakopmund. And when it gets unbearably hot, he'll even let you swim in his reservoir.

I was sad to bypass the delights of Swakopmund, but time was against us and our trajectory led north and east. We took the steep mountain pass through Spreethoogte and the Auas Mountains to enter Windhoek through the back door.

The history of Namibia is that of the subcontinent in microcosm. For millennia the San lived here – hunting, gathering, painting on rocks and smoking the local dagga. Then about 500 years ago Bantu-speaking people arrived from the north. They came with cattle and didn't appreciate the San's 'raiding', so they roughed them up badly, chasing them into the deserts and mountains.

Things really hotted up with the arrival of missionaries, traders and colonists. It was survival of the fittest and the San came off worst. The Germans ruled *Südwest* with an iron fist, crushing local rebellions while expropriating the best farmland and exploiting the diamond fields along the southern coast.

Then came the First World War and with Germany's defeat, South West Africa was entrusted to South Africa by the League of Nations to 'promote to the utmost the material and moral well-being of its inhabitants'. South Africans were determined to make South West their own and brought with them their notions of race separation. A 30-year guerrilla struggle ensued which often flared into outright war on the northern border and only ended with the country's independence in 1990. The Namibians inherited a relatively prosperous and well-organised nation with good infrastructure, which is still running pretty well.

Windhoek, like Cape Town, is often described as un-African, whatever that may mean. Sure, some of the architecture bears a German colonial stamp and the city centre is filled with continental-style confectionaries, but it's as African as any other city on the continent. Both Robyn and I were ready for a bit of rest and recovery, so our priority was finding a laid-back backpackers' lodge where we could enjoy a few days free of the spooling road.

We discovered the Cardboard Box, a destination – it turned out – for like-minded African overlanders. There was Phil, heading north for the umpteenth time on his old BMW 1000, and the young Polish couple with visas and vague plans to travel through Angola. Whenever you start thinking your travels are hard-core, just mix with the folks at any international backpackers' and you're brought right back down to earth. The stories of their adventures can inspire slack-jawed awe. The information shared and camaraderie is like a drug to any keen traveller. We met one mad Englishman who'd just crossed the Namib on foot from the coast to Dead Vlei. It took him four days and he carried everything, including 15 litres of water. He'd navigated by compass, but told us the iron content in the dunes is so high it often played havoc with the needle, so he had to carry a GPS as backup. The Namib was the first of six desert crossings he was doing for the Discovery Channel (12 were being researched for suitability) and it seemed likely the next one would be the Kalahari.

We ate good Italian food at Sardinia Restaurant, spent time kicking back and shooting the breeze . . . and discovered that Windhoek's nightclubs were still unofficially segregated: Chez Ntemba for black people, La Di Da for coloureds and Pentagon for the whities.

The day before we left town, I celebrated a rather lonely wedding anniversary. I reflected on how everything in life depends on balance. But, like children on a see-saw, who wants to stay motionless in the middle all the time? The real fun is in the highs and lows of the ride.

At Okahandja I took a wrong turn and we ended up on the B2 to Swakopmund – perhaps subconsciously I was just too keen to see the lovely seaside town. Robyn didn't buy it, but rather than turn back, we decided to go where the road took us and ended up driving north through Omaruru. Oddly enough, the little town has a wine estate and, coming from wine-crazy Paarl, I cajoled Robyn into stopping for a tasting.

Herr Helmuth Kluge is the energetic Kellermeister at Kristall Kellerei. It's amazing what he's achieved with just four hectares of grapes. His vineyards are planted along the banks of the usually dry Omaruru River. There he fights a lonely battle against frost and marauding kudus in order to produce a colombard, ruby cabernet and cabernet sauvignon. Helmuth is a mechanical whizz and has built his own press and crusher, while his state-of-the-art, jacketed stainless-steel fermenting tanks were imported from South Africa. The operation is housed in an old-fashioned cellar where you can taste or buy, and enjoy traditional German cuisine. In a good year he makes 5 000 litres of a wine that's flavourful and intensely dark – in this harsh climate the skins are very thick and full of colour and tannins.

The road to Etosha National Park was, like most others in Namibia, quiet and a dream to drive. It's easy to understand why the country is experiencing a tourist boom. So many African parks have become playgrounds for wealthy overseas visitors – bearers of all-conquering Western currencies. But at Etosha blasé local Suidwesters, who've been going there every year for decades, rub shoulders with South Africans up for the school holidays. And shushing everybody at the waterholes because they're so excited to be in Africa are the northern Europeans, dressed in regulation safari gear bought specially for the trip.

Charles Andersson, an explorer, hunter and trader who documented his travels in the early 1850s, was one of the first Europeans to visit Ethosha Pan. Other hunters came to exploit the game until, in 1907, the governor of German South West Africa, Von Lindequist, proclaimed a reserve. It is to South Africa's discredit that the reserve shrank in size under its mandate.

We booked into Okaukuejo and, after selecting a campsite, headed for the waterhole just over the fence. What a pleasure to watch game from a bench with binoculars in one hand and a cold Namibian beer in the other! When the sun sets, spotlights come on to give you a 24-hour show. We sat for ages, watching the coming and going of animals as they all took turns, according to rank and size, to slake their thirst. The elephants made a mess of the water. Like naughty children, they splashed and muddied the place, while smaller fry, such as wildebeest, nervously waited their turn. Jackals jumped the queue and slunk in when no one was looking. The giraffes needed to feel safe before they were prepared to spread those two long front legs and lower their necks to the water. Among the most elusive were the rhinos, but late that night a mother and calf came down to drink. I celebrated with some of Herr Kluge's potent red wine.

The next day we drove east through the park, kicking up a fine, insidious dust as we made our way from waterhole to waterhole. There were some lions, but we would probably have seen more by remaining in camp and watching our waterhole. We didn't stay at Halali, the most modern camp in Etosha, but rather pressed on to Namutoni, centred around a fort with watchtower and waving palms. Built about a hundred years ago by the Germans, it was the most northerly police outpost in their colony and was intended to control the restive Ovambos. It was so far off any beaten track that camels were used for transport and patrols. In January 1904 a force of 500 Ovambo warriors attacked the fort. Inside were seven German soldiers who defended all day, then managed to escape during the night. Namutoni was set alight and partially destroyed, but later restored and strengthened. Now it's a guesthouse and I wondered how many visitors know of its violent history as they drift off to sleep with the howls of African scavengers in their ears.

In Namutoni's campsite we met the crews and passengers of several overland trucks. Some were on a grand circuit of Namibia, others were travelling through southern Africa, but the really dusty and disreputable-looking ones were trans-African veterans. All seemed to be well organised – a tame, contented bunch. There appeared to be none of the rowdiness that used to be associated with the overland trucking fraternity, no nights of drunken debauchery keeping fellow campers awake – behaviour that had them banished from many respectable camps.

We left Etosha and on our way to Tsumeb stopped at Otjikoto, an enormous sinkhole sometimes referred to as a 'bottomless lake'. Exploratory dives have yielded interesting finds, notably a

large quantity of weapons dumped by retreating German forces during the First World War. At Otjikoto's entrance we studied a tank full of the lake's endemic fish, while eland, kudu and warthogs wandered about in enclosures outside. A good collection of local semi-precious stones was also on display, along with the usual carvings and curios. A tourist trap for sure, but a damn nice one.

The road north to Rundu on the Kavango River was good, straight and dull, with only lively Katatura township-jive thumping from the radio to slightly alleviate our boredom. Thorn trees made way for makalani palms, and local bars with names like

Okavango Love Station, Hot & Cool and The Bruce Lee Bar lined the highway. The monotony of the road belied the tempestuous past of this corner of Namibia. This was, until fairly recently, wild pioneer country. The intrepid Charles Andersson first opened up the trail with ox-wagons. His route followed the dry Omatako River in a northeasterly direction from Windhoek and ran for 450 kilometres through inhospitable country. When the railway did eventually come it ran only as far as Grootfontein, and even after the Second World War the only way north was still along Andersson's dusty pioneer trail.

Rundu: $5 prostitutes, gun-runners, begging Aids orphans and roadside butchers selling fly-blown meat next to flourishing wholesalers that supply Caprivi Strip inhabitants, as well as people from across the river in Angola. But when we motored through town it was Sunday-dead, so we took a detour down to the river and came upon the pretty Sarasunga River Lodge. The grassy campsites were shaded, there was a swimming pool and the bar had a pool table – what more could we wish for? And when I actually beat Robyn, who's a pretty mean striker of the white ball, I was very satisfied with life.

A frontier atmosphere pervades these northern reaches, and the oddest characters wash up here. Take Obie: *'Ek's disleksies, maar moenie dink ek's dom nie'* ('I'm dyslexic, but don't think I'm stupid'), a stranded biker from Windhoek who was trying to fix his old 500 Yamaha so he could get back home to his gang, the Left-to-Righters. Sprawled on the lawn alongside the pool, he and I passed a well-used Spanish wineskin back and forth while he talked: 'My buddies and me used to drive our bikes into Windhoek bars and get lekker plastered. Hell man, we used to pick some fights too . . .' He whistled through his teeth. I'm sure there was a tear in his eye, helped, no doubt, by the sweet Mocador liqueur. 'You know, before joining the Left-to-Righters I was really *teruggetrokke* (introverted). But now I just can't stand most people.'

That night we ate another perfunctory meal: camp cuisine was never going to be a highlight of the Cape to Cairo safari. Neither Robyn nor I could be bothered with doing much cooking, so a typical evening meal was rice, to which we'd add a tin of tomato-and-onion mix and a tin of meat. Breakfasts were easy – muesli, tea and rusks – and lunch was usually a couple of cheese-tomato-and-onion sandwiches. Nice and simple. Biltong and beer were treats between meals and, thank goodness, my stash of Paarl wines was still holding up.

Next morning Rundu's shops were open and we stocked up for a detour into the Kaudom Game Reserve. We were a bit paranoid about the safety of the vehicle and its contents, so we shopped in relays, one of us always standing guard. I find that the further north I travel, the safer it feels. But only north of Kenya would I really start to relax.

About 115 kilometres east of Rundu a faded sign announced the turn-off to Kaudom. This isolated national park is bordered by Botswana in the east and Bushmanland to the south. Its Kalahari dunes are criss-crossed by *omurambas* – dry riverbeds concealing a flow of underground water that occasionally pops up in the shape of life-giving waterholes. As we turned off the tar the Land Rover was almost immediately into deep sand, so we stopped to deflate the tyres. This, combined with the vehicle's good traction and high clearance, allowed us to claw our way down to the park without any difficulties. The tyre tracks were so deep that when we encountered other vehicles it was quite a struggle to get out of the ruts and allow them to pass.

Teak and mopane trees thrive in this arid area and the grazing looked good, so we kept our eyes peeled for game as we detoured south. We arrived tired and dirty at the heavily fortified camp office. We'd heard that the elephants there were wild and belligerent, but this was ridiculous – was the moat around the building really necessary?

'What's all this?' I asked the game warden. 'Surely it's a bit much?'

'You'd be surprised,' he said. 'Be careful when approaching our *ndovu* (elephant), and watch out tonight. They always raid the campsite to see what they can steal. These guys are lekker mal (nice and crazy), but don't you worry, we'll be there to protect you.'

Later Robyn and I did a circular game drive that took us down to the confluence of the Kaudom and Cwiba omurambas, back up the Cwiba and then across a field of dunes to the camp. Out on the sandy game track I spotted something in the distance, small and dark. Heat waves distorted the image. Our Land Rover laboured in low gear, drawing the tiny speck closer. Its shape and colour were confusing. Then it came into focus.

Stumbling towards us was a baby elephant. It was thin from hunger, its sunken eyes glassy. Our first reaction was 'Oh, cute', and then 'Oh, hell' as we thought the rest of the herd might be close and aggressive. The helpless animal mistook the Land Rover for its mother and approached us, trying desperately to suckle from the vehicle. Our eyes scanned the surrounding bush for danger. But we were alone in this corner of the vast Kaudom and the youngster was obviously lost. It snuffled around the 4x4 until the heat and smell of the engine made it whirl away. Slowly the baby elephant retreated into the mopane bush, searching for its mother, towards certain death.

We drove on until we came to a sandy ridge overlooking a waterhole in the dry Kaudom omuramba, where we watched a group of elephants loitering. Like gangsters on an inner-city street, they caused trouble with everyone and everything that came their way. Other animals were chased off and made to wait for a chance to drink the muddy water they'd churned up. Any vehicle that dared get too close was likely to be charged. When night came, they set off to cause mischief in the neighbourhood.

On our return to camp we found there was no shortage of firewood (from elephant uprootings), so we built a blazing fire and feasted on braaied sosaties, baked potatoes and sweetcorn. After a much-needed hot shower we went to bed early with the sound of roistering coming from the waterhole. But sleep didn't come easily, for soon the cat-and-mouse game between rangers and pachyderms began. Like a bunch of looters, the elephants were determined to get at the goodies in camp, while the rangers were equally determined to keep them out. Armed only with clashing dustbin lids and protected by roaring fires, the rangers spent the whole night holding the elephants at bay. The men knew that if they weren't successful in their defence of the camp, they'd spend the day repairing damage instead of resting up to be ready for the next night's campaign.

We retraced our tracks back through the thick sand to the main road and pumped our tyres again. Our route now led into the Caprivi proper and the road was long, quiet and straight: endless rolling blacktop all the way to the bridge across the Kavango

River. It's difficult to believe that this river, after it crosses into Botswana, feeds the Okavango Delta's wide panhandle, its shallow triangle beyond and a maze of swampy tentacles. At its limit, the advancing water comes face to face with the parched Kalahari Desert – and simply disappears. It's one of nature's greatest smoke-and-mirror acts and provides among the finest of wildlife arenas on earth. But all this lay to the south and we were Zambia-bound.

Robyn slipped JJ Cale into the deck as we sped eastward. 'They call me the breeze, I keep blowing ev'ry road, I ain't got me nobody, I ain't carrying no load.' There and then I decided to christen the Land Rover, which had somehow remained nameless thus far. From now on, in my head anyway, it would be known as *The Breeze*.

The Caprivi Strip (along with the small, but strategic island of Heligoland in the North Sea) was ceded to Germany by Britain in 1890 in exchange for sovereignty over Zanzibar. This gave Germany access to the Zambezi, as well as a better shot at linking up with its East African colony, Tanganyika (Tanzania). The Zambezi, it was hoped, would give them an outlet to the Indian Ocean. The very notion infuriated that arch-imperialist Rhodes. He needn't have worried, as there was the small matter of Northern Rhodesia (Zambia) blocking the Germans' path to Tanganyika. Besides, Victoria Falls and the Kariba Gorge would have given any German captain an interesting riverboat journey down the Zambezi.

As for the Caprivi, it's remained a forsaken and wild corridor of marginal land. Poachers, fugitives from the law and escaped prisoners-of-war found refuge there. If the authorities came looking for them, it was easy to nip across into Angola, Bechuanaland (Botswana) or Southern Rhodesia (Zimbabwe) or Northern Rhodesia. The Namibian independence struggle turned it into a war zone during the 1970s and '80s – contested ground where South Africans, Portuguese, Angolans, Cubans and Namibians fell during a protracted bush war. With conflict having become a way of life in these parts, Caprivi inhabitants (with the clandestine support of Botswana) have recently been agitating for independence. One can only hope this endeavour will not see the locals dusting off their old AK47s again.

We made a slight deviation to the south to view Popa Falls, more of a cascade or series of rapids than a waterfall. Young boys offered to paddle us across to the other side in their leaky *mokoro* (dug-out canoe), claiming that the view was better from there, but I declined as the game-rich area south of Kongola beckoned and we still had a good few kilometres to cover that day.

The B8 carried us east to the Kwando crossing. This river-with-four-names starts out as the Kwando, becomes the Mashi, then the Linyanti and finally joins the Zambezi at Kazungula as the Chobe – all very confusing. The reason for our keen haste was that we'd been offered accommodation at the Namushasha Lodge. Standing on a high bank overlooking the Kwando River, the chalets all face a little Eden of aquatic wildlife.

Later we relaxed on the deck with hosts Henk and Angelique, sipping cool, strong Urbocks. Angelique kept interrupting the conversation to point out another delight: open-billed storks roosting nearby, a buffalo herd passing or elephants mangling vegetation on the floodplain below. Directly in front of us, three kingfisher species worked the same patch of water. It was idyllic and the road weariness drained from us.

The next morning Henk offered to take us in his boat to a spot where a colony of migrant carmine bee-eaters nested in the riverbank. We set off early, hippos huffing and puffing on either side of us as we motored cautiously past. Tell-tale bubble trails warned of others lurking below. Wattled cranes foraged in the shallows while fish eagles circled overhead. The fattest crocs had already booked all the best sandbars, while flattened reed beds indicated recent elephant activity.

None of this prepared us for the sight of almost a thousand rainbow-coloured carmine bee-eaters filling the air as we rounded a bend in the river. Henk cut the motor and we drifted silently down on them. The magnificent little creatures flitted in and out of their nests. 'If the nests are built high up the bank, it predicts a very wet season,' explained Henk. Nearby white-fronted bee-eaters – usually a favourite – were hardly noticed as they went about their business like bit-players, upstaged by their colourful cousins.

Katimo Mulilo is one of those far-flung outposts that some colonial power once thought important, like Etosha's Namutoni Fort a century earlier. They were usually isolated dumps of no interest to anybody, other than the poor suckers sent there to guard the empire. Sandbags dating back to the 1980s, when Katimo last assumed strategic importance during the Namibian independence struggle, still lie around. In those days thousands of South African troops were stationed there, or passed through on the way to cross-border campaigns in Angola.

We restocked at Katimo's supermarket and fuel station for the journey into remote western Zambia, and crossed at another easy-going border post. Our luck was holding. Past the ferry docking point at Sesheke, the road kept to the Zambezi's western bank, following the well-wooded course of the river.

We were now finally, and officially, off the beaten track. We'd have to be more self-reliant, as this was travelling without a safety net. Even the Landy seemed happy to be entering the wilderness fringes, hopping and skipping over the potholes and ruts. This was also baobab country. The tree is a bloated, fantastic hobgoblin, sometimes referred to as the elephant of the plant world. Livingstone was more prosaic in his description of it as 'a carrot planted upside down'. Used for its medicinal value, for water storage in times of drought and even as pulp to make paper, these prehistoric botanical monuments would punctuate our journey from here onwards as far as Ethiopia.

Mutemwa Lodge, run by former Springbok rugby player Gavin Johnson, was about 50 kilometres up the road and a welcome oasis in this isolated region. Gavin was away on business, but we were made welcome by his brother, Howard, and Anissa de Bruin, who told us of their efforts to promote Barotseland, this forgotten corner of western Zambia. Best of all was an e-mail connection through Bushmail (ours was still playing up and both of us were keen to contact home base). Communication had its pros and cons. On the positive side, it was great to keep in touch with family and friends, but on the negative, if we didn't cut ourselves off sufficiently from our lives back home, then we'd find it difficult to immerse ourselves in the road experience. It was tempting – but limiting – to travel in a comfortable, well-connected cocoon.

At 6.30 the next morning we were bobbing along on the Zambezi heading for a little-known tributary called the Njoko. Our boat avoided a large crocodile – which had already taken two of the lodge's dogs – and skimmed across a river which was wide, shallow and smooth. The banks were so heavily wooded that it was difficult to spot the side stream. But Howard knew his way, and we were soon snaking up a narrow, swift-flowing channel. After about 30 minutes, we turned around and drifted back with the current. It was utterly still and peaceful, but the amazing absence of bird or animal sounds bothered me. Barotseland is poor and its hungry people, it seems, eat what they can.

Roads in Zambia are shoddily maintained. In some commercial agricultural areas, the farmers might donate the diesel and offer a little 'incentive' to the driver of a government grader to maintain their local roads, but out here in the wilds of Barotseland the tracks probably hadn't seen a road gang since their construction. For drivers, it's a case of survival of the most cautious. Consequently we needed low range a lot of the time and the going was painfully slow.

Ngonye Waterfall, about 77 kilometres north of Mutemwa, was our goal. Eventually Robyn spotted a hand-painted sign that read 'The Real Ngonye Falls' and we took the turn down to the river. Here a group of boys offered comprehensive guarding-and-guiding services: one lot would keep an eye on our vehicle, another would row us to the other side and a third group would guide us to the best lookout point. After prolonged but good-natured negotiations over payment for the full package we set off.

The leaking dug-out made it across to where a young guide was waiting. A 40-minute walk brought us to the edge of the main cataract. An avalanche of water turned to roaring white as it foamed over the rocks, then regained its green pallor in the maelstrom below. Spray hurtled into the air, and the water's thunder drowned all other sound. While Robyn and I struggled to absorb this attack on the senses, our guide just yawned – he'd seen it too many times before. Sitting watching the cascading water, I couldn't help but feel sorry for Ngonye and its people. With Victoria Falls further downstream how could this place hope to compete? Were it not Vic Falls, international tourists would doubtless be beating a path to Ngonye.

Robyn met two young geologists fly-fishing below the falls. They'd taken time off from mapping the area for a mining company and were doing what many men dream about – camping, drinking beer and angling for tiger fish. They'd found an abandoned lodge a few kilometres downstream and had set up camp. It was Huck Finn stuff.

Beside a deep pool in the Zambezi stretched a shimmering white beach overlooked by a circle of tumbledown huts. This was Maziba Bay. The place was picture perfect and a small fee to Feliciano, the watchman, got us our choice of campsites. As attractive as the beach looked, we were warned: no swimming. Monster crocs lurked about the pool waiting for careless overlanders. But I couldn't resist at least having a good wash, and found a relatively safe spot between the rocks to bathe. Just a moment's dunk in the river made me feel so much cleaner and fresher and got the heart beating a lot faster!

The two geologists arrived to show off a beautiful 3.5-kilogram tiger fish. A bonfire was lit on the beach, onions and potatoes were wrapped in tin foil and tossed in the fire, and soon the fish was sizzling over the coals. Then, under an almost full moon, stories of the road and bush were spun deep into the night.

Strong coffee got us going the next morning. We were headed for the crossing point at Sitoti. Fortunately the ferry was temporarily out of action, a heavily laden truck stuck halfway up the ramp. I say fortunately, as it gave us time to relax and absorb the scenery and riverside pageant. Mekoro drifted by on the stream, briefly disturbing the hard-working pied kingfishers. Children splashed about in the shallows, their wet bodies glistening in the sun, while their parents waited patiently for the ferry to resume its service. The flimsy stick structures of a small market clung to the bank, the stalls offering everything from torch batteries to dried fish.

As the queue for the ferry lengthened, soldiers lounged around their truck, glad of the chance to enjoy a smoke in the shade. Meanwhile a fancy new UN Land Cruiser revved impatiently, its fashionably dressed occupants ensconced in air-conditioned comfort. A lone missionary, delving into his store of holy patience, sat meditating in a battered Land Rover. The rest of us simply loitered. Advice was shouted at the struggling truck driver while old acquaintances were renewed and new ones made. I was in no hurry; this sort of situation is what I travel the continent for.

The stricken truck was being horribly abused. Overloaded and ill-treated, lorries are the modern pack animals of Africa; the only difference is that when they die, the hyenas and vultures can't clean up, so metal carcasses litter the landscape. Eventually the truck was manhandled onto the ferry, which immediately backed out into the current, puttered across the stream and beached itself on the opposite bank. The lorry then crunched off the ramp, freeing the ferry for duty again.

Now it was our turn. It needed care and low-range to get us down the bank and up the ramp, but soon the Land Rover was safely aboard and rubbing bumpers with its new friends, the army truck, UN Land Cruiser and old missionary vehicle. Passengers streamed aboard, some pushing heavily laden bicycles, others carrying goods on their heads. In rural Africa locals seldom travel with merely a destination in mind – there's usually some business to be done along the way. Maize is cheaper in the countryside, while cloth can be bought in the city and sold at a profit in the outlying villages. And so goods are distributed and modest profits made. This trade is impossible to quantify, but it makes a mockery of official commerce figures.

After all the excitement, the ferry ride was over far too quickly. A clanging of chains, roar from the engine, billowing of black smoke... and we had crossed this important divide, leaving the south behind.

We jolted off the ferry and churned up the sandy bank. Our goal was Mongu, capital of Barotseland province. Another poorly maintained road carried us there – badly potholed tar is better than badly potholed dirt, I suppose, but only just. Our bouncing bodies certainly registered the ride.

Barotseland covers the floodplains of the upper Zambezi and is home to the Lozi people and their king, the Litunga. Formerly subjects of a British protectorate, the Lozi were granted more autonomy by the colonial authorities than any other ethnic group in Zambia. This position of pre-eminence helped them preserve their culture and traditions, most notably the Ku-omboka ceremony. This takes place every year around Easter, just before full moon, and follows the king's annual trek from his dry-season royal kraal at Lealui to the higher-lying kraal at Limulunga. As the plains begin to flood, royal war drums summon the people from miles around to watch the king embarking on his royal barge and, accompanied by musicians and attendant vessels, being paddled to his new abode. It's one of the subcontinent's oldest and most colourful ceremonies.

It's funny how an obscure little town in the middle of nowhere assumes grander proportions when you've been starved of amenities. Mongu was like a metropolis. Hell, there was a supermarket and a petrol station! We were like kids in a toyshop. The feeling soon wore off though, and we were happy to be on the road again, bound for Kafue National Park.

Piles of roughly-hewn logs lined the highway through western Zambia. Tens of thousands of trees had been chopped down. But where was all this magnificent wood going, I wondered, and could the landscape survive even another year? Smaller trees were being turned into charcoal and what remained of the once mighty forests was going up in flames so that patches of cassava could struggle in the poor, sandy soil left behind after the devastation. Deforestation is a common problem in Africa, and finding a solution is complicated by need and greed.

Kafue is enormous – more than 22 000 square kilometres. Bisected by the Great West Road that runs between Mongu and Lusaka, the park is split into a northern and southern section. Over the past two decades, during which few tourists visited Zambia, controls were lax and poaching became a severe problem. Fortunately, visitor numbers are up and better enforcement has allowed game numbers to bounce back. Most of the wildlife was still very shy, however, and the elephants in particular were restless and aggressive.

Lufupa, a rustic camp in the northern section of the reserve, lies on the banks of the Kafue River. The buildings are plain and there is no electricity in the rondavels, but this is a serious operation with good game viewing – a bush experience rather than a luxury lodge.

Our game drive early the next morning produced an exciting first for me – a pack of wild dogs squabbling over a kill. Robyn is a keen wildlife photographer and she began snapping away. The dozen healthy-looking dogs fought for chunks of a bushbuck carcass to the gruesome sound of crunching bones. Their coats were splashes of colour and blended perfectly with the undergrowth. The dominant male was hostile, intermittently growling at the vehicle while we silently endured the bites of tsetse flies.

Later, a lazy boat ride on the river yielded crocs, hippos and a variety of aquatic birdlife. A fish eagle was enticed to snatch a fish thrown by the boatman. It's a pretty cheap trick, but impressive on film if you're quick enough.

Our inboard engine chugged us quietly past the trees of a riverine forest where monkeys swung lazily from branch to branch and sinuous water monitors sunned themselves on logs. The heat of the sun made us all drowsy. We'd been travelling hard, and now, as Robyn's journey was drawing to a close, it was good to relax in surroundings so quintessentially wild.

For the night drive that evening we bundled up warmly and meandered along, quietly absorbing the sights and sounds of the bush. Nightjars flitted in and out of our headlights and frogs croaked noisily in the wetlands. A zillion stars shimmered overhead. Fields of anthills on the plains loomed like tombstones and it felt as though we were driving through a graveyard. The sombre mood was heightened when we came across a lonely, doomed lion with a wire snare attached to its leg, cutting into the flesh with each step.

The worst potholed road in the world ushered us into Lusaka. Thank goodness it was a sedate Sunday with little traffic. We joined the capital's main thoroughfare and headed for Eureka Camp, about ten kilometres south of the city. Finally we were able to unwind. No glitches so far: no run-ins with police, no border hassles, no breakdowns, not even a puncture. This trans-Africa thing was starting to look like a doddle. Could it last? I was excited about the great game parks of East Africa ahead, and Zanzibar, and beautiful Ethiopia – my favourite. Then the wide-open spaces of the Sudan and the hectic pace of Cairo. Bring it on, I thought, hungry for road.

While Robyn eagerly packed for her flight home, I used the time to clean and repack most of our gear. I re-sorted my music collection. Judith Sephuma, Eric Clapton, JJ Cale and Hugh Masekela had got us so far; now it was the turn of Ethiopia's Hamalmal Abate and great West African musicians like Fela Kuti and Ishmaël Lo. I wondered what my next travelling companion, Cameron, would be like.

So, it was one leg down, three to go. I drove Robyn to the airport along the aptly named Cairo Road. She had the escape hatch before her, but for me there was still a helluva long way to go up that road. It was only the end of the beginning.

LUSAKA TO NAIROBI

Shooting the East African breeze

Cameron Ewart-Smith

2 October 2002, somewhere over Zambia . . .

Africa is alight. From 12 000 metres the entire continent north of Johannesburg seems to be smouldering, clouds of smoke reaching up to the heavens. It's as if earth-dwellers have decided to compete with God . . . and from where I'm sitting, row 18A on a British Airways daily to Lusaka, it's still anybody's game. Great cumulus clouds form the anvils of the Almighty's effort, towers of smoke the human offering.

In some ways it's the age-old African battle. Ever since a few snooty australopithecines with lofty ideals began to consider their place in it all, they've grappled with God. For if there's one continent that should question the modern Bible's version of an all-loving God, it is Africa.

I collected my bags from the carousel, dodged two young women dressed in luminous orange who were helping arriving passengers connect their cellular telephones to a local network, deftly negotiated immigration and customs . . . and burst out into the midday heat of Lusaka. Mike and the Land Rover were nowhere to be found. All that greeted me was a cluster of taxi drivers who finally lost interest when I insisted they couldn't take me anywhere. I grabbed a piece of pavement in the sun and lay back to await Mike's arrival. It wasn't long before the characteristic grumble of our diesel engine interrupted my daydreams.

The grey stubble on Mike's chin made him look older than I remembered from previous meetings (only weeks earlier). He jumped out the vehicle and strode around extending his hand in welcome while pushing his cap – already perched at a rakish angle – to an even more tenuous position. A khaki trekking shirt hung from his wiry frame, an ever-present notebook was jammed into the thigh pocket of his shorts and his bandy legs were thrust into a pair of tired-looking sandals.

'We've got some shopping to do and I've got someone looking at the radio because it's stuffed, but I'm hoping we can get out of Lusaka this afternoon,' he said while tossing my kit onboard. We edged into the capital's sea of people, bicycles, cars and buses.

'Lock your door, this place can be pretty dodgy,' he said, giving me a knowing look.

I did as he said and we roared down Cairo Road to Mike's radio repairman, only to find the place closed for lunch. While we waited Mike filled me in on the plans, elegant in their simplicity. We'd stock up on enough food here to last us a couple of days because, he said, it's better to re-provision along the way with fresh vegetables than carry a whole vehicle load of supplies. Then we'd hit the Great North Road to Tanzania. From the border we'd cut across on the Tanzam Highway to Dar es Salaam on the coast. From there, try to get to Zanzibar. Then head back inland through the great parks of East Africa – Ngorongoro, Serengeti, Masai Mara. We'd hopefully get to stick our feet in Lake Victoria before turning northeast and ending the leg in Nairobi.

It sounded hurried – all this in little more than three weeks – and bloody expensive. East Africans are masters at milking tourist dollars. Our budget of roughly R13 000 was limited, so we'd need to live frugally: water rather than cold drinks, simple meals, the cheapest accommodation we could find and no more than a beer or two a night . . . except on special occasions.

Mike's radio guru eventually showed up and, after much fiddling, declared our radio repaired. He quickly reinstalled it, murmured something in a thick German accent about reverse dipoles, antennae length and frequency modulation, while throwing us suspicious glances from behind a drooping eyelid ideally suited to a monocle. Eventually, satisfied that everything was installed correctly, he slapped us both on the back and wished us well.

And so it was that we found ourselves on the road with a repaired radio, supplies garnered from the shiny new Shoprite at Mandla Hills and a full tank of fuel. Mike drove while I gazed out the windows. The clutter of urban life receded and soon the Land Rover was humming along through neat smallholdings and cultivated lands. Today's run was short – our plan was to put only a hundred or so kilometres between us and Lusaka before sunset. Mike had heard from some bush-wise backpackers that Fringilla Farm Lodge would be ideally situated for our plans.

We swung off the road at the black-and-white cow-shaped sign and drove slowly beside a stream of children coming and going along a dirt track leading to the farm. Those heading towards the homestead laughed and joked, nonchalantly carrying an assortment of empty containers; those going in the opposite direction carried bottles full to the brim with milk, furiously concentrating so as not to spill.

Jannie van der Berg was similarly intent on not spilling as he stared into a double 'Klippies' and Coke in Fringilla's bar later that evening. He was one of a group of South African expatriate farmers living in Zambia. This evening, however, Jannie's mind wasn't on farming. At the rate the bottle of Klipdrift was diminishing it was amazing his mind was on anything at all.

Jannie was a large man – the product of Bekker Agricultural School near the Magaliesberg. I was schooled nearby and have painful memories of rugby encounters against the 'plaasjapies' from Bekker, who relished the opportunity of increasing their season's points tally against the 'rooinekke' from Krugersdorp High School. The humiliation was often severe – especially when they'd stop kicking conversions as it wasted too much try-scoring time.

Mind you, this particular product of Bekker High wasn't quite how I remembered them. Jannie was clad in surfing board shorts, a duo-tone khaki shirt and long socks stuffed into newfangled boots, the likes of which would create a stir at mampoer festivals everywhere. He looked every bit a cross between Herman Charles Bosman and a Spice Girl.

While fashion sense wasn't Jannie's most valuable contribution to Zambia, his farming know-how certainly was. The country is blessed with fertile soil and a relatively benign climate. Unfortunately a colonial legacy, mismanagement and a complete lack of skills development has left the land largely unproductive. Hence the need for the package of talents that men like Jannie could offer. Especially as back home in South Africa there's a surplus of qualified farmers and work was hard to find. The call to dinner interrupted Jannie's Klipdrift-tinted memories and Mike and I slipped away while the two other guests, Eskom workers expanding South Africa's electricity network northwards, headed for their dinner. We returned to our camp and the remains of a passable chicken stew that Mike had cooked the previous night.

3 OCTOBER 2002, THE GREAT NORTH ROAD . . .

No time for dallying this morning, after a brisk bowl of muesli we aimed the Landy north. Now, truly, we were leaving city influence behind, passing through vast unkempt tracts of land, some of which smouldered from chitmane fires (slash-and-burn) set by villagers to improve the quality of grazing, provide space for crops and reduce mosquito habitats.

Zambia is a large country with a relatively small population, yet every few kilometres the road bisected neat villages comprising square mud-brick houses or rondavels with thatched roofs and swept courtyards. Children beamed and waved as we passed. We caught glimpses of everyday life – women carrying water, children dressed in an assortment of uniforms, a father walking his daughter to school. Here and there men held up makeshift cages fashioned from twigs containing parrots for sale. It was heart-breaking – the tiny cages were barely large enough for the birds and many looked terminally ill.

'Should we buy a few and set them free?' Mike asked, sounding exasperated. I shook my head. 'Nah, that'll just encourage the hunters. I'll bet loads of travellers try that.' Mike mumbled something about shotguns and we continued in a stony, uncomfortable silence. All one could realistically hope for was that the government, encouraged by sensible conservation initiatives, would realise that a bird in the bush is worth two in the hand, so to speak. For the parrots in those cages it was probably too late; maybe even for the whole species. But it wasn't too late to help others. For their sake, and ultimately for the bird catchers themselves, educated conservation practices and law enforcement would hopefully come to the rescue.

A checkpoint appeared up ahead. A boom blocked the road, complete with a chicane of spikes to prevent any would-be criminal from bursting through; a small sign telling visitors to 'phone this number' if they witnessed any money changing hands flapped in the wind. It was a welcome indication of the government's attempt to come to grips with corruption. A beautiful policewoman, hair drawn back from her face in stylish dreadlocks, was in command.

'Eishhh!' she exclaimed when Mike explained our route. 'It's too far . . . but at least you have the vehicle for it,' she laughed, circling our 4x4 and examining all its paraphernalia. Long-distance overlanders were clearly nothing new to her and she wore the expression of someone content with her lot and amused at our folly. To her, travelling all the way to Cairo was madness. Long journeys were only worth enduring for important occasions, such as weddings and funerals. She waved us on with a smile, her submachine-gun swaying nonchalantly on its strap as she moved her arm. I looked back, but the officers had lost interest in us and were already interrogating the occupants of the next car.

The Great North Road was in fairly good condition and although roadworks slowed us on certain stretches, we were mostly able to cruise along at 120 kilometres an hour. It was comfortable travelling. Mike tapped his wedding ring on the steering wheel in time to a blues CD as we sailed northwards. Regiments of clouds massed, waiting for the call to bombard the land with their life-giving munitions.

We turned off the road towards Kundallila Falls, following a narrow track that wove through a landscape of miombo woodland. Between the trees, knee-high grass formed a carpet under the greens, reds and browns of a leafy canopy. Cicadas filled the air with a directionless sound that seemed to project from inside my head all the way to the horizon, like some bizarre torture device.

As we turned into a small parking area near the falls, a guy on a bicycle came careering after us. He threw himself off the bike in a cloud of dust – an elaborate stopping procedure necessitated by a lack of brakes. The cyclist's name was Samuel Kamfwa and he was Kundallila's curator, guide and walking ticket office. We handed over the $6 fee and made ourselves a sandwich while Samuel laboriously issued a receipt in meticulous copperplate script.

His administrative duties complete, he led us along a path to a rickety bridge that spanned the Kaombe River. 'The last bridge was washed away,' he said, noticing our incredulous stares. 'But this one has a *wire* cable, so it will be fine. Yes, yes, very fine.'

I was not convinced and hurried across, even though, being the dry season, a collapsed bridge would only result in a wet boot or two. From the top of the falls we peered over a 30-metre drop, watching the water cascade into space. Unfortunately, Kundallila wasn't as majestic as I'd hoped. It doubtless needed a heavenly delivery.

When we got back to the vehicle we had a quick look round the falls campsite. 'Pretty shitty place to overnight. Should we go on?' Mike asked, echoing my thoughts. I agreed, and after a rapid guidebook consultation we decided to make for Kapishya Hot Springs on the historic Shiwa Ng'andu Estate.

'Look on the bright side,' said Mike, 'even if it's a bit of a drive and we arrive late, we can wallow in the hot springs first thing in the morning.' No further argument was required.

Anxious to make Kapishya, Mike pushed hard through the scorching afternoon. We resorted to the air conditioner which, combined with Mike's JJ Cale CD, provided a cool, laid-back atmosphere: 'It don't matter what you say or do; it just seems to work out, if you want it to; carry on, carry on.'

Darkness had already drawn a cloak over the landscape when we took the tree-lined road to Shiwa Ng'andu. The faint glow of a light flickering through the trees led us to Kapishya Lodge. Mike asked the guard where to camp and, rather than explain, he motioned us to follow him. He ran in front of the vehicle with his flashlight to guide us round a copse, before pointing out a road down to the campsite.

It lay in a grassy glade surrounded by trees. A few other campers were already hunkered down over their fires when we pulled up. Mike recognised two brothers he'd met earlier in the journey. They'd leapfrogged us while Mike waited for me in Lusaka. We wandered across with beers in hand to check on their news and, ever calculating, to steal a bit of their fire seeing they'd finished cooking for the evening.

Rob and Scott had been travelling in their old Series III Land Rover for a few months already and, notwithstanding the odd mishap here and there, had negotiated some pretty rough terrain. They were overlanding sedately and in style . . . slow and steady, with time to chill in places such as Kapishya. It was the complete antithesis of our journey with spanking new vehicle and time constraints.

Mike quizzed them on roads, borders, provisions and the like. I made a hurried meal of canned green beans and a roll of boerewors and then we set about pitching our tents for the evening. For Mike this was a formality. With nearly a month behind him, pitching his rooftop tent had become a cinch, but in the darkness I had to grapple with the complexities of a dome tent. And this, it seemed, had become possessed by demons somewhere between Fringilla and here.

'You need a hand?' Mike sniggered, sucking on a beer.

'Nope, I'm fine,' I snapped. Every time I got one pole lodged it would jump free as I tried to place the other. Eventually, the colour-coded poles had all been slotted in the right sleeves and my shelter took shape. Mike gave a round of applause and I tossed my gear through the flaps.

4 OCTOBER 2002, SUBMERGED AT FIRST LIGHT...

The photographer's tendency to wake at first light is both bounty and burden. I love that pre-dawn anticipation: the landscape is always alive, expectant – like a Parisian street-café owner cracking crisp tablecloths in readiness for the customary onslaught. The burden is my internal clock, which triggers my senses at dawn when I'm travelling.

When I poked my head out through the flaps it was pitch dark. To make matters worse my bed, which had seemed so welcoming the previous evening, had revolted during the night. It now had two strange lumps and a definite slope, which meant that lying back and waiting for the dawn proved long and frustrating. The sun eventually managed to wrestle control from darkness and light flooded our glade. I woke Mike and we headed to the springs for a dawn photo session in the warm waters.

Generally, I'm not a fan of hot springs. The water is usually sulphurous and it takes cajoling to convince me that I'm not going to succumb to the noxious fumes. Kapishya was pleasantly different. Clean, non-sulphurous, bath-temperature water bubbled up through soft white sand in a spring surrounded by lush vegetation. Raffia palms draped their leaves into the water. Steam rose from the surface, forming clouds in the cool air. I clicked away, getting Mike – for lack of a more comely model – to pose. Eventually he lost his patience with my artistic whims and yelled, 'Put the fucking camera away and let me wallow in peace!'

Good muesli, it must be said, is reliant on good, cold milk, and as I scrunched through my bowl I wondered how travellers like Livingstone and Selous handled life on the road without an onboard fridge. Our Land Rover was of course kitted to the hilt, but as far as I was concerned most of it could have remained behind. Our travelling fridge, however, seemed to me the pinnacle of human invention. Cold milk aside, I suppose Livingstone would have been astounded at the speed and distances of our modest expedition. That two men in one vehicle could travel hundreds of kilometres a day through the heart of Africa would have blown his missionary mind.

Wherever we went, travellers marvelled at all our toys. They would stand around whistling reassuringly or clucking worriedly, while offering opinions on everything from tyre-tread patterns to the validity of snorkels (the plastic tube that lifts the engine's air intake to roof height). Not being very technically minded, all Mike and I could do was nod approvingly and mention snippets we'd picked up from the previous petrol-heads' observations. These generally seemed to do the trick and we soon became adept at convincing people we were de facto off-road experts when in reality neither of us knew where the carburettor was.

In our defence, we had got the knack of most of our onboard technology. Since Lusaka we'd properly got the hang of Bushmail and, what with regular snippets from home and BBC Africa, world developments were hard to escape. It also meant work was never far away as we were required to provide updates for the *Getaway* website, including replies to a selection of goodwill messages and general queries from readers. Mike and I shared these duties, which often involved trying to allay uninitiated readers' fears of impassable roads, landmines and fatal diseases.

After breakfast Mike went off to gather more intelligence from Rob and Scott, especially GPS co-ordinates, which were Mike's particular travel passion. He never tired of gathering titbits for his Cape-to-Cairo guidebook. Meanwhile I wandered down to the river, which cut across a corner of the campsite, to chat with some workers busy on a contraption that resembled the step machines one normally associates with city gyms.

Bright Katongo toiled away, maintaining a steady, high-stepping gait on the machine. This powered a small piston which sucked water from the nearby river and forced it uphill to storage tanks above the ablutions on the far side of the campsite. Feeling a little road-weary and in need of some exercise, I asked whether I could give it a try. Much to the gathered workers' amusement, I mounted the steps and carried on where Bright left off. Their bemusement turned to discomfort, though, as I continued 'climbing' away, enjoying my exercise, while they sat about doing nothing. Eventually, and much to their relief, I relinquished my spot, aware that the 'mzungu' was causing some angst by doing their morning's task for them.

I asked Bright a little about life on the farm and we were soon talking about our respective wives and his three kids. The oldest was five and would soon be ready for school. 'Education is so very important,' he confided. 'Without it what future does my child have?'

I nodded at the rhetorical question. In theory Zambia has a good record as far as education goes and the country provides free schooling at junior levels. Alas, the economics don't quite match the ideology.

'It would be better if I had some land of my own,' Bright continued. 'But at least we have a small area near our house where we can plant some crops. I'm happy here and we are treated well.'

I wanted to continue chatting, but Mike was making ready to leave. As I headed back to the vehicle, I marvelled at the burning reverence Bright had for schooling. Ultimately, survival in an educated world depended on one's ability to gain that education, but how trigonometry and Latin were going to help a Zambian school kid in the middle of nowhere posed some interesting questions.

We pulled out of camp and headed to Shiwa Ng'andu's manor house, stopping at a majestic gatehouse guarding a tree-lined avenue. After much haggling, we purchased two tickets for a house tour, a loaf of bread and a big bag of fresh peanuts. Mike convinced the fastidious gatekeeper to allow us to take our vehicle up to the house. After a wrong turn and an unintentional tour past a collection of red-brick workers' cottages, we pulled up at the main building. Compared to the desolate countryside we'd passed through the previous day, the colonial opulence before us seemed wholly out of place.

Shiwa Ng'andu had obviously seen better days, but renovations were in full swing. Men scurried about bearing boards heaped with plaster, roofing materials and an assortment of tools. Even in its state of semi-repair, the building held its dignity with a stiff upper lip. The place resembled a Victorian country estate in the south of England. Above the red-brick walls between white balustrades dangled a rusting coat of arms. The lawn was immaculate and bordered by beds overflowing with purple verbenas and rose bushes that bore the season's last tattered blooms.

As we approached the front entrance, a well-spoken young man wearing an apron welcomed us. 'Ah yes. The gate phoned to say you were coming up.' He laughed, stretching out a hand, a broad smile on his round face. 'I'm Bright Sikana, the housekeeper-cum-tour-guide at Shiwa Ng'andu. Unfortunately, I'm busy with another party right at the moment. Please be patient and I'll come for you as soon as I've finished with them. It shouldn't take more than 20 minutes or so.'

When Bright reappeared, he led us through a small side door into the chapel. 'Shiwa Ng'andu is the creation of Stewart Gore-Brown. The young gentleman fell in love with Africa after being appointed to the Anglo-Belgian Boundary Commission in 1911, while those two nations divvied up the spoils of their colonial imperialism,' Bright began in his very formal manner. 'Upon completion of his commission duties, he returned to the area with an entourage of 30 porters, looking for a piece of land to buy. Eventually he stumbled across what he considered the perfect spot on the slopes of the hill which you saw behind the house overlooking the lake. He purchased 10 000 acres and named the estate after the lake, Ishiba Ng'andu, meaning "lake of the royal crocodile".'

The local villagers were relatively recent arrivals in the area and were apparently friendly. Legend has it that the tribe, which was originally from the Congo, had come across a dead crocodile on the banks and, deciding this was a good omen, settled here.

Gore-Brown was an industrious man and set about carving a farm from the surrounding wilds. However, almost immediately all work was stopped while he returned to serve with the British forces in the First World War. Six years later he was back, and the farm began to take shape. It was obvious that the isolation from world markets and absence of an efficient transport system would require a novel approach and he initially set about farming citrus and extracting essential oils. This was ideal, as the resultant product was relatively valuable per unit mass, requiring minimum bulk transportation.

Work was also started on the manor house. Armed with a military building manual and the ingenuity to make all the materials he required, Gore-Brown trained carpenters and blacksmiths. Finally, in 1932, work was completed and the new lord of the manor started importing the appropriate furniture and fittings from England. These were shipped out and transported overland in ox-wagons along the rough dirt tracks which were slowly threading like veins across the middle of the Dark Continent.

Bright led us through the main house. Faded, sepia-toned pictures adorned the walls, their subjects staring down with watery eyes. One photograph featured Gore-Brown with two dead lions; in another he sat beside Kenneth Kaunda. I poked my head through a door leading into the dining room where one place was laid for lunch – sterling-silver cutlery and lead crystal on an enormous hardwood table. Among the valuable Victorian crystal on the shelves of the server I glimpsed a Snackwich toaster, which somehow epitomised the incongruity of the place.

Our guide told us that it was Gore-Brown's grandchildren, the Harveys (tour operators in nearby North Luangwa National Park), who were busy restoring Shiwa Ng'andu to its former glory. These days it's run as a guesthouse for Europeans yearning to recapture a colonial past. The only guest during our visit was a German big-game hunter. No doubt somewhere a doe-eyed trophy was keeping him from his lunch.

Bright offered to walk us up to the graves of Gore-Brown's children, who'd been murdered on a nearby farm. 'The perpetrators were never found, but rumours say it was a group of poachers annoyed with the Harveys' conservation efforts,' Bright told us solemnly as he struck off at a fast pace.

'My grandparents worked for Gore-Brown, my parents were born on the farm and worked here all their lives,' he said as we huffed after him. 'But I am planning to go to college. I finished grade 12 and I'm hoping that the Harveys might help me get to teachers' training college. Otherwise I will work here until I've enough money. Then I'll go.

'You know, they say many good things about Chipembele – or 'rhino', as the people called Gore-Brown after he killed one. But he was a harsh man. Fair but hard . . . but he could have been much worse. We could have had someone like Cecil John Rhodes. . . Tell me, is it true Rhodes stole Zimbabwe from the Matabele?'

I considered the question and wondered how best to answer. Eventually, I shrugged my shoulders and nodded. 'Yes, in a way I suppose he did.'

I asked Bright what he thought of the current farm invasions going on in that country.

'Well, it's good for business. We'll surely get more tourists. Also, suddenly we're the stable nation in the region along with South Africa. That must be good for us. I don't think anything like that will happen here though – we have enough space in Zambia for everyone.' I smiled at the answer. It was characteristic of Zambians to be unfailingly welcoming and friendly. Could their relatively painless road to independence have had something to do with it?

Covered in sweat, we finally arrived at a low, chain-link fence surrounding four neat graves overlooking Gore-Brown's beloved estate. In the distance Ishiba Ng'andu glittered in the midday sunlight. Standing there, I could see exactly why that soldier, son of England and Knight of the Realm, had traded Britain for the Zambian wilds.

Mike braked suddenly, bringing the Landy to a halt, and threw it into reverse. 'What's up?' I asked, looking up from the guidebook I was scrutinising to find somewhere to spend the night.

'Two white women hitching on the side of the road,' said Mike. 'Thought I'd investigate.'

I smiled: typical Mike. He never missed a chance and I could only imagine what fantastic scenes were playing out in his head as we roared back the hundred or so metres.

'Hi theeer,' one of the women greeted us with an American drawl. 'We were wonderin' if you'd be able to give us a lift up the road. We're Peace Corps volunteers headin' back to Isoka.'

'Well, in that case, get stuffed,' I replied. Then, thinking they might not get my irony, I leapt out to help load their dusty packs onto the roof.

'Would you have space for all three of us?' she asked, pointing to a young villager standing on the verge. 'Carson here has got to go to the dentist.' The boy looked less than enthusiastic at the prospect, his eyes large with fear.

'Sure, sure,' Mike fussed, 'just be careful of our radio.' This was positioned behind the centre console in the passenger's foot well. We rearranged the back seat, moving camera gear and bags out of the way. Then the women climbed in, sandwiching Carson between them. 'Keep your feet off the radio, Carson, otherwise you'll break it,' Mike urged, a concerned note in his voice.

Liz Scriven and Alexa Panagoulis had been living in this part of Zambia for two years and were teaching villagers how to farm fish. Normally Peace Corps volunteers and aid workers get under my skin pretty quickly with their self-righteousness. And it didn't take long before conversation turned to the merits of foreign volunteerism and aid in Africa. After all, my argument ran, if the programmes weren't initiated by the villagers themselves, what chance did they stand of being continued after the mzungus pulled out?

To my surprise Liz nodded in agreement. 'You know, one of the problems with the Peace Corps is that youngsters come here thinkin' they're gonna change the world. They're . . . I mean we're, just not. Honestly though, I feel that my two years here won't be wasted. For one, I have gained terrifically by bein' associated with a culture outside of my own . . . and you know, in truth, if I leave one individual better off when I go home, well then I think I've been kinda successful.'

This wasn't the usual rhetoric of the Peace Corpsniks I'd bumped into elsewhere. In fact, Liz had a point. Sure, in the greater scheme of things the projects have a so-so success rate, but if one does break it down to individuals . . .

I pondered this as Mike asked them more about where they stayed, how many volunteers were in the area, what sort of fish they were farming. As they answered, my respect for these two began to grow. After only three months' basic training they're dumped in, I mean assigned to, villages. There they live and work alone, separated from their compatriots. In anyone's book, it must be pretty tough to land up thousands of miles from home in an area as culturally different as these African villages must seem to them.

We pulled into Isoka and deposited our passengers at their friend's place, which turned out to be the local butcher. On their advice, Mike and I decided to buy meat for the next night's braai. The butcher waved away the clouds of flies that descended on her meat the moment she lifted the fridge lid. Mike ordered two T-bone steaks and, after much discussion with an assistant, she chopped the piece of meat, dropped two slabs into a plastic bag and said, 'That'll be 4 900 kwacha' ($1).

We bade Liz, Carson and Alexa goodbye and headed off in search of a general dealer to stock up on basics. We found the tiny Shopleft – a playful dig at Shoprite, the big South African supermarket chain expanding into this part of Africa. Although the store was no bigger than a shipping container, the shelves were tightly packed with a surprising array of goods and we bought spaghetti, Mazoe Orange, cans of beans and tins of tomatoes. Although money was tight, we splashed out – for Mike a milkshake and for me a Coke.

'By the way,' I said, back in the vehicle, 'did you notice the price of Cokes at Shopleft is half that at Shiwa Ng'andu . . . and they're even cold?'

My driving companion smiled and said, 'That, young man, is the price we travellers pay for tourism.'

Mike didn't start shouting until the large woman, dressed in a flower-print dress which gave her a remarkable resemblance to a giant frangipani, crossed her arms and refused to allow us into Tanzania. No matter what tack we took, she simply wouldn't budge. It was a $20 temporary import permit for our vehicle or a night spent in the no man's land between Zambia and Tanzania.

Borders in Africa are never quiet places. There's always a crowd of 'facilitators' trying to convince you to employ them to help you through the intricacies of border bureaucracy. It's as if they've decided there's no way a tourist could possibly understand the complexities of the forms and procedures required. And often they're right.

Mike and I had already spent more than an hour at Taduma border post. Admittedly, I should have familiarised myself with border requirements for this leg of the journey. But at that moment all I could do was shrug my shoulders and frantically page through the guidebooks trying to work out whether Mike was justified in losing his temper. He was convinced we were being fleeced. Every time we turned round it seemed there was another tax, admin fee or insurance levy. The temporary import permit had been the last straw.

'I tell you, they're ripping us off,' Mike insisted, while I ham-fistedly tried the old line: 'Your minister of tourism is a personal friend of mine.' But it was to no avail. When I agreed to pay as long as she gave me her name and rank, she flatly refused. 'Stuff it!' shouted Mike. 'What's wrong with you? Can't you see how bad this is for tourism?'

The woman stared back balefully and I got the inkling Mike may have just crossed some invisible line. She stormed out with our passports and, when she eventually returned, I was relieved it wasn't with the machine-gun-toting guard who was patrolling the fence.

'Okay, okay,' I sighed, 'here's your $20. But,' and here I raised myself to my full but modest height, 'I'm going to discuss this with my friend the minister!'

It had been our intention from the start to avoid travelling at night and as darkness rolled across Tanzania we felt our way along uneven tar. For the first time on the trip I was truly concerned. I sat in the passenger seat peering into the gloom created by our headlights. '*Bicycle!*' I'd yell, as one would veer into our path, seemingly oblivious to our presence. Drunks, trucks, unlit cars and hundreds of pedestrians streamed along the road in both directions. Driving faster than 30 kilometres an hour would have been suicidal. And so it was that we crawled into Mbeya and, after asking directions at two fuel stations, located a little hotel a short distance from the main road.

Holiday Lodge and Restaurant was a dreary place inspired by the most proletarian East German design. We found the proprietor seated behind glass in a small kiosk and sweating profusely. Mike enquired whether there were rooms available and, after a lengthy consultation with his ledger, the man confided that he just might have space for the two of us. In the restaurant behind us a television blared and the sound of laughter accompanied the clinking of beer bottles as patrons tucked into their daily dish of *nama choma* (an assortment of grilled meat).

Mike went off to bring the Land Rover into a small courtyard filled with vehicles. It was a real who's who of the African road. Here was a *matatu* held together with bits of wire, a sedan car in reasonable condition, a white Toyota Land Cruiser with World Health Organisation stickers on the doors . . . and our safari vehicle.

We were ushered to the second floor and into a small room with a musty odour and paint peeling off the walls. It had a desk and two beds over which dangled a pair of tatty mosquito nets. We lugged up our gear and, while Mike wrote an e-mail home, I heated a can of sweet corn and leftover boerewors.

'Haven't we got any beers in the fridge?' I asked. Mike looked up from his typing and in a flash he'd disappeared downstairs. He soon returned with two ice-cold Zambezi lagers. And while we sat down to our humble fare, we chatted about the route ahead. We were more than a day's drive from Dar, so we'd need to find another overnight spot somewhere along the road.

'It shouldn't be that tricky,' said Mike. 'The guidebook has loads of places. And besides, we can always ask along the way.'

'More importantly,' I offered, 'what are we going to do about these bloody Tanzanian park entrance fees? I don't think we can afford to go to Ruaha *and* the Serengeti. Also, we haven't a clue how much Zanzibar is going to cost. According to the guidebooks it looks pretty stiff.'

Mike remained silent, then continued with the philosophical tack he'd taken every time I'd brought up finances, saying, 'We'll just have to see what happens, won't we?'

That wasn't good enough for me and while Mike lovingly transcribed the GPS co-ordinates he'd taken during the day, I sat worrying about the money. Shillings, dollars, exchange rates, receipts, ledgers – it was semi-organised chaos. Keeping tabs on cash is not my forte. I generally find that I always seem to have less than I thought I should have at the end of the month, yet here I was the designated book-keeper and stasher of cash. So I re-counted everything, fiddling with my calculator and trying to work out how much we could spend. Every now and again I'd say something like, 'Hey Mike, I reckon it's a hundred bucks a day from here on,' only to be met with disinterested grunts from the other side of the room.

5 OCTOBER 2002, SWEATING IT OUT IN MBEYA . . .

After a fitful night plagued by dreams of mosquitoes fashioned out of $100 bills, I was surprised how pleasant the little hotel appeared in the soft morning light. Reproaching myself for my initial prejudice I wandered to the bathroom to install my contact lenses, only to realise, with vision restored, that my reaction the night before was probably an underestimate. If anything the hotel looks worse in the morning light. So now I'm headed for a run to get the stale, musty air out of my lungs.

I grabbed my running shoes and, leaving Mike sound asleep, hit the roads of Mbeya. The sun was slanting in at a jaunty angle, filling the shopfronts with golden light that greatly improved the dreary town. People were emerging onto the streets and already the odd stall in the market was preparing for the day's trading.

I ran on, an anomaly creating much interest from locals, who stared at me in wonder. At first I thought it was because I was a mzungu on the run. But then, after passing other joggers, I began to realise it probably had more to do with how I was dressed. I had donned a pair of skimpy running shorts and a light vest – standard running garb where I come from. But the runners I passed were all dressed to the gills, like something out of a Rocky movie. Full tracksuits with hoods were obligatory and towels draped over the shoulders seemed to come highly recommended.

I tried to keep pace with the locals, but stood little chance as they disappeared into the distance, intent on their workouts. Eventually I turned for home, bathed in sweat. The sun now carried more meaning and already the temperature was fast rising towards 30 degrees. How those joggers coped in their garb I'll never know.

We pulled out of Mbeya and eased back onto the Tanzam Highway. Mike looked across and said, 'By the way, I didn't realise the minister is a friend of yours. That could be very useful you know.'

6 OCTOBER 2002, THE MORNING AFTER THE NIGHT BEFORE . . .

'Aaah, this is what death is like.' As I opened my eyes a crack the light streamed into my vacant mind and exploded as if a laser had struck a room full of mirrors. I vainly tried to clamp my eyes shut to block any further pain . . . to no avail. The owner of Baobab Campsite had welcomed us warmly the night before and, unfortunately, that welcome had spilled into the bar.

One of the downsides of being a travel journalist is that hosts sometimes think the drunker they get you, the better their write-up will be. Of course one tries to avoid such complications by declining offers of free-flowing alcohol. That is, of course, unless the place is pretty groovy right from the start. Then the review is going to be favourable anyway, so why not share the owner's enthusiasm for his establishment while piling into the secret store that always seems to materialise from behind the bar after the other guests have retired.

Situated roughly midway between the border and Dar es Salaam, Baobab had been recommended to us earlier in the day by the owners of another stopover – Kisolanza Farm. A few kilometres past the turnoff to Iringa, the Tanzam Highway sweeps down into the surprisingly steep Ruaha River valley and follows the course of the great Ruaha until it rises once more out of the baobab-studded valley on the far side. We slowed the vehicle, beginning to recognise the landmarks we'd been told about. A short dirt road led us to the camp, situated on the northern bank of the Ruaha.

'Excuse the appearance, but I've been in the village building a school,' owner Darren Coetzee explained, with the faintest Australian accent. He was in his early 30s, barefoot with reddish blond hair and dressed in a holed shirt and dirty shorts.

'You can park wherever you want. We're expecting only one overland truck and they always take the grassy patch over there, so park on the far side of the ablutions.' He pointed at a large baobab surrounded by a tall grass screen. We found an ideal spot far enough away from the overlanders – a usually loud and often loutish bunch – and pitched camp under a magnificent baobab with a girth wider than our vehicle.

We'd finished our last two beers the night before, so Mike dug around in the back of the vehicle and emerged with a bottle of shiraz – one of a case he'd packed before leaving Cape Town. He opened the bottle and, with much deliberate ceremony, let it breathe while washing the dregs of Mazoe Orange out of the stainless steel beakers – now transformed to wine glasses – which came with our camping cutlery-and-crockery set.

I chopped veggies while Mike went off to organise wood for a fire. Soon he had a merry blaze going, poured our wine and there we sat, watching the fire slowly die to coals and talking about the endless African road, distant wives and the comforts of home, pleasantly avoiding the regular 'where to stay, what to do and whether we can afford it' conversations.

I fetched the meat and laid it on the chopping board. 'Say Mike, isn't T-bone called T-bone 'cause of the T-bone?' He wandered over and surveyed the slabs of red meat.

'Um, I think you might be right. Maybe it's rump.'

We looked more closely at the cut, but it didn't resemble any rump steak I'd ever eaten. 'Nope, I don't think so, but never mind, let's get it on the fire. How do you like yours? Rare-medium-rare?'

Mike nodded as I slapped the steak onto the grid. A satisfying hisssh, accompanied by the spicy smell of grilling steak, filled the evening air.

The meat scorched on the hot fire and I turned it after a few moments. We piled our plates with fresh green beans and potatoes purchased from Kisolanza Farm's stall and added the steaks, cooked to perfection.

'Hmm – this knife seems a little blunt, Mike,' I said, struggling to force the blade through the flesh. 'Mine too,' Mike replied.

Trying to chew a morsel I'd eventually managed to slice, confirmed my worst suspicions. This was no T-bone, rump or any other kind of steak cut. This was probably a transverse slice through the hind leg of a very old cow, which was now doing its best to imitate good Italian leather. Eventually I swallowed the gristly lump. We ate in silence, diligently chewing away, although this seemed to have little effect on the meat.

'Not very good, is it?' I ventured. Mike nodded, his mouth full. I watched a lump slide down his throat, like an ostrich swallowing something too large for its neck.

'Doesn't taste all that bad though,' Mike replied, laughing at the crushed look on my face.

For two days since purchasing the steak, we'd been enthusing about how great it was going to be. Now I simply pushed the remains of the cooked shoe to the far side of the plate and finished off the vegetables, grumbling under my breath.

To drown our sorrows we headed for a nightcap in the bar just as the overland truck arrived, disgorging a collection of anxious foreigners. While they went about pitching tents and getting supper on the go, Mike and I drank a beer, compliments of Darren, who sympathised with the meat issue, having had some experience with local butchers.

But, as with most of the new breed of adventurers setting up businesses in Africa, overcoming adversity was part of the challenge. Darren was a prime example, and as he talked about the local school they were building to contribute to the development of his neighbouring villagers, I began to imagine that this time round possibly, just possibly, these neo-colonialists may be getting it right.

'I've shot the camel,' Darren said solemnly. This was much, much later, after the overlanders had turned in exhausted by their first day in the 'wilds'. I looked up from my beer, noting the serious look in Darren's steel-coloured eyes.

'How do you mean?' I asked.

'I mean I'm here to stay. This is my home and when I die, they can take me up there on that hill and bury me.' I studied the determined face, squarely set jaw and thought about how history had treated previous settlers, many who'd displayed equal or greater fortitude.

I stumbled back to my tent sometime after 2 a.m., cursing the labyrinth of tents set by the overlanders to test my navigation skills. Having tripped over two guy-ropes and woken one couple, who probably thought I was a lion, I found my dome-shaped home and crawled into bed.

The first barrage announced itself with a splat on the windscreen the size of a particularly large bug. Another followed closely, then another, until the windscreen wipers did little more than offer momentary glimpses of the road ahead. We were entering the outskirts of Dar es Salaam and already the vegetation had changed from dry acacia savanna to the lush green of a tropical coastline. The rain, which had been threatening all the way from Lusaka, now seemed intent on making up for lost time.

It was hot and humid. People were everywhere, dashing between showers or cowering under umbrellas that seemed, in most cases, too small to prevent a solid drenching. Some simply ignored the deluge and walked on as if oblivious to the torrent. We skirted the city, heading north towards one of the campsites on Bahiri Beach.

When we found the ocean it was cordoned off behind a high barbed-wire fence patrolled by armed guards. One rushed across and opened a boom, allowing us to enter a sandy compound containing four or five overland trucks, enough to suggest we needed to get out of there, fast. Mike, however, seemed intent on staying, so we hopped out to investigate costs and, when the rain let up, take a gander at the Indian Ocean.

On the beach I discovered a collection of rosy-red Europeans who'd emerged after the downpour. A German couple stalked past wearing the burn-lines of new arrivals. The water was a murky, unpleasant brown but there were nevertheless a handful of tourists frolicking in the gentle surf. I flopped onto the sand to wait for Mike and watch the mzungus enjoying the water.

He joined me about half an hour later, beaming with anticipation. 'So what 'ya think? It's not that expensive. Should we stay?'

I looked up sharply. 'Are you kidding me, Mike? This place sucks, big time. Too many people, overland trucks, shit beach . . . need I go on? I reckon we move on to Bagamoyo. It's only an hour or so north of here.'

Mike sat down looking deflated. 'But . . . but, why not stay here and then head there tomorrow. Besides, didn't you say something about a contact in Dar who could get us to Zanzibar.'

I'd met a representative from Zanzibar at a travel show who'd enthusiastically offered to help us. However, I was reluctant to take up the offer. Generally the touristy spots are expensive and my contact would probably arrange a posh hotel. It wasn't the point of the trip and I decided not to pursue it. Mike looked perplexed as his vision of fluffy white gowns and room service disintegrated.

'I think you're crazy,' he said, shaking his head. 'But if you insist, let's hit Bagamoyo and check it out.'

The city invaded my senses as we headed north once more. It was a heady mixture – pleasant and vaguely nauseating in one breath: stagnant water, piles of oranges, grilling nama choma, roasting corn-cobs, mounds of trash. Curiously, a profusion of plant nurseries lined the road. It seemed there must be huge business in gardening. Collections of cuttings from the numerous bushes and trees that thrive in these idyllic conditions were stuffed into old cans.

The gatekeeper at Bagamoyo's Traveller's Lodge pointed us towards a shady spot under towering coconut palms surrounded by chalets. A handful of tourists were already enjoying sundowners in the bar and the sound of laughter wafted down to us as we set up camp. This was more like it, I thought. Even Mike accepted it'd been the correct decision to get clear of the city.

Tropical evenings don't hang around and night descended on our camp. Having learnt our lesson with the steak, we prepared a vegetable stir-fry from the remains of our Kisolanza shopping. The humidity of the day's rain hung in the air. Bob Marley wailed from the CD. Life was good. We'd decided to chill a little in Bagamoyo, take a break from the road, tighten the odd bolt which had worked itself loose (vehicle and otherwise) and tend to our various housekeeping duties. We also needed to find a way of getting to Zanzibar on the cheap.

Our guidebook stated categorically that catching a dhow from Bagamoyo to Zanzibar was both illegal and dangerous. But with Dar's ferries charging prices aimed at dollar-rich tourists, we had no option but to investigate this alternative. The first inkling that it might even be possible had come from Marcel, the jolly-faced manager at Traveller's Lodge.

'Some of the backpackers take that route,' the Dutchman told us over a beer. 'But don't go down there and jump on the first boat you find. I'll get one of my guys to come and see you in the morning. He'll make sure you're not ripped off. Oh, and that you get a decent skipper who's likely to get you *all* the way there. You shouldn't pay much more than $6 or so a person each way. But,' he said, beckoning one of his staff nearer, 'Gregory here will find out more.'

He quickly explained to Gregory Muyango, one of the lodge's waiters, what was required and arranged for him to come by in the morning to discuss things further.

7 OCTOBER 2002, NO RELIGION PLEASE, I'M SLEEPING . . .

'Crikey, that's commitment!' At 4.15 a.m. – well, so my watch said – the local imam began calling the faithful to prayer. I tried to drown out the sound with my pillow, but it had little effect. Then the Catholics, not to be outdone, began ringing their bells too.

For a few minutes the morning peace of this coastal town was ripped apart as the two religions vied for souls. Further sleep was impossible, so I got out of bed and set off for a run along the beach. The sun raised itself slowly, also seeming a little startled by the noise.

Gregory, no longer in his uniform but decked out in a pair of smart blue flannels and a maroon-collared shirt, was discussing arrangements for our dhow trip with Mike when I returned. He then set off to negotiate with the skippers on our behalf. We did our washing and then I sat down with a book to enjoy the sun. Mike tinkered with his notes and was in the middle of typing an e-mail when an attractive young woman walked across to us.

'Is this a real safari vehicle?' She had a thick Scandinavian accent. The sunlight pouring over her shoulder caught in her locks of golden hair. Her piercing blue eyes had a sparkle and she wore an innocent smile. She cast her eye slowly over our camp, taking in the washing strung between a nearby tree and our vehicle's roof rack, gas stove, fold-up chairs and table. I glanced at the line and was relieved to see a pair of shorts obscuring my threadbare jocks.

'Er, well yes... I mean no... I mean we're on our way from Cape Town to Cairo. We're sort of journalists,' said Mike.

The blue eyes came back to rest on Mike. 'Oh, I see. Can you take us on safari?' she asked, pointing to a friend who'd wandered over to join her. 'I'm Elisabeth by the way, and this is Katrina.' The friend was shorter and had tightly curled auburn hair. Her honey-brown eyes smiled in welcome. 'We're dancers from Stockholm University... in Sweden.'

'Well, unfortunately we're going to Zanzibar,' I said. 'But how long are you here for? We're heading to the Serengeti in a couple of days' time when we get back from Zanzibar. And you'd be more than welcome to join us then.' Mike nodded enthusiastically in agreement.

'Oh,' said Katrina, an uncertain note in her voice. 'What's the Serengeti? Is it close?' Mike and I looked at each other, not sure how exactly to reply.

'This is our first visit to Africa. We're exchange students working at Tanzania's only music school,' Katrina explained. This happened to be located in Bagamoyo and they'd flown directly into Dar es Salaam. 'We're here for two weeks, but we work every morning so we could join you for an afternoon. I've always wanted to see an elephant,' she continued excitedly. In her mind's eye she envisaged that beyond the city limits Wild Africa roamed.

We explained the logistics and, looking crestfallen, the two departed for their classes. I glanced across at Mike. 'Can you think of anywhere where we could take them?'

He shook his head and returned to his e-mail, saying, 'But, I'm sure going to think hard about it.'

Later that afternoon Gregory returned, informing us he'd found a skipper who could be trusted. 'We need to go to Customs House now, to speak with the customs officer and have your passports stamped,' he told us.

We gathered our documents and followed him through town.

Bagamoyo was slowly falling to pieces. We passed magnificently carved doors, similar to those one associates with Zanzibari tourism brochures. The wood was turning grey from constant sun and little care. People came and went through the intricately worked doorways, seemingly oblivious to the masterpieces framing them. Thank goodness a few concerned citizens are initiating projects to protect and restore parts of the historic old town – if not to their former glory, at least to their former infamy. Bagamoyo was, after all, one of East Africa's slave-trading capitals in the 19th century.

In its heyday Bagamoyo was a flourishing centre and huge caravans arriving from or setting off for the interior were everyday occurrences. Explorers such as Burton, Speke, Stanley and Livingstone all passed through the town on their African adventures. The name Bagamoyo, it is thought, derives from the caravan porters – a corruption of *bwagamoyo*, which means 'to throw off melancholy'. Ironically bagamoyo means 'crush your heart' – entirely fitting when one considers that 50 000 slaves a year arrived there destined for the Zanzibari slave markets.

Bowing to British pressure, the Sultan of Zanzibar eventually outlawed slaving. Without it, Bagamoyo's importance began to decline. Even the Germans, who initially thought the town ideal for their colonial headquarters, decided to move south to Dar es Salaam and take advantage of its better anchorage. These days, all that remains of the German influence are a few decaying buildings, the impressive Customs House and a very big mission.

A collection of dhows lay keeled over on wide tidal flats that stretched out from the foot of Customs House. We pushed through a throng of people and caught snippets of a heated discussion in Swahili. 'They're haggling over shipping charges for their produce,' Gregory explained. 'Everything is a negotiation in Tanzania, it's the way we do things. So *never* accept the first price asked.'

The customs official was a large man, as his status no doubt required. He beamed at us as we entered, his smile startlingly white in a face of rough-hewn coal. 'So what is your purpose for going to Zanzibar,' he asked, a crease forming on his brow.

'We're tourists,' Mike and I replied together.

'Ah. Good. Good. You know that we cannot be held responsible if the boat sinks or you are killed while crossing,' he continued in a confidential, business-like manner. 'You will have to sign a declaration to that effect.' The officer scratched in his drawer before producing a sheet of paper. He then proceeded to write out a rough indemnity form and handed it over to Mike to fill in our names and passport details. The customs man signed it with a flourish and then, as if an afterthought, smashed his stamp onto the page. After subjecting our passports to similar treatment he stood up and wished us well, a broad smile returning to his face.

'How much does that cost?' I asked, digging in my pocket for the roll of Tanzanian shillings. He looked confused. 'There is no charge for this service – just have a safe journey.'

'*Asante sana*' ('thank you'), Mike and I replied together and retreated into the crowd which had come no closer to reaching an agreement on shipping charges. If anything, the argument was in stalemate, each waiting for the other to concede, while the tide grew ever closer to the boats. And therein lay their skill as negotiators. They would remain cool right to the last minute, arguing all day if need be. Until eventually, with only moments to spare before the high tide returned to prevent any further loading of the dhows, a deal would be struck. Then the cargo would be loaded with alacrity and the boat prepared for sea.

Gregory led us through the crowd until he found our skipper. Juma Ali Hamisi was a tall, thin man with an angular jaw. His face was pocked with acne scars and his front teeth were stained yellow and chipped. He couldn't speak a word of English. Gregory assured us he was the best skipper in town and could be trusted not to toss us overboard once we'd reached open water. This was, according to Gregory, a favourite trick of some of the less savoury characters who ply the Bagamoyo-to-Zanzibar route.

With Gregory interpreting, we negotiated to meet at 10 p.m. Juma wanted a deposit, but I refused, saying I'd pay him the entire amount when we reached Zanzibar. After a few moments of haggling we agreed on a price: $10 a person each way, which was more than we wanted to spend, but significantly less than the ferry.

Our negotiations complete, we packed up camp and stashed our valuables in the relative safety of Marcel's office. Then we headed for the beach to enjoy the last hours of sunshine. The Swedish dancers were already there, tanning in their bikinis. They waved hello as we laid our towels on the sand nearby. I hauled out my book and Mike worked on his notes. Eventually, the soporific effects of the sun had my head dipping and I dozed off.

I was woken by a quick inhalation of breath from Mike. Looking up I saw that Katrina was practising some of the dance steps she'd been working on. With eyes closed she glided over the sand. Two fishermen re-caulking their dhow nearby stopped work, spellbound. All eyes feasted on the lithe apparition ghosting across the beach.

Suddenly Katrina opened her eyes with a start, returning from the stage in her mind, and shot me a coy glance. For a moment she looked directly at me and, just when the horizon began to shift, she broke away, returning to her towel.

'It's going to be a long journey,' Mike hissed under his breath. 'A very long journey indeed.'

Juma led us through a darkened town. Deon and Susan van Zyl, two South Africans we'd met earlier in the day, tagged along, also keen to avoid the exorbitant fees charged by the ferry operators. The place was almost deserted and shafts of light spilled into the street from windows. In the distance a dog warned of our passing, but no one paid it any attention.

The tide was still some way out, yet close enough to make the sand damp. Shallow depressions were filling, the water table now only centimetres below the surface. Juma helped us aboard, and gestured for us to wait. Another crew member appeared out of the dark and told us to make ourselves comfortable, it would be a few hours yet before there was enough water to float the boats.

Now that we were aboard, the dhow appeared far smaller than it had in the sunlight. It was piled with palms covered with a tarpaulin and passengers lay about wrapped in jackets, fast asleep. As most of the flat areas were already taken, we settled down as best we could. I found myself a relatively comfortable spot lying in the groove between two logs and tried to get a little sleep.

The various dhow crews whispered loudly as they waited for the tide. A drum beat rhythmically in the distance. I drifted off, only to be woken by a burst of laughter or a hacked cough from a nearby vessel. I snuggled into my polar fleece as a cool wind coated everything in a salty dampness.

After what seemed like an age I was woken by frenetic activity. The tide had come in and our boat had righted itself, bobbing gently at anchor. With much shouting and cajoling the crews untangled their anchor lines and set sail, pointing their noses towards a featureless horizon.

I stared at a heaven full of stars burning with unfamiliar intensity. The crew tacked to catch the faint breeze, rigging their triangular lateen sail to grab every breath. The night wind had almost completely died by the time the sun began painting the east. We tacked again and this time I got up and moved to the front of the boat, aware that any further attempt at sleeping was futile. The crew were locked in discussion and at Juma's urging they dug out a little motor from below the tarpaulin and rigged it over the stern.

With a few splutterings and lots of pull-starting the engine eventually coughed awake. Our crew dropped the sail and we chugged into the dawn. Juma pointed out a low smudge in the distance, simply saying 'Zanzibar'. It was still too early to make out any of the legendary spice island's features, but the sun soon raced into the sky, drenching our boat and the isle in orange light.

The crew took it in turns to go about their morning ablutions. Each one would go to the barrel of fresh water stored in the stern, dip a mug and brush his teeth, sharing the boat's communal toothbrush. He would then have a gargle, spit over the side and swallow the rest of the water before passing toothbrush and mug to the next in line.

The crew nursed every knot out of the overworked engine and

the excitement on board grew as we neared the harbour. The other passengers (four Zanzibaris returning home) readied themselves for arrival, while we simply sat watching Stone Town grow out of the Indian Ocean. The water was clean and blue. Shallow coral reefs reached up from the white sand below the keel. Every so often schools of baitfish would skip across the surface, their bodies catapulting from the water in panic. Flying fish launched themselves from under the bow and sailed off downwind before splashing back into an azure ocean.

8 OCTOBER 2002, STONE TOWN . . .

Zanzibar, it is said, was built from equal quantities of mortar and human blood.

In the 1800s it was a busy place with ships of many nationalities visiting what was essentially the most important centre of overseas commerce along the entire East African coast. Far and away its most significant commodity was human. Thousands of slaves were sold in the markets of Zanzibar and British and French efforts to halt it initially had little effect.

When Richard Burton arrived in 1856 on his first expedition to solve the riddle of the source of the Nile, he found the market in full swing. Even though the sultan had outlawed the export of slaves nearly ten years earlier, Burton described 'lines of Negroes, like beasts; a broker calling for bids'.

The presence of British and French warships simply made the conditions worse for slaves being smuggled through the blockades. Prices increased dramatically and it became worthwhile for slavers to cram their human cargoes below decks in ghastly conditions: '18 inches between decks and a pint of water a day,' as Burton bitterly noted.

East Africa was a hostile place. Few people of the interior had encountered Europeans, although many were familiar with Arab traders and slavers who'd been working the east coast since the days of Mohammed. Into this space stepped the explorers. Some, such as Livingstone, came to do God's bidding; others, like Burton, Speke, Stanley and Emin Pasha, for the greater glory of Queen Victoria and the monarchs of Europe. In many cases it was the Royal Geographical Society's quest for knowledge that guided the explorers.

In Zanzibar, expeditions were provisioned, porters were enlisted, and the blessings of the sultan sought before departure for Bagamoyo and the interior. Today Zanzibar is economically less vibrant and most travellers come to enjoy the sunshine, the island's white beaches, or to potter about in Stone Town's history-laden streets with their noses in guidebooks: Livingstone slept here... The sultan kept his harem in such and such a palace... Slaves were stored there...

Our entry into Stone Town's harbour was hailed with much joviality. The skippers who had already docked turned from their off-loading duties to berate our crew for their tardiness. The gist was obvious: who taught our crew to sail? Their mothers? Finally our boat bumped gently into one of the other dhows crowding the landing and was tied fast, the passengers quickly disappearing into the crowd as if they'd merely alighted from a taxi.

I found Juma, paid him, and then anxiously tried to explain to Bhatista, the only crew member who spoke a bit of English, that we'd be back in two days' time – 'on Thursday... Thursday, understand?' They all nodded. But, having already encountered Swahili time – essentially the day begins at sunrise, meaning that midday according to our clock is 6 a.m. on theirs – I didn't know what they might do to the days of the week. Everyone, however, seemed in agreement and with a glance over my shoulder we followed the other passengers, stepping from dhow to dhow.

One big advantage of taking the slow boat to Zanzibar, it turned out, was the complete lack of touts. As Mike and I walked over to the passport office we noticed a ferry disgorging passengers in the distance. The *mzungus* were swallowed by a crowd of Zanzibaris who grabbed luggage and offered their services as guides. All knew of great hotels, the best spice routes, unique colobus monkey tours . . . and no one understood the word 'no'.

Our passports were stamped – a formality revered by islanders as a last remnant of their independence from the mainland – and we emerged from customs just as the first tourists began trickling through, each trailing a phalanx of 'facilitators'. I hailed a taxi and, following Mike's advice (he'd visited Stone Town on his previous perambulations across the continent), set off for the cheapest hotel in town.

However, our damp ground-floor room, complete with peeling paint and mouldy, spore-ridden air, cost an exorbitant $20. 'But,' the overweight proprietor informed us happily, 'that includes breakfast.' Considering the state of the room, breakfast, it must be said, was a prospect that didn't inspire me.

While Mike went in search of a cup of coffee, I stripped down for a shower. The bathroom was small and gloomy, illuminated by a naked bulb, flummoxed in its attempt to fill the shadows. Eventually, after burning for a few minutes (just enough time for me to work out there was no hot water), the bulb died. But the cold shower *was* refreshing in the tropical heat. The nozzle rained over the toilet and sink and soon the entire room was an inch deep in water. I waded out, and shouted down the hall to Mike that the shower was open.

Clean at last, we found a taxi driver who offered, for a fee, to speak to a contact of his whose brother had a cousin who ran spice tours – 'best price', of course. We headed out of town to the Kidichi Baths and the nearby spice farm.

'These buildings were constructed for Sultan Bin Said's wife, Binte Irich Mirza, the granddaughter of the Shah of Persia,' said Abdullah Kheys (our driver's contact's brother's cousin) as we wandered through baths surrounded by white stucco walls. Back then, of course, Abdullah's head would have been delivered to the palace door for allowing disreputable strangers to enter. We emerged into the sunlight and wandered across the road to the Kidichi Spice Farm, leaving Abdullah perplexed by our indifference to the baths. He was milking his guiding services for all they were worth, which in our opinion wasn't much.

At the spice farm two brothers, Abdullah and Lamask Said, had collected the most important herbs, spices and fruits of the island on a small plot to show tourists: cinnamon, ginger, cloves, turmeric, manioc, mangoes, cardamom, pineapples, chillies, coconuts and ten or so species of banana. Our tour culminated in a demonstration by a Mr Butterfly who fetched coconuts from the palm tops 20 metres above our heads, accompanied by much singing and performing from his lofty stage. Tourists love it and his return to the ground precipitated a shower of notes – dollars, pounds and euros. Meanwhile two assistants on the ground fashioned garments from coconut fronds or chopped off the tops of coconuts, presenting the sweet milk for tasting. It was a slick performance, even though it felt a little like 'Coconut World'.

If the look on his face was anything to gauge by, strangling his first-born son could hardly have caused our taxi driver more anguish than when Mike told him we required no further guiding. His mouth opened and closed like a goldfish as he stammered, 'But, but the beaches-islands-monkeys-south-north...'

That evening, anxious to avoid Stone Town's expensive restaurants, we threaded our way into its dingy heart. This was the Stone Town people could still afford to live, eat, work, sleep, play and, alas, watch television in. The offending box poured out a cheap science-fiction movie from its perch in the corner of a packed square.

The younger generation sat enthralled by a multi-headed demon savaging a scantily-clad spacewoman who'd been a little slow drawing her ray gun. Young women, their heads wrapped in bright scarves, stared up in wonder at a universe so recognisably American – and so lacking in dignity. The older generation preferred checkers, and a crowd had gathered in one corner of the square to cheer a particularly spirited game between two grey-bearded opponents.

We slipped into a café for dinner. The young owner was dressed in shorts and a Manchester United football jersey with 'Beckham' printed boldly across his back above the number seven. He shooed away two regulars occupying the only table in the place. They grabbed their cups of *chai* (tea) and moved off with annoyed glances at us. We ordered fish cakes, a collection of local dishes and some fish that I couldn't name. All excellent.

The walls were covered with football posters – England, Manchester United, Brazil, Real Madrid, Juventus – and I asked which teams were his favourite. Finding mutual ground, conversation soon flowed freely. Was it true Zidane was out? Was Beckham leaving Manchester? And so it went: global concern for the masters of a little round ball. Eventually, after a discourse on the future of Tanzanian football, and many cups of chai, we wended our way back through the echoing streets to our dungeon.

9 OCTOBER 2002, SOMEWHERE DOWN THE ROAD WITHOUT ANY PETROL . . .

This morning we hired a motor scooter and are heading off to tour the island.

Mike drove and I perched on the back, shooting pictures. We swept along tar roads lined with impossibly tall palms, their crowns forming a roof above us. Some potholes were avoidable, others less so, and we bounced through the bigger ones.

The aroma of cloves hung in the air. They're one of the island's most important exports and the trade is strictly controlled and regulated. In every village there were cloves drying on woven reed mats – colourful mosaics in red, green and black indicating different stages in the drying process. The villagers, it seemed, harvest seeds from trees surrounding their homes and dry them in the sun before selling them to licensed operators who drive around the island collecting the crop. The cloves are then shipped to the mainland and thence the world, destined for my mom's gammon at Christmas-time and other places.

Each village we passed evoked the same response: kids screaming 'Mzuuunguuu' and waving madly. The adults, too, seemed friendly and looked up from the day's chores – coconuting, weaving, sewing – and nodded in greeting. Further from Stone Town the roads deteriorated. The corrugations were transmitted through the poor suspension of our scooter, making my backside feel like I'd been to the headmaster for six of the best. Mike, occupying the comfy seat, had no idea of the pain he was causing and every time I fidgeted, making the scooter swerve, he'd look over his shoulder in annoyance.

We finally arrived in the town of Nungwi, whose lighthouse marks the island's northernmost point. Fancy tourist lodges dotted the shoreline. We wandered through one or two remarkably un-Zanzibari establishments so Mike could make some jottings, then jumped back onto the scooter.

The dangerous thing about guidebook maps is they're horribly small. So small, in fact, that your eyes sometimes mistake the distances between places. This realisation struck me when all of a sudden our scooter's engine missed a beat, lurched, caught again, lurched and then stopped.

'Are we out of gas?' I asked, getting off the scooter.

'Nope, there's still a little in here,' Mike answered, shaking the bike while peering into the tank. 'But, it's not very full . . . actually it's practically empty. I'm not sure we'll make it home.'

We had taken an alternative, less-popular route down the eastern side of the island through a forest of concrete abominations constructed by the benevolence of some Soviet-era government. If you'd ever needed a reason to support the Cold War, this should be sufficient. Gaunt grey, multi-storey apartment blocks were overfilled by Zanzibaris living in squalor. It was a blight on paradise. How could people give up their elegant reed houses for that, I wondered? Past the monstrosities, we were now on a deserted stretch of road leading to the southern resorts.

I dug out the guidebook and peered at the map again.

'It's not far to Tungu,' I said.

Mike shook his head, 'How about Kitogani? There must be fuel there.' We weighed up the fuel possibilities of the two dots on the map and finally resolved the dilemma with the flip of a coin. Of course fate doesn't always work in your favour. And, as it turned out, Madame Luck had turned her attention elsewhere. When we ghosted in on residual fumes we discovered there wasn't a fuel station in Kitogani. With no other option, we headed to a nearby restaurant to see if they served beer and to use their phone. Unfortunately no beer and no phone.

Returning to the scooter, we heard a shout from behind us. The restaurant owner approached in a tattered yellow vest, his bearded face lit by a self-congratulatory grin. In his hands was a yellow 25-litre drum with liquid splashing about in the bottom.

'I asked one of the local fishermen if he didn't have any spare,' he said proudly, holding up the drum.

I unscrewed the cap and peered inside. There must've been about two litres of petrol covering a thick layer of beach sand.

'You can have that for $2,' he said.

'Two dollars!' Mike replied incredulously. 'No way. I'll give you one.'

The owner shook his head, looking offended by Mike's hard bargaining.

'Done deal,' I said, quickly terminating the negotiation and handing over the cash. I wasn't about to risk a sudden change of heart. 'And besides,' I turned to Mike. 'It's a helluva lot cheaper than spending the night here.'

Mike mumbled something about charity, fools and money under his breath and snatched the fuel drum, pouring it into the tank and trying to avoid the sand.

'At least it's a rental,' he laughed and kicked the starter. With one splutter it took to life.

'Home, Mike?' I asked.

'Home indeed!'

That evening as we wandered around the narrow streets of Stone Town young women sailed past wrapped in chadors, their perfume lingering in the alleys. We walked on, marvelling at doors armed with imposing studs and hanging in elaborately carved frames. As we passed the Africa House we heard a shout from above.

'Hey you two, come join us for a drink.' Deon and Susan from our dhow were leaning over the balcony waving. They were freshly laundered in clean khaki outfits. The deck was full of tourists – Italians, French, Germans, Brits – all gathered to toast the sun's demise. At the critical moment, 20 or so moved forward, clutching an array of instamatics and video cameras and lined the railing in a futile attempt to capture the moment.

After a few drinks in the Africa House, which in its heyday used to be the home of the British Club, Mike and I excused ourselves and made for Forodhani Gardens on the sea-front. Although this was crowded and not that cheap, being aimed largely at the foreign market, I'd been told not to miss out on its lively food stalls. So we scrummed with other tourists to sample the fair – prawns, fish, beef kebabs – grilled on glowing coals while you waited.

'The calamari's tough,' moaned Mike. 'I told you we should've gone back to the café we ate at last night.' I nodded, too busy chewing to argue.

10 OCTOBER 2002, A DHOW BACK TO THE CONTINENT . . .

Thank goodness, my concerns were baseless. If anyone's been worrying, it's the crew who stood to lose $20 if we failed to pitch. They've waited all along, and, it seems, negotiated cargoes, visited girlfriends and so on.

A brisk wind was whipping the ocean into a confusion when we entered the dhow harbour. Juma stepped out of the crowd, grabbed my bag and pumped our hands vigorously while talking away in Swahili. They had waited patiently for us but now that we were there, they seemed anxious to get us on board lest we decide to elope with another skipper.

We clambered aboard an empty dhow and I asked Bhatista what the drill was. 'They still discussing price of shipping the cargo to Bagamoyo. But no worry, we leave one o' clock sharp-sharp. Good wind then.'

I looked at my watch – it was already noon and I could see Juma and a stranger arguing furiously on the harbour wall. A small crowd had gathered and seemed to be taking one side of the argument at one moment, another the next. From the look of things, it appeared that even locals weren't immune to the ubiquitous facilitators.

Slowly other passengers clambered aboard. They were dressed in their finest, but once on the dhow they stripped down, packing their good clothes away and pulling on older garments. We lay about in the sun enjoying the bustle of the harbour. At 12.30, the arguing on shore reached a crescendo and, all of a sudden, Juma and the stranger shook hands and the man disappeared.

Moments later he returned in a truck piled with large, hessian-covered bales of Iranian cumin, which were carefully loaded into our dhow. We squeezed onto the stern to remain out of the way. A crowd once again formed to offer verbal input, although no one actually lent a hand. Even when one of the crew nearly overbalanced with his load while stepping between two dhows, they merely laughed and teased.

Eventually the cargo was loaded and ten other passengers were safely on board. We cast off and pointed the bows for Bagamoyo, like so many adventurers and slavers before us.

Our dhow heeled into the wind. Waves splashed over the gunwale, drenching all the occupants except Juma, who sat in the stern, tiller braced under an arm, his face wrapped in a huge grin. The sweet, clove-like smell of damp cumin issued from the bales. Water sang along the side and the rigging groaned like an old man carrying a heavy load, the sail taut, describing a graceful arc. Meanwhile, an elderly woman was ill, intermittently vomiting into her yellow scarf.

Mike and I sat in the prow enjoying the refreshing spray that tempered the mid-afternoon heat. We had a fair wind in the sails and our course set. Beyond the horizon the great game reserves of East Africa lay in wait.

11 October 2002, gateway to 'safaridom' . . .

We've bumped into two expatriates quite by accident. They recognised our Western Province licence plates and sticker-festooned Landy and flagged us down. Malcolm, a robust, red-cheeked man with square, wire-framed glasses and greying hair works for South African Breweries. I'm not sure I remember exactly how that crucial bit of info came up . . . All I remember is one moment we're driving along looking for a loaf of bread and the next we're knocking back a selection of beers at Arusha Country Club's 19th hole.

Tanzania is in pretty bad economic shape. Under strong Soviet and Chinese influence – partly in response to the country's former European colonial masters – Julius Nyerere took Tanzania down the socialist road after achieving independence in 1964. Everything was nationalised. Production quotas fell and profits were usurped by corrupt officials. Ordinary citizens simply had to accept the government's line, but possibly the worst ignominy of all came when they were forced to stomach the introduction of foreign beer after the collapse of the nationalised Tanzania Breweries.

Luckily, after the demise of apartheid, help was at hand. South African companies are now good business partners and things are slowly improving. One of the first companies to the 'rescue' was SAB (South African Breweries), which bought controlling shares in Tanzania Breweries. Under this new profit-driven enterprise the pride of the country – Kilimanjaro lager – was soon flowing freely again. At least, that's how the managers of the SAB plant in Arusha explained the region's recent history to us.

'The Castle [SAB's flagship beer] we brew here is the best in the world,' Malcolm boasted, sliding a couple of bottles across the bar for Mike and me to try. By this time, however, my mouth and mind were both rather affected by sampling Kilimanjaro, Ndovu, Safari, Big Bingwa and the like.

The next morning started slowly. Fortunately, all we'd planned was a visit to Shoprite to re-provision for the next leg. Mike browsed up and down the aisles, gathering food prices for his guidebook while I got down to the business of shopping, 'um'ing and 'ah'ing over how much bacon we'd need to get us through the Serengeti.

With a well-stocked fridge and two dozen bottles of beer clinking in the back – compliments of Tanzania Breweries – we headed out of town, proudly wearing our new Ndovu lager caps. The road deteriorated as we headed west towards the Ngorogoro Crater Conservation Area. We bumped along potholed blacktop and seemingly endless, psychotically inspired detours that crisscrossed the new artery of tar. Almost the entire stretch was being resurfaced or re-built with Japanese aid, and every few kilometres we'd pass signboards proudly sporting the rising-sun flag. Despite my scepticism about foreign aid, after a few hundred kilometres of shocking roads I was ready to kiss the first Japanese engineer I saw. My rear end, still sore from our adventures on Zanzibar, was now taking a beating, compliments of the hard suspension of the Land Rover.

12 OCTOBER 2002, THE CELESTIAL STADIUM . . .

If the gods are ever seeking a stadium in which to stage a celestial football match, they need look no further than Ngorongoro Crater. With more than 200 square kilometres of turf and excellent natural grandstands, they should be able to knock it around quite nicely here. Of course, they'd have to remove the animals first and, as the crater houses some of the densest populations of ungulates anywhere on the planet, this may prove more than a little tricky. They could, however, always schedule their games in migration season when most of the ungulates play away from home.

The crater forms the centrepiece of the Ngorongoro Conservation Area, some 8 000 square kilometres of land which is split between the local farmers, the Maasai and the game reserve. Today it is all that remains of a peak that once rivalled Kilimanjaro. This was formed, along with the other mountains in the area, by volcanic activity during the shifting and fracturing process which brought the Great Rift Valley into being.

Ngorongoro's volcanic origins were the reason we looked like bakers covered with flour by the time we arrived on the crater floor. Fine, white, volcanic dust billowed out from under our tyres, creeping between seals and settling over everything in the vehicle. By lunch time it was in our teeth and we crunched sandwiches with equal quantities of sand and cheese, mindful of the circling yellow-billed kites. They have learnt to steal tourists' lunches at all the popular stops. You expose food at your peril. The raptors are sly and constantly work to get into position behind your head. Just when you think it's safe to take a bite, wham! If you're lucky, you only lose the sandwich; otherwise their powerful talons may rip into your hand. Mike and I ate shielding our meal from view and standing with our backs against the Landy. This seemed to have the desired effect and the kites slipped away on the breeze to hover over a young Japanese tourist who was eating some way off. The youngster's mother looked up and, noticing the bird's attentions, shouted at their guide who in turn mouthed off at it in Swahili – these were, after all, East African kites. It seemed to do the trick and the raptor drifted off.

Our visit coincided with the dry season and so we missed the concentration of game associated with the crater floor. Most had trekked further west in search of the greener pastures of the Masai Mara. Those that stayed behind plodded through the short, dry grass, kicking up puffs of dust with each footfall. Even the hippos were battling and had to turn over every few minutes to prevent their backs from burning. It was comical watching these two-ton animals playing roly-poly in the few shallow pools that remained at the heart of the crater.

'Hey Mike, this is what an ant in a fruit bowl must feel like,' I joked. Mike grunted, scanning the surroundings with his binoculars. 'You know, apparently there are no giraffes down here because the crater's sides are too steep. Can you believe that?' I continued, bored with the slow sighting rate. 'And you don't see many cheetahs here either according to the guidebook – something to do with competition from lions.'

We had driven to a part of the crater where its steep slopes rose menacingly beside us. 'Sssh,' hissed Mike. A herd of elephants suddenly crashed through the yellow fever trees nearby, their tusks gleaming in the light. We watched as they meticulously stripped leaves and bark with their trunks before nimbly popping the greens into their mouths.

Eventually my companion broke the silence: 'It'd be great to see a rhino.'

'Unfortunately, there aren't many left in the Ngorongoro 'cause of poaching,' I said. 'Mind you, the populations have been increasing, so maybe we'll get lucky.'

Reluctantly, with the sun slipping below the crater, we made our way up a steep exit road and navigated around the rim until we found Simba Camp. The little campsite, which commands a majestic view over Ngorongoro, was peppered with tents. Driver-guides hurried about, busily pitching tents and heating water so their precious cargos could wash off the dust before dinner. Some of the tents were simple dome affairs like mine; others were lofty fabric mansions complete with separate shower cubicles. After their charges were safely ensconced in their overnight homes, the drivers hurried off to prepare dinner.

At first I found it strange that the guides didn't stay with their clients, but it soon became clear why. Once we'd sorted out a site right on the crater rim, I ambled across to their kitchen. There must've been about 15 guys gathered there, deep in conversation as they chopped onions, stirred pots and fried vegetables. It was welcoming and social – unlike the cold separateness of their European guests. Of course, these were old hands and probably knew each other well. And this was their time to swap gossip about the latest peculiarities of their charges and to compare sightings, ensuring the clients got to see the animals they'd paid top dollar for.

One driver was play-acting for the others, who were laughing along loudly at the scene. I couldn't understand the Swahili but from the pantomime it was clear: one of his female passengers had needed to step out for a pee, only to reappear from behind the bush with her pants around her knees. I don't know what scared her, but clearly the drivers found it terrifically amusing. Probably a tortoise.

We helped ourselves to a cold 'Kili' from the fridge and fried up a collection of vegetables and the remains of a chicken we'd roasted in tinfoil the night before in Arusha. A cool wind whipped across the crater rim and slowly the cloud base descended, covering the entire camp in thick mist. I hauled out the laptop, but the atmospherics were such that our radio wouldn't connect on any frequency.

It was still misty early the next morning when I wandered across to the toilet. I've done more than my fair share of longdrops, but this was by far the worst – and the most expensive. As I sat there thinking pleasant thoughts, trying to avoid gagging on the smell, I wondered where exactly the $20 a person a day goes – certainly not on camp facilities.

13 OCTOBER 2002, SERENGETI . . .

On the road between Ngorongoro and the Serengeti, down a small dirt track you could easily miss, is one of the world's most important archaeological sites. Oldupai (or, as it was incorrectly named by the first Europeans, Olduvai) is the Maasai word for sisal, which grows in abundance in the area. Olduvai Gorge is a dry river-course that cuts through five million years of sediments. It's here that in 1959 Mary Leakey, wife of famous palaeo-anthropologist Louis Leakey, found one of our oldest ancestors.

Interestingly, it isn't just the skulls and fossil-bone fragments which make this site so critically important, but also the discovery of a set of fossilised footprints at adjacent Laetoli. These finally proved what many palaeontologists had for long hypothesised – that *Australopithecus* walked upright in a manner not dissimilar to a rugby front-row forward. The track of ancient footsteps, housed in a little prefabricated museum, is less than inspiring and looks like a newly-laid pavement defaced by neighbourhood kids.

'Lucky it wasn't us who stumbled across it, hey Mike,' I whispered. 'We'd have walked right by without a second glance.'

Mike nodded and checked his watch.

'I hate to break this up,' he said, 'but if we want to avoid paying for another day in Ngorongoro we'd better fly. It's still some distance to the Serengeti gate and you know what these bastards are like – one minute late and they'll charge us for another 24 hours.'

We left the unassuming museum behind us in billowing dust.

'Thank heavens for Africa, Mike,' I shouted over the rattling. 'Imagine what the Americans would do to a place like that.'

Mike grinned and shouted back, 'What, you don't like the ring of Olduvai World, entrance $50? And what about Australopithecine ice-cream and Mammoth lollies?'

There's no fence around Ngorongoro. The road simply passes through a large arch that spans the road . . . and you're into the Serengeti. Almost immediately we started to see more and more animals. How they knew where the boundary lay was anyone's guess. We banged towards the exit gate as fast as the road would allow, becoming increasingly anxious about making the park office in time. Tourist minibuses whizzed past us. Few of the pale faces looked up from their books, or from their dozing, completely reliant on the driver to direct their gaze to all the essential fauna and flora.

The road stretched across wide, golden plains dotted with game. We bounced along, the corrugations playing havoc with Sade's voice, my backside and the bolts holding our snorkel in place. These eventually surrendered and we had to do a rapid repair job with cable ties.

We arrived at the Serengeti offices with five minutes to spare. I handed over a large percentage of our remaining money and we left brandishing a collection of coloured papers – entrance tickets, camping permits, gate passes and forex receipts.

Drenched in sweat, we pulled into Seronera at lunchtime. The heat left us little option but to search out some shade. We decided to head for Dik-Dik Campsite, claim a decent spot and make some lunch before resting until the evening's game drive. The place had little to recommend it: a stony clearing surrounding a large acacia, two thatched bomas which served as kitchen and dining room, an over-full longdrop and a shower without water. While I was pitching my tent one of the drivers came over to chat, intrigued by our Land Rover.

'This model's not yet available in Tanzania,' he said.

While scrabbling on the ground inspecting our suspension and giving the vehicle a good going-over, he told us absent-mindedly that 20 lions had been spotted earlier near Simba Hills to the east of camp. He also warned us to be on the lookout for a leopard that had been hanging around over the past couple of weeks.

We followed his advice and headed for Simba Hills later that afternoon. Without a driver to spot the game, we drifted along, eyes peeled, letting the torque of the diesel engine pull us slowly forward. The Simba Hills are a series of granite koppies which pop out of the surrounding knee-high grass like the lost marbles of some celestial giant. Trees had taken root within the cracks and crevices, their branches stretching up the sides into the sun. Black streaks, stains left by running water, scored the deep grey of the rock. A gentle breeze teased the grass, which rustled with the sound of rice poured into a pan.

We turned off the track at a well-used detour and made for a copse of low acacias. It was immediately obvious why so many drivers had bundu-bashed along this route before us. Two young lionesses with four or five cubs lay about enjoying the coolness of the shade. We remained with the lions for an hour or so until, tiring of the immobile cats, we went in search of other sightings. Rounding the end of a nearby koppie, I glimpsed an unmistakable tail swish of feline annoyance out the corner of my eye.

'Leopard!' I hissed at Mike, who braked, eased the vehicle into reverse and pulled off the track, positioning us so we'd get a good view. The cat lay on a round boulder 20 metres from the road, regally surveying its surroundings and enjoying the late afternoon sunshine. Mike killed the engine and we sat quietly absorbing the scene. After its initial irritation at our intrusion, the leopard resolutely ignored us as only cats can. Suddenly our fridge kicked in, whirring loudly, and it shot us a venomous glance, tail flashing displeasure. Luckily the fridge stopped almost as soon as it started and the leopard returned to its musings.

In the Serengeti you can see for vast distances and a halted vehicle unfortunately signals a sighting to others. Generally you can gauge how good the sighting is by the length of time a vehicle stops, so it wasn't long before our koppie was crawling with minibuses. The pattern was always the same – and quite comical. A vehicle would arrive and the driver would catch sight of what we were looking at. Heads would pop out of the open top like gophers on ground-hog day. Cameras clicked, videos whirred. Ultimately it got too much for 'our' leopard. It lost patience with the intruders, slipped off the rock and disappeared.

Dik-Dik was crowded with tents when we returned that evening. Once again drivers scurried about while the tourists sat back in their camp chairs sucking beers like babies on a teat. And in some ways this was how their minders saw them. Self-drive overlanders like Mike and I were viewed as an enigma. Remarkably, we cooked our own food, cleaned, fixed our vehicle, pitched tents without the help of a guide. But this self-reliance meant we found ourselves in no man's land. The tourists seemed to look down on us, yet we were not fully welcomed into the drivers' set either. The closest thing to acceptance we got was the occasional offer of hot water from their catering-sized kettles, or an invitation to sit by their fires for a while.

14 OCTOBER 2002, DEATH OF A TOMMY . . .

It's well before dawn and we've packed up our camp to head out in search of more sightings. Once again, we have a long distance to travel to clear the Serengeti before attracting extra fees. As our brights cut the darkness into slices of light, a family of spotted hyenas lopes beside the road; shadows in the night.

After sunrise we saw a lioness padding along the banks of a dry river and turned for a better look. A small herd of Thomson's gazelles eyed her passing suspiciously, but she moved on, ignoring them. Mike and I drove across to the other side of the river and positioned our vehicle so that she was now moving towards us. The cat was the picture of nonchalance. In fact, she was being downright blatant in advertising her presence to the nearest herd. Then we lost sight of her as she slipped into a patch of thick green grass in the riverbed. On the far side another herd of gazelles nervously stamped their hooves.

Suddenly she burst from the grass – a tawny blur – and the gazelles scattered... except one, which remained locked in the vice grip of her jaws, its neck broken by the force of the bite. The lioness sat up, issuing a rough, growling purr from deep in her throat. Immediately two cubs responded. They'd been hiding nearby, waiting for a signal from mother and now they bounded over, licking her enthusiastically before settling down to the meal provided. The presence of the cubs showed just how premeditated the attack had been. Their mother left them hiding while circling away far down-river in order to surprise the prey close to the cubs' hideout.

Aware of the exposed location of her kill, she rose and, much to the annoyance of her cubs, dragged the gazelle into the long grass nearby, quickly disappearing from view. The last we saw of her was a long tail scything through the grass, her cubs in hot pursuit.

Instinct and first impressions are often right.

John Hanning Speke's first impression, when he stumbled across the vast expanse of Lake Victoria, was that he'd found that objective of so many explorers before him: the source of the White Nile. Burton, his partner on this exploration, was not convinced, claiming that the legendary Mountains of the Moon would block any flow north from Victoria. History would vindicate Speke.

We were glad we'd followed our instinct and headed for Speke Bay. Our reward wasn't fame and fortune, simply a hot shower and a chance to get rid of the dirt of the last few days from beneath our fingernails.

Lake Victoria beggars description. It's a sheet of water so large the movements of the moon and sun affect it, albeit by a 'tide' of only 20-odd centimetres. As I sat on a deck overlooking the lake and watching the sun dropping towards the horizon a juvenile fish eagle, in response to its parent's urgings, was testing its wings. A strong breeze whipped up the surface of the lake and the resultant wavelets lapped the shore a few metres below my chair. Every now and again the fish eagle would brave a short flight over the water, the wind lifting its body out of the nest as soon as its wings were angled for elevation. Out it would soar until it realised the finality of the situation and hurriedly retreated to its nest, much to the disapproving squawks of its parents – a far cry from the regal calls that reverberate around African waterways.

Speke Bay Lodge gave us an opportunity to refill our water tank, which was running dangerously low. Owner Jan – a tall, heavy Hollander who patrolled the place on a mountain bike, white socks stuffed into his sandals – had created one of the best water purifying systems this side of the Rift Valley. 'He's got the works,' reported Mike after touring the establishment. 'It's unbelievable. Sand filters, microfilament filters, UV filters and God knows what else.'

I'd already been for a shower while Mike was having his tour, and was impressed by the ablutions: hot and cold water on tap for a mere fraction of what the parks were charging. Wherever private enterprise took root hereabouts, it seemed to flourish. Hell, the Tanzanian Parks Board should simply lease their two campsites to Jan and they'd be world class before you could say 'pass the zebra biltong'. For all of Speke Bay Lodge's comforts, we had to tear ourselves away early the next morning. Time was now precious. My replacement, Justin, was flying into Nairobi in two days' time and we still had to find our way across the border and through the Masai Mara.

15 OCTOBER, THE 'LONG' ROOM . . .

Mid-morning. We've arrived at the boisterous border post of Kisumu. A dank, fishy smell hangs over the place, emanating from the capenta – tiny fish caught in enormous numbers in Lake Victoria – that are being wheeled around in huge sacks on the carriers of bikes. These, along with sacks of rice, are on their way to market in Nairobi, each sack carefully marked so the recipient in town will know whose it is.

We strolled into an office on the Tanzanian side of the border where, after a long wait, a harassed official burst in, apologising for the delay.

'You know, this is the "long room",' he confided once he'd got his stamps and forms sorted. 'And do you know why we call it that?' We shook our heads in unison.

'It's because of the wait,' the official said, laughing loudly at his own joke. Incredible, I thought, a border official with a sense of humour. He spent a few minutes pawing through our documents before tearing out those pages he required from our carnet. Then he wished us well on our travels: 'Safari njema.'

The Kenyans were speedy by comparison and we were soon on the road to the Masai Mara. We had decided to enter the park on the little-used western approach and bundu-bashed along some pretty rough roads towards Talek Gate. As we drove, the game numbers increased. During the migration, animals flood into the Mara across its unfenced boundaries. It's one of Africa's great spectacles.

Park guards liberated us of the required fees. Now, all the cash that remained was enough to buy fuel to get us to our final destination and, with luck, a bit left over to have slap-up venison steaks at Nairobi's Carnivore Restaurant.

The Masai Mara is a small reserve – really a pocket-sized extension of the larger Serengeti National Park across the border in Tanzania. In the spring migration season it is also unquestionably the best place to view wildlife anywhere in Africa. Great herds of wildebeest assemble in phalanxes and march off the dry plains into the

Mara to enjoy the sweet new grass, which sprouts after the seasonal rains. Two million or more animals congregate in these cramped plains, mowing the grass until all that's left is a low stubble, as if the landscape had forgotten to shave. Everywhere we looked there were animals and the air was thick with the ripe smell of decaying flesh, churned mud and processed grass.

We nosed our way through the herds and made for our evening's campsite. A gentle rain dulled the incessant 'gnu'ing of the beasts – a sound like that which escapes your lungs after the school bully has punched you in the solar plexus. Our campsite, situated in a stand of trees a little way from the road, was perfect – evocative of the wild Africa of old. There were no fences and no facilities (other than a small canvas-sided longdrop which had been freshly dug). Mike built a fire from a pile of wood that had been provided and we set about pitching tents in the drizzle. Occasionally we'd catch the sound of a tourist bus heading towards a nearby lodge, but even that eventually died away as daylight abandoned us to a primeval world.

This is the East Africa I've sought throughout our journey. The mythical Africa everyone – me, Mike, the tourists in their minibuses – likes to pretend is the real McCoy, is not. This is a small campsite in a small reserve isolated from the destruction humans have meted out almost everywhere else. In the past it was Europeans who were largely responsible for the rapid demise of Africa's wilderness. Unfortunately, today no amount of European aid, conservation initiatives or anti-poaching incentives will undo the original wrongs of the emissaries of God, king and country. But these thoughts only distract me from the thrill of being surrounded by countless wild animals, just a hair's breadth away in the pressing dark under countless stars.

Tomorrow we'll head to Nairobi and from there, for me, home. For Mike the African carpet stretches out ahead.

NAIROBI TO ADDIS ABABA

Rummaging through Africa's attic

Justin Fox

I stood in the hot rain outside Nairobi's Jomo Kenyatta International Airport circled by touts, waiting for Mike. 'You want taxi? You want hotel, bus, guide, hire car? What you want?' Nairobi's air smelled strange, tinny, like earth or danger, and seemed as thick as soup. 'What you want?'

Eventually the Land Rover emerged from behind a row of palms, mud-spattered and looking the part. 'Hey, hop in Justin, let's hit it,' said Mike with a smile. I tossed my luggage in the back and we were off, squeezing into downtown traffic. 'Cameron got the hell out early to be with his wife, poor bastard. Champing at the bit to get laid. You looking forward to this?'

'Sure,' I said. 'So long as the shiftas don't get us. . .'

After a night in Ed's palatial home we threaded through Nairobi's rush-hour traffic along an avenue of glass high-rise where marabou storks stalked between the cars like businessmen. Mike pulled up at a supermarket to grab the last provisions. 'Robyn always wanted bloody fizzy drinks, Cameron was fine drinking water and beer. What do you want?' asked Mike.

'Um, I think I'll be fine with water and beer too, thanks Mike,' I said, resolving to buy Cokes on the sly with my pin money.

The road led north out of town through coffee and banana plantations. Plots were neat and fertile. Jacaranda blossoms decked the ground like a purple carpet. A boy walking a sheep on a lead was overtaken by a man in a white suit on a bicycle, the wheel flicking mud expressionistically across his back. Oncoming traffic seemed adrift in the road, gliding this way and that to avoid pedestrians, livestock and cavernous potholes disguised as puddles.

Later, and free of Nairobi's sprawl, we cruised for ages beside Mount Kenya's conical base – the rest, if it existed, was lost in cloud. There were checkpoints comprising metal spikes laid in the road and policemen fidgeting with semi-automatic rifles. Then a plateau that suddenly fell away to the west, revealing scored valleys and blue mountains far, far away.

One never thinks of Kenya's north being desert. Savanna yes, undulating grasslands maybe, but not merciless waste. The old Northern Frontier District is a wild place and not to be tackled without a pinch of humour and a little recklessness. It's criss-crossed with ancient migratory routes and sparsely peopled by nomadic Samburu, Rendille, Turkana and Somali herders.

The north is not safe for travellers, and certainly not those in flashy 4x4s. Highway robbers, rebellious Somalis, refugees from war-torn Sudan and a tendency towards bellicosity among the locals make for a jittery journey. You get the feeling your bullet-holed body would blend quickly with the landscape and hardly be remarked upon by passers-by. An erratic military presence and armed escorts are the norm hereabouts. One guidebook was in no uncertain terms about venturing into these parched parts: 'If you're thinking of heading out beyond Isiolo to the far northeast, however, take careful advice: this is one region where the rest of the country's traditional fear and ignorance is no longer just prejudice.'

We passed isolated groups of Rendille warriors dressed in tribal costume: red kikoi, beaded necklaces, plugs in their ears, red-dyed hair and ubiquitous spear. The men seemed on display, like live curios waiting by the roadside for passing tourists to stop and pay to take their photo.

Isiolo was a scruffy town bustling with people from half a dozen tribes. Women sold vegetables harvested from irrigated shambas, men passed the time of day at the livestock market and chewed sprigs of *miraa* (a narcotic leaf) while hawkers fished for customers. At the fuel station we were surrounded by a group selling Somali swords in leather scabbards and bracelets of copper, brass and aluminium. 'I am blacksmith and I make this myself,' said one, thrusting a handful of bangles through the window. 'Look, I must twist metal like this,' he said, showing me a half-finished effort.

'Very nice, but I'm not buying,' I said, but the price kept plummeting as the fuel filled our tanks and in the end I felt compelled to purchase a couple as we pulled away. This created a riot among the sellers, who followed us down the road at a trot shouting a descending avalanche of prices – the whole bargaining negotiation, which they could not forego, compressed into a few seconds. 'Must be bloody hard times,' muttered Mike as the town and its hawkers dissolved into dust.

After Isiolo the police roadblocks became more haphazard affairs, almost indistinguishable from the ambushes I feared. We crossed the dry Ewaso Nyiro River and passed through Archer's Post, just a row of *dukas* (shops) and a straggle of shacks. The flat-topped Ol Olokwe Mountain became a compass point on the horizon. Then we were into the Kaisut Desert, dry and endless and peopled only, it seemed, by the odd shaggy baboon and flocks of vulturine guineafowl with their distinctive cobalt chests. This was full-blooded bandit country and I had the Dutch-accented voice of our Nairobi host in my ears. Ed had talked about the hijackers on this road . . . and the English girl who'd had her limbs hacked off and then been set alight . . . and nasty Lake Turkana with its seven-metre crocodiles and giant carbon dioxide bubbles that rise to the surface with enough gas to snuff out an entire village.

Did we really want the north road, I wondered? How important was it in the bigger scheme of things. Like our lives, for instance. 'It can be a dark place if you let it get to you,' Ed had said. So we'd just have to make sure it didn't. The road and its constant spooling motion helped: at least we could say, 'Shiftas hereabouts? Well by tomorrow we'll be 500 kilometres away.'

The longest road in Africa. It was big, open, empty country and hot as hell. We passed isolated hamlets and small herds of cattle, goats and camels led by boys wrapped in red sarongs, their hair in braids and decorated with copper ornaments. Women wore bangles halfway up their arms, a lasso of necklaces and robes in the brightest colours. When we stopped to take photographs a chorus of 'no' sent us scurrying back to the vehicle. Even my gifts of pens and hats prised only one or two reluctant shots before the session was peremptorily ended. They all had the air of Naomi Campbell on a grumpy day.

It was late afternoon when we reached Laisamis, a mission station in the middle of nothing. The Italian Father Fernando pointed to a patch of ground near his house where we could camp. Mike climbed onto the Land Rover's roof and opened his tent like a concertina. I tried to hammer the pegs of my dome tent into unforgiving ground. After bending three in half, I gave up; so what if it blew away with me inside in the night? While Mike settled in a camping chair to jot his notes and watch the sun simmer away, I went looking for pictures. A group of pretty teenagers on their way to church were happy to have their photograph taken. But just then two young men rushed over. 'Why you take pictures?' asked one aggressively.

Before I could reply the other cut in, 'You exploiting the children! You go make money from these children. They're innocent.'

His rhetoric took me by surprise and I was just beginning to think that at an ideological level he had a point. In post-colonial terms I could be, theoretically, in hot water. I mean, a white man with an intrusive lens crafting a vision of Africa without remunerating or consulting with locals is a tricky thing indeed. But the young Nkrumah blew his argument somewhat with his next leap of logic: 'You give me money!'

I recognised the green slime between his teeth and noticed his cohort rhythmically chewing on a stick. Their eyes were glazed and they were clearly buzzing on miraa. Despite attempts to explain my position, it was obvious they wanted dollars for my camera's indiscretion. I refused and retreated to the vehicle, but the men followed, hurling abuse and threatening to call the police. 'That's fine with me,' I said. 'Please go and call the police.'

'Okay, I will,' fumed the agitator, and they staggered down the road. I figured they'd have at least a 50-kilometre walk through the desert at night to reach the nearest police post. But this was not the last of the hostility. In the coming days there were a number of tense encounters. The Turkana, Samburu and Borena live in a near-lawless wilderness with murder, stock theft and raids from Somali shiftas a constant threat. Even herdboys hereabouts carry AK47s.

The two photo-terrorists soured Laisamis for me. However, I was cheered up a little later when reading Philip Briggs' excellent guide to Ethiopia in which he described the habits of 'plonkers' like the two I had just encountered and was to meet repeatedly on the trip. Briggs writes, 'Plonkers will latch onto you, accompany you uninvited to your hotel or wherever you are going, then demand money, ask to be your guide, expect you to marry his sister, or something equally inappropriate . . . They are always male, and generally deadly earnest (and equally banal), relatively educated, and out of work. Nine times out of ten, the worst a plonker will do is bore you for a couple of hours and then expect to be paid for it; sometimes they might also expect you to send them to university in your home country, or to find them a job . . . Plonkers are not a threat: they are just quite appalling company and entirely immune to subtle dissuasion.'

In the coming weeks we'd get to know the signs. You could spot a plonker locking on to you from a long way off. And the brief, or not so brief, encounter would be a dance whose steps were rehearsed to the point of despair. There'd be the friendly questioning as to where we were going, what we were doing, whether we needed assistance. There'd be our back-pedalling and reserved cordiality. Eventually the questioning and the demands would be more insistent and the ingratiation more pointed. If we tried to direct the conversation away from the inevitable request for payment, it would get rudely snapped back into line. Didn't we know the rules? It was all pre-ordained and seemingly impossible to circumvent. We were rich *faranjis* (foreigners) passing through and we had 'meal ticket' written all over our faces. These brief road encounters summed up much of Africa's relationship with the developed world. Our white skins and the nature of this kind of journey forced us into roles we couldn't easily escape.

It was sweltering hot as the two of us ate our spaghetti, chopped vegetables and mince cooked over the gas. We sat on camp chairs under a moonless sky resplendent with stars. Distant mountains and inselberg outcrops jutted from the plain like a row of teeth that needed dentistry.

I crawled into my tent beneath a tree hung with weaver nests, the Italian Father's television burbling in the dark. But the heat made sleep impossible. I stripped to my briefs and lay on top of the sleeping bag with my head at the tent opening, listening to frustrated mosquitoes hurling themselves at the gauze netting. A dog barked, tearing the stillness at regular intervals. Later it began to howl.

I woke to a cacophony of pigeons, crows, weavers and chickens. Mike poked his head into my tent and said he was off to the church whose bell was tinkling from an adjacent yard. Soon Kiswahili voices issued from the mission, then the sonorous voice of Father Fernando leading his flock in prayer. I dozed through the service, letting waves of ecclesiastical sound intermittently rouse me.

Beyond Laisamis we happened upon a tanker and trailer stuck in mud, the result of a flash shower in an otherwise cloud-free sky. In trying to extricate himself, the driver had gouged deep grooves in the road. Mike pulled over to video the scene, but when we returned to the Land Rover, it refused to start. The ignition was dead. We looked at each other in consternation. This was the worst possible place to break down. It would probably take a mechanic days to reach us and besides, we were sitting ducks for shiftas.

Mike checked the fuses, scratched his head, then checked the fuses again. Consternation turned to despair. Not being mechanically minded yet wanting to help, I kicked a tyre. The men who'd been riding on the tanker's cab came over to commiserate ... and did we have any cigarettes, food, maybe a drop of water to spare? We stood around in the mud for a while, then Mike checked the fuses yet again. After jiggling what looked like a loose connection, he turned the ignition and the Landy coughed to life. With enormous smiles of relief and a blast of the hooter we were northbound again, leaving the trucker and his crew to wait until the mousse round his tyres had dried.

We coursed through acacia desert, passing outposts festooned with plastic packets impaled on thorn trees. Nomads were on the move everywhere, their caravans of camels, cattle, goats and donkeys stretching over many kilometres. Herdsmen on the flanks carried spears or semi-automatic weapons. Cattle trucks with Turkana tribesmen riding shotgun on the roof eased out of their grooves and slid across the road towards us. We headed for the ditch and were swallowed by their dust. Hours of desert driving, then a tank piled with troops, or a camel train ghosting in a mirage.

The lonely track to Lake Turkana entailed a two-day detour but we wanted to see Africa's Jade Sea. Just before Marsabit ('place of cold') we turned west. The road was jagged stone and boulder madness. Our vehicle wound down the side of an escarpment, a descent marked by an umbrella thorn standing iconic against the plains beyond. Two ostriches jogged beside us for a while, trailed by a family of 15 chicks. For a couple of hours we saw not a soul; then a speck on the horizon materialised into a motorbike mounted by two herders. If they broke down out here, their bush knowledge and ability to find food and water would have to be pretty canny.

Somewhere in the flatlands there was a loud pop and hiss, and then a sudden slewing across stones. Blow-out.

There we were, toiling in the midday sun, jack and grease, sweat and swearing. The dinky jack-spanner arrangement took forever to lift the vehicle clear of the ground. And now the question, what to do? The road to Turkana was diabolical and almost certain bandit territory. With the tyre a virtual right-off we were down to only one spare. The other three tyres had been badly chewed on the rocks and had pocked walls and chunks missing from the tread. A week in the Chalbi waiting for a recovery truck held little allure, so we reluctantly turned the Land Rover round and headed for the safer option of Marsabit. Later we heard that an overland vehicle ahead of us on that road had been stopped and stripped by shiftas. So the blow-out was, after all, a blessing.

Marsabit is an island of green hills that rise a thousand metres above the desert plains. It's an oasis of forests and volcanic craters swathed in clouds which keep it cool. The town is the capital of the largest administrative district in Kenya and a centre for livestock trade. I wandered around the market while Mike went to refuel. It was heaving: Boran selling short-horn cattle, stalls packed with women wearing Somali printed cloth, and 'window-shopping' Rendille clad only in skins. I soon had a teenage plonker on each arm telling me about the delights of the dustbowl. My camera was causing a disturbance and I didn't try to take pictures of the market-goers for fear of giving offence. Even photographing a building elicited an angry response from the shopkeeper.

Mike picked me up and we made straight for Marsabit National Park, whose entrance was on a hillside at the edge of town. Studded with craters, it's home to a surprisingly large number of bigger game, such as elephant, buffalo and reticulated giraffe. The gatekeeper informed us we'd be the only visitors in the reserve that night. Dense vegetation pressed in on the road and the trees were decorated with Spanish moss and twisted lianas. Fallen giants lay beside the track, suffocated by strangler figs. We were on the lookout for anything big or hairy, but were not rewarded.

At the first crater lake we stopped to check out the lodge, but the price was discouraging so we pressed on to the second lake. We made camp on a grassy patch beside Gof Sokorte Guda (Lake

Paradise) in the bowl of a volcanic sphere. There were no amenities and no sign that anyone had camped there before. It was a magical, if eerie, spot: a dark pool set in a steep-sided crater. Spoonbills waded in the shallows and sentry-like fish eagles called from treetop perches. The presence of the Big Five, possible shiftas, and the location of our camp, lent menace to the encroaching shadows.

A herd of long-tusked red elephants stepped from a seemingly impenetrable wall of hardwoods, their ivory glowing yellow in the last rays of the sun. They seemed nervous, trunks tasting the air for danger. Then they waded into the lake, the little ones splashing and spraying water at each other. These were the descendants of Ahmed, a bull with legendary tusks granted presidential protection by Jomo Kenyatta in 1970 and guarded 24-hours a day to discourage poachers.

Darkness seeped from the shadows as we chopped vegetables for our macaroni and mince. Tiresome moths, plonkers of the insect world, threw themselves into our food. Two Tusker beers later saw us munching on unknown bodies scooped from our plates in the dark.

In the absence of a disco it was early to bed. A chorus of sounds enveloped us, echoing round the bowl. I woke on and off during the night, listening: it was the most complex, most complete sound I'd ever heard. Africa unplugged. If I were a religious man, I'd talk about the voice of a Maker. That's almost what it sounded like . . . that's what it *felt* like.

Lying in my tent, I thought about how the noises had matured. At dusk I'd been more aware than usual of the sounds: ducks squabbling, shrill crickets, pulsing frogs, the splash of elephants cooling themselves. Those fish-eagle cries were, now that I considered it, more evocative than ever before. Perhaps it was the shape of the crater that trapped the sounds, making them echo off its walls, and gave them an enchanting ring.

I'm normally not good with noise, especially when trying to sleep. Traffic, barking dogs, television sets, mating pigeons mewing on my windowsill. But this was something altogether different. The guinea-fowl made the point. Normally their staccato clucking in the early morning irritates. But here, from afar, moulded by the shape of the crater and modulated to fit the other noises, it was acceptable, necessary even. Tree castanets, oboe frogs, wind instruments in the high leaves, the static hiss of insects, bird calls – all were in harmony.

I left my tent flap open and kept waking to marvel at the perfect sound. It changed through the night: different movements in a long symphony. It was varied and complex; no instrument took control or overbore.

The shock came just before dawn. I snapped upright, terrified. Waap! Waap! Waap! 'Bandits' was my first thought, expecting the crackle of AK47 fire, glass shattering, metal puncturing in pops like hail on tin. In those sleep-fuddled moments, I imaged Mike shot and me running in my briefs, without spectacles, into the dark forest, bullets whistling around me.

The Land Rover alarm was deafening. Mike, trapped in the rooftop tent, cursed loudly, fumbling for the remote button. 'Fuck! Fuck! Fuck!' Waap! Waap! Waap!

The alarm had ruined everything, silencing the creatures. But after a while one brave frog began a tentative croak, just a clearing of the throat really, and slowly each instrument rejoined, building for the dawn crescendo.

I emerged from my tent into thick mist and we broke camp in the rain, after a bowl of watery cornflakes and coffee sprinkled with tasty ants. Tendrils of mist snaked between trunks whose higher branches were whited out. The Land Rover slid along sodden tracks. A startled buffalo faced us head-on in the road. Snorted. Then turned and was immediately swallowed whole by the vegetation.

The roads of Marsabit had turned to waterways and we coursed a wake down the main street. People were wading knee-deep to market and we parted a herd of white cattle whose rumps were branded with a makeshift X. At a checkpoint on the outskirts of town a policeman chewing miraa told us we'd need an armed escort for the road to Moyale. 'Many, many shifta. They shoot you dead,' he said.

'No, no, we don't need,' said Mike. 'We'll be, eh, fine.'

'But sir, you must have escort!'

'Thank you, but no,' said Mike accelerating away. 'They're just looking for a big tip when we get to Moyale. I'm pretty sure the road is fine. Probably just a scam.'

'Still, shouldn't we wait for a convoy?' I suggested nervously.

'Nah, that could be hours. It'll be fine, Justin, trust me.'

I had that famous-last-words feeling as we sped north on the God-forsaken run to Ethiopia. Mike's foot flat on the pedal we hurtled across the black stone of Ngaso Plain. It was a scary, bone-jangling ride. Nomads, curious human-sized piles of stones and domed huts made from branches stood like ciphers, contorting in the heat haze. Pale jackals and the occasional camel train were the only things that punctured the monotony.

We rumbled into the moonscape of the Dida Galgut Desert. Remoter still. It was hot and the wasteland stretched to the horizon. Shimmering brown earth, stones, sparse thorn trees and nothingness. Hours passed and gradually the Ethiopian hills, a first hint of the highlands beyond, lifted from the plain.

This was the road followed by South African forces advancing on the Italians in the Second World War. Mussolini had invaded Ethiopia in 1935 to avenge the defeat of the Italians at Adwa in 1896. In so doing he set wheels in motion that would propel Europe into the worst war in history. In typical uncompromising fashion Winston Churchill had tried to dissuade the Italian dictator: 'To cast an army of nearly a quarter of a million men, embodying the flower of Italian manhood, upon a barren shore two thousand miles from home, against the goodwill of the whole world and without command of the sea, and then in this position embark upon what may well be a series of campaigns against a people and in regions which no conqueror in four thousand years ever thought it worthwhile to subdue, is to give hostages to fortune unparalleled in all history.'

Mussolini didn't listen. His modern army completely outclassed the Ethiopians and his air force dropped illegal mustard gas which decimated the ranks of the African soldiers, as well as towns and farms. Haile Selassie fled the country and made an impassioned appeal to the League of Nations, but it fell on deaf ears. Unofficially the Second World War had begun.

When Il Duce teamed up with Hitler in 1940, Allied forces made ready to attack his African possessions in the horn of Africa, where he threatened the Suez Canal and British Egypt. In the early stages, South African armoured car and truck columns probed along the very road Mike and I were driving. Radiators boiled over as they struggled through the desert, encountering occasional resistance. Things hadn't changed much – like us, they were fearful of ambushes. More than 40 000 South African troops headed north, and the route our Land Rover would follow through Ethiopia intersected, in many places, that of the South Africans'. Marsabit had been the Kenyan base for initial operations. The heavily defended border towns of Moyale and Mega were their objectives. They were ours too.

South Africa's Ethiopian victory was the first unequivocal Allied success of the war, and provided Churchill with a much-needed morale booster in the dark days of 1941. Apart from having an interest in South Africa's invasion, I had some family involvement in the campaign. My uncle, Uys Krige, was a war correspondent 'embedded' with the troops and wrote about his experiences in articles and letters home, and later in short stories, plays and poems. As an Afrikaner with strong anti-fascist convictions he'd been asked to serve in Jan Smuts's War Office, helping to compose and broadcast counter-propaganda to the Nazi radio station Zeesen. But when the South African armed forces set sail from Durban for Mombasa, he started to get itchy feet. Uys went to see 'Oom Jannie' (the president was an uncle by marriage) and asked permission to go north and report from the frontlines. Smuts agreed.

Uys Krige (third from left) during the Abyssinian campaign in 1940.

Uys Krige and Ethiopian tribesmen pose in front of a South African armoured car.

Nearing the border, our route became more hilly. A scrubby excuse for vegetation returned. It was here, just north of the Turbi Hills and hemmed in by thicker bush, that the South African columns encountered heavier resistance. Armoured cars advanced through the bush – one falling into a tank trap and another crashing into a tree – to overwhelm the enemy machine-gun nests.

The South African columns didn't try to take Moyale, but instead launched an outflanking manoeuvre westward through the Chalbi Desert to attack Mega. Uys hitched a ride: 'The convoy spread out. While it kicked open a road through the burning red desert sand and surrounding naked thorn trees, armoured cars raced up and down the sides of the convoy, sometimes ploughing through the soft sand like destroyers . . . The thick red sand twisted skywards. Sometimes you couldn't see a yard in front of you.'

Our last stretch before the border hills was across a plain that had seen rain only hours previously. The road was a mess and punctuated by muddy pools whose depth we had no way of guessing. Neither of us felt inclined to get out and wade. I was at the wheel and Mike hauled out the video camera to record the fun through the windscreen as brown water cascaded over our bonnet. I kept the speed up, largely for dramatic filmic purposes. The result was a thrilling ride, the 4x4 slewing this way and that like a raft in white water, spray flying.

The outskirts of Moyale were dotted with the houses of Burji farmers – Boran nomads who'd given up their wandering existence. It was time to get rid of our Kenyan shillings, so we stopped to refuel. Moyale straddles the border, and there was clearly not much to the Kenyan side: a few dukas and bars, a camel halt, post office and police station. The town had been shelled and bombed by the South Africans during the war and didn't seem to have recovered. Its border post was the most happening place in town and that's where we wended our way.

At the customs building I was approached by a man with a

heavy jaw and a faraway, slightly crazed look in his eyes. Clothes hung on his substantial frame by threads and his beard looked moth-eaten. 'Excuse me, sir, a moment of your time please,' he began. 'My name is Bebelzabehe Belethe. I am an Ethiopian. I have been living here, in no man's land, between the borders of these two countries, for two years.' He pointed at a bridge that led to the Ethiopian post on the other side of a valley.

'I was kidnapped by government forces and they held me captive. They took my leg. Look.' He pulled up his trousers to show a wooden leg. 'It was a ground mine, but it was their fault. They knew I had a satellite telephone. You must get a message to the International Red Cross. Tell them my father's people are not warlike.' He was distracted, continually looking over his shoulder to the Ethiopian side of the valley. 'In the riverbed for two years I have lived. On the mercy of Samaritans I have relied. Please put in a good word for me and my leg that has been taken by the ground mine.'

I felt that Bebelzabehe, or Beelzebub as I took to calling him in my head, was the keeper of the border, and a foretaste of the strange land we were about to enter. He needed to be appeased if our journey into Ethiopia was to be a success. We gave him some of our food and assured him that yes, we would mention his name if we met any Red Cross officials or United Nations envoys that could alleviate his plight. Never cross Beelzebub, particularly not at a border crossing, I figured. In the realm of plonkers, I thought as we pulled away, this man was undisputed king.

The Kenyan side had been a breeze, but the Ethiopians were more officious. Two Capetonians on a trans-Africa adventure and a Dutch couple in a converted ambulance painted with flowers, paw prints and lines of poetry were plodding through the paperwork ahead of us. Mike was dispatched to photocopy our documents while I started filling out a dozen or so forms.

When a charming customs woman finally stamped my passport, I noticed that the date was wrong, by quite a few years. I was about to point this out when I remembered that Ethiopia runs on a pre-Christian calendar based on the flooding of the Nile in ancient Egypt. The Western world abandoned the Julian calendar in favour of the Gregorian in 1582, but Ethiopia, never big on change or tradition-tampering, stuck to it. As a consequence, Ethiopia is nearly eight years 'behind' us, although at times it seems more like eight centuries. Oh, and just to make things more confusing, because Christ was allegedly born on a Wednesday, the Ethiopian week starts on a Wednesday.

The customs woman then asked me for serial numbers. 'For what?' I asked.

'Everything,' she said with an apologetic smile.

So I went searching for the numbers of our chassis, engine, cameras, lenses, laptop. Then she asked to have a look at the vehicle. 'Please will you unpack your Land Rover?' she said.

'What would you like to see?' I asked.

'Everything,' she said.

Half an hour later the contents of three overland vehicles were strewn across the parking lot and a crowd of children had gathered to admire our stuff. Slowly she worked her way through bags, boxes and coolers, asking sweetly, 'And what is in this one... and this one... and this one?'

While she went through the kit, we swapped overlanding stories. The Dutch had joined a convoy from Marsabit when they heard of recent bandit activity in the Chalbi Desert. The South African guys had given a lift to a local nun as protection. She was the perfect person to have at the Kenyan checkpoints: the police invariably waved them through when the nun was spotted. On another occasion, a group of wild-looking ruffians with rifles had stepped from the bush in front of their vehicle. When they saw the nun, they simply stepped back into the foliage. She'd probably taught some of them religious instruction...

Clearly every overlander in these parts needs a talismanic nun. Perhaps 4x4s should be fitted with game-tracker chairs on the bonnet, so your onboard nun could be seen from afar and there'd be no need to decelerate when approaching a police or shifta roadblock. Maybe nuns could replace carnets de passage, even passports.

But for the official's pleasant demeanour, we would have been seething at the endless checks. Fortunately there was no sign of corruption this side of the border, not a hint of soliciting a bribe to speed up formalities. Just a mountain of bureaucracy that had to be climbed. The cost of the entire process – including importation of a vehicle, levies and tourist fees for both of us – was one dollar.

We extricated ourselves from the money-changers and headed into town, easing over onto the right-hand side of the road. Men chewing *chat* (another version of miraa) sat by the roadside while goats nibbled the stalks of discarded branches, then ambled into the middle of the road to chill out, stoned off their floppy heads. Hooting wouldn't budge them, so the Landy wove between them.

Ethiopia is Mike's favourite country in Africa and he was grinning from ear to ear. Moyale lay on a slope and we drove up the long main drag past hole-in-the-hut shops and a market packing up for the day. We found an inn with bungalows in a garden. I grabbed a cold shower and washed layers of red earth off me as though my entire body was bleeding, then shaved patchily in the electricity-free bathroom.

At supper that night Mike wanted me to try some of the local beer – St George was an immediate hit – and the 'national food' he'd been raving about since we left Nairobi. First a man led us to a back room where he poured water from a tin can for us to wash: we'd be eating with our right hands, Muslim-style. When it came, the *injera* (unleavened bread made from dough left to ferment for three days) looked like a spongy pizza. On it were arranged little piles of *wot*, a spicy stew made from vegetables or meat, *gomon* (spinach) and *kitfo* (raw mince). There were also some darker mounds of lethal *beriberi* (peppers and spices) into which we dipped our food for lift-off. The conversation went something like this:

'You must try some wot,' suggested Mike.

'What?' I said.

'Wot.'

'That's what I said - what.'

'No, no, some wot.'
'Don't be ridiculous.'
'Wot, Spelt w-o-t.'
'So you can't spell either.'
'Stop playing stupid, wot!'
'My name's not what.'
'Whatnot then?'
'Piss off.'
It had been a long day and we were overtired.

I woke early to amplified chanting coming from a nearby church. Were it not for the strains sung in ancient Ge'ez – the Ethiopian church's equivalent of Latin – I'd have said it was a muezzin calling the faithful to prayer. Indeed, as we'd find throughout our Abyssinian travels, Islam had left many marks on this brand of Christianity. After all, the highlands have been surrounded by Muslim lowlands for centuries.

'Whey ho hey ho ho howo heyee hoo ho ha fa wha whey hey haa ha ha.' The chant soared and dipped and kept up its wailing for more than an hour. I was driven from bed and went photographing in the market, which was buzzing, even at that early hour. Women sat behind their wares: piles of spices, flour, beans, tef. Donkeys and camels milled about, loaded with goods. A truck arrived with plastic buckets of milk and was immediately surrounded by a throng of Borena women clad in the brightest sarongs, like butterflies alighting on a branch. Tailors sat at outdoor sewing machines, older men with red-dyed beards relaxed on dilapidated armchairs, having their shoes shined and watching the bustle.

Children called out 'Faranji' and pointed at the curiosity that was me, or shouted 'you-you-you' like a chant. Mike explained that it could be a shortening of 'How are you?' But the chorus, which accompanies tourists around Ethiopia, eventually grates. I took to calling 'you-you-you' in response, or the Ethiopian word for you, *ante*, which drew either laughter or baffled looks.

A yellow-billed kite put on an audacious flying display in the middle of the market. Every now and then it would drop from the sky like a stone, wings folded. Just before ploughing to a certain death, it would slam on air brakes, lower its undercarriage to grab a morsel of offal, bank hard to avoid a wall, stretch both wings and soar skyward like a rocket. I was stunned. No one else seemed to notice.

Beyond Moyale the land lay under a grey mantle, but the blacktop was straight and pothole-free – a dream after the Kenyan north. Vulturine guinea-fowl gathered on the road in clusters and had to be hooted onto the verges. One plucky fellow stood tall, sizing up the oncoming Land Rover and spoiling for a fight. Just when I thought we'd have spatchcocked dinner on the engine grill, it fluttered clucking from our path.

Square huts were the rule here: mud-and-dung walls built around a wooden frame with a porch supported on tree-trunk pillars. Roofs were nearly a metre thick and constructed from a mixture of mud and plants. Goats and chickens lived up there and their excretions made the roof more fertile, resulting in a thick growth of insulating vegetation. Some huts were more rooftop garden than family home.

The hills around Moyale had been heavily defended by the Italians with a battalion of troops, many machine-gun nests and artillery batteries. But the westward thrust by the South Africans meant these defences were never really tested and the Italians were forced to withdraw from Moyale without a fight once Mega had fallen.

To attack Mega from the west, the South African engineers had constructed a 250-kilometre road through the Chalbi Desert, climbing more than a thousand metres into uncharted territory. General Cunningham called it the most remarkable engineering feat of the campaign. Meanwhile the South African Air Force (SAAF) bombed artillery positions and Italian airfields in southern Ethiopia and flew survey flights to help the engineers with their road building.

Approaching Mega, soldiers of the Third Transvaal Scottish and the SA Irish pushed forward under cover of artillery and bombing by the SAAF. Rain turned the ground to mud. This was the first time Uncle Uys came under artillery fire and he vividly describes his and his countrymen's fear. Uys also had to deal with the death of a young lad he'd befriended. He kept thinking of 'the seventeen-year-old boy from the Transvaal platteland whom we had buried there in the reddish gold Mega earth in his brown veld blanket; and of his young half-section who, when Frans Fourie's grave lay level with the ground, suddenly bent down, carefully removed a stone as big as a man's fist from the fresh earth lying over the grave, and then, with his gaze fixed on the grave, half whispered: '*Slaap sag, Fransie* . . .' ('Sleep softly, Fransie . . .').

Our Land Rover coasted past the ruined fort at Mega which caught a shaft of sunlight breaking through the clouds. Set on a verdant slope it looked like a Cistercian abbey on a Scottish moor. It appeared now just as it must have to the South African troops as they charged the defences with fixed bayonets on the afternoon of 18 February 1941. The episode is described in the military's official history: 'At this crucial moment, the rain came down in torrents, but both the Transvaal Scottish and the SA Irish pushed on towards the substantial stone walls of the large fort squatting solidly on the level of the grassy plateau which formed the bottom of a wide basin beyond the crests of the surrounding hills. Through gaps in the mist and clouds they intermittently caught glimpses of the objective ahead of them. Over to the left of the Transvaal Scottish as they forced the wire, the SA Irish had broken through and were streaming down the spurs east of the fort and the Residency, where all resistance was collapsing . . .

'White flags fluttered from the straggling collection of hutments and shacks that was Mega, and the scene in the courtyard of the big stone fort made an indelible impression on the victors – weary, mud-bespattered but very confident South Africans, dejected prisoners by the score beneath battlements reminiscent of a bygone age.'

Those South Africans, one of them perhaps Uys, were chilled to the bone, short on rations, plagued by ticks, but reassured in the conclusion of their first important battle. They welcomed the blankets, warm coats and food provided of their own volition by the Italian prisoners.

Uys was struck by the kindness and humanity of the soldiers he was travelling with and wrote from Mega: 'In the constant company of those men [probably the Natal Carbineers] for about a month, I got to know them well. Most of them came from the Border districts, that is to say the Eastern Province, Transkei or certain country districts of southern Natal. Almost all of them were tall, broad-shouldered, bonily built and very quiet men. Only when they opened their mouths, could I distinguish who was Afrikaans- and who English-speaking. If I had to choose a single word to characterise them, it would have been "gentle".'

This pause at Mega was a happy, but brief respite in the advance. Many South Africans would be killed in the highlands, and many more would be captured or perish in the battles still to come in the Sahara before the Axis forces were finally chased from African soil.

Fields of red termite mounds lined the northward road. Some of them were fat and squat, others were tapering giants standing more than ten metres tall. With dead soldiers still on my mind, I wondered whether these mounds were the inspiration for the funerary stelae we encountered all over Ethiopia? Indeed, some were topped by vultures, reinforcing the death motif.

We drove through lovely undulating countryside, lush with plantations of coffee and *enset* (false banana). Square architecture was replaced by *tukuls* (rondavels) whose wooden walls were plastered with mud or hung with reed matting. The roofs were of thatched grass or banana leaves, the latter looking like fish scales, particularly when the old leaves dried to shingle silver. Between the hamlets lay village greens, or commonages, where children played soccer, passing the ball between unperturbed cattle. It seemed a land of bounty, far removed from the television images of desert and famine the world had grown to expect. How could this be the same Ethiopia?

The Arcadian atmosphere was marred in one village when we passed a young woman with aquiline features asleep on a bed beside the road. 'Bier, not bed,' said Mike. 'And she isn't asleep.' A group of men lifted her wooden 'bed' and bore her away. She lay on her side, both hands beneath her chin, the picture of peace. Within seconds the image flashed by, but it nagged round the corners of my mind for the rest of the journey.

Both Mike and I wanted to visit a field of 1 200 stelae known as Tututi. Villagers directed us to a road that wound up a hill which, they assured us, led to Tututi. It turned into a cattle track eroded with dongas. After some tricky negotiation the vehicle could go no further and we continued on foot. Soon we had an entourage of 30-odd, many calling the customary 'you-you-you' as we trudged upward. A prophet-like elder with a shaved head and long beard took the lead. He was barefoot, clad only in a black coat and shorts with holes. This Moses paused now and then to lean on his staff and wait for the slowcoach faranjis, offering encouragement in an unfamiliar tongue, probably Oromigna. Ethiopia has 83 languages and 200 dialects, so making yourself understood in remote parts is always a challenge.

As we progressed, the thin air began to smell decidedly rank. After another hundred metres it became almost unbearable and we pulled our shirts over our mouths, which the children mimicked, with much amusement. The charnel house, when we drew level, was a simple clearing next to the path piled with carcasses, skins and entrails. A flock of feeding vultures took to the air at the last moment, flapping just above our heads with great beating wings.

Exhausted, we reached the top to find an open-air market, but no sign of the stelae field. Surrounded by hundreds of people, we were becoming the centre of too much attention. A pocket Mussolini brandishing a stick at his subjects addressed the crowd and then pointed at us. Even with Mike's rudimentary knowledge of Amharic, we had no idea what he was saying. From the tone, it didn't sound like a completely positive introduction. People started laughing at us. We tried to ask about the stelae, but no one spoke a word of English, other than 'you'. Mike wanted to find Tututi on his own, but the stick-wielding leader would have nothing of it, shouting at us and shaking his head. Mike tried to push his way through a sea of people that wouldn't part.

'Um, Mike. I think we should give the stelae a miss. I wasn't *that* keen anyway and we need to get to Dila before dark.'

My travelling partner was still trying to part the masses.

'Mike!' I said rather harshly. 'Those carcasses at the charnel house were lost faranjis and I'm getting the hell outta here.'

Next thing, we were descending the hill at a decidedly brisk pace, Moses struggling to keep up with a hobbling gait. This time the vultures didn't budge as we passed, shooting us withering looks. We were practically running now, and had put a good distance between ourselves and our entourage. But when Mike stopped for a pee he was quickly surrounded by gapers. I pressed on, hopped into the Land Rover and put it through a wheel-spinning five-point turn. Mike had broken into a trot, followed by two dozen guides who felt entitled to a small tip for their efforts. The vehicle was already rolling when Mike dragged himself into the cab.

I too needed to take a leak, so after driving a little way, I pulled the car over and got out. I was just beginning to relieve myself against a tree when I heard the distant sound of what seemed like cheering. Looking back up the track I saw our friends hurtling towards us. They'd regrettably surmised that our conscience had got the better of us and we'd stopped to distribute gifts and alms for the needy, perhaps even an airline ticket or two. I nipped my leak in the bud, so to speak, and sprinted for the door. Having learnt his lesson, Mike knew an awkward moment when he saw one and had moved into the driver's seat. It was my turn to throw myself into the cab just as the acolytes drew level. Tears of laughter or mild hysteria poured down our cheeks as the vehicle skidded away.

We passed through villages where children's greetings were sirens which rose and faded: 'YouyouyouYOUYOUYOUyouyouyou,' punctuated by the staccato shouts of 'Faranji! Faranji!' Mike turned up his Hugh Masekela CD and we steamed on.

By evening we'd reached the commercial town of Dila where we found a quiet *pension* in a back street. It was early to bed and early to rise for the leg to Addis Ababa. The road dropped off a plateau into the Rift Valley and the temperature climbed accordingly. Vegetation turned from a lush green back to the drier acacia woodland of Kenya. The valley floor was dotted with lakes that culminate in Turkana in the far southwestern corner of the country. This great Rift is a relatively new feature on the planet's surface and some geologists attribute it to an asteroid impact, perhaps the same one that ended the age of the dinosaurs. Major volcanic activity raised highlands on both sides of Africa's long gash, and volcanoes occasionally broke through the valley floor. In Ethiopia some of these are still active and hot springs bubble from the earth's depths.

At mid-morning on market day we arrived at the lake and town of Awasa, set in a volcanic caldera. Horse- and donkey-drawn *garis* (carts) in their dozens negotiated the narrow streets, piled with produce. Some garis were elaborate affairs with bonnet and bells, husband and wife in their market finest trotting into town like a scene from a Western. Fiat buses disgorging diesel fumes tried to overtake carts already in the process of passing pedestrian traffic. It was good-natured mayhem.

We stopped to stretch our legs at the Wabe Shebele Hotel on the shores of Lake Awasa. It was a lovely spot filled with shrill avian life. I took a walk along a dyke separating the hotel garden from the lake. Abyssinian ground hornbills clashed beaks as if applauding, lovebirds and parrots squawked, reed and white-breasted cormorants watched the water for movement while pied kingfishers made attacks on surface minnows. There were storks, egrets, geese, ibises, hamerkops, crakes, terns and fish eagles. I could easily have whiled away the morning there with bird book, binoculars and a longish drink. But Addis beckoned.

North of Awasa we drove between Rift lakes – Shala, Abijata, Langano, Ziway – through a yellow land patrolled by dust devils. Driving grew more taxing as we neared the capital. The road itself was good blacktop, but its users kept us on our toes. Crippled horses that had been discarded to fend for themselves would stagger into the road. One donkey even walked up the centre, parting traffic. Trucks swerved into the ditch to avoid Eeyore, but the commotion hardly ruffled his jauntily angled ears.

After Mojo we joined a stream of lorries doing the Djibouti to Addis run. Then we got stuck in traffic on a ring road being built by the Chinese: the sections didn't quite fit together and the in-between bits had become a potholed racetrack free-for-all. Bemused Ethiopian workmen in wide-brimmed straw hats watched the mêlée.

I thought of Uncle Uys and the entry of the South African army into Addis 61 years before. It was the first Axis capital city to fall during the war and official history records that it was a group of jovial war correspondents who were the first to enter Addis, not the army. Uys was one of them. As they motored into the centre Italians lined the streets giving the Fascist salute. The arrival of this motley bunch at the Emperor's Palace, serving as Governor Aosta's vice-regal residence, must have been something of a letdown for the immaculately turned-out Italians.

There were joyous celebrations in Addis. The five years of Italian rule had been brutal. Viceroy Graziani had crushed resistance with chilling efficiency. After an attempt on Graziani's life, his Blackshirts took revenge on the capital, going on a three-day orgy of rampage, murder and arson. Innocent people were disembowelled or decapitated, and it is claimed that up to 30 000 citizens were massacred, among them all the young, educated Ethiopians the Italians could lay their hands on.

While he was at it, Graziani ordered that all hermits, soothsayers and travelling minstrels be rounded up and shot. He was also convinced that high church officials, particularly the monks at Debre Libanos, had known about the plot on his life. He ordered the destruction of this ancient monastery, which had been the political centre of the Church for four centuries. Its 297 monks, along with a hundred young deacons, were shot. Hundreds of other clergy were sent to concentration camps.

By the time the Allied forces liberated Addis, they could congratulate themselves on a successful campaign. The East Africa Force had advanced 2 760 kilometres in 53 days over difficult terrain and in the face of demolitions, bad weather and appalling roads against an enemy that was numerically superior. With the fall of Addis and the reinstatement of Emperor Haile Selassie, it was hoped that all Italian resistance would crumble. However, some of the hardest fighting awaited the South Africans north of the capital.

Addis Ababa started life as a royal encampment. King Menelik II chose the verdant hills below the Shoan tableland for his capital and called it Addis Ababa or 'new flower'. Named after legendary King Menelik I (the son of Solomon and the Queen of Sheba) the new leader expanded his kingdom from here, eventually proclaiming himself Emperor of Ethiopia in 1889. Ethiopia had for long been a name given to this region of Africa (Homer and Herodotus refer to *aethiops* as burnt/black-faced people), but official use of the word, and the conscious forging of an Ethiopian national identity, are Menelik's doing.

Like Johannesburg, it's a young African metropolis. A visitor to the new capital at the turn of the 20th century would have found green hills and valleys of mimosa and newly-imported eucalyptus trees (to solve the capital's firewood problem). The land was dotted with huts, but there were no streets and only a handful of stone buildings. It was a sprawling, glorified kraal.

Menelik's dynasty continued down to Haile Selassie (a baptismal name meaning 'power of the trinity'). Selassie's given name was Tafari, but he was simply known as Ras (Duke) Tafari until his coronation in 1930. From his name stems the Caribbean Rastafarian cult, which venerates Selassie as supreme ruler of all black people and seeks their return to Africa. Although not as godlike as the Rastas would have us believe, Selassie *was* one of Ethiopia's most illustrious leaders, an autocrat intent on modernising the country and doing away with feudalism and the power of regional princes.

At his coronation he took the title of His Majesty, Haile Selassie the First, King of Kings, Conquering Lion of the Tribe of Judah, Elect of God, Emperor of Ethiopia. He delayed his crowning by seven months in order to invite the world's leaders and turn it into a spectacle the like of which had never been seen in Africa's highlands. Addis Ababa underwent months of cleaning and painting. Golden headgear was fashioned for the ras, pearl-studded coronets and crowns for royalty, headgear from lion's manes interlaced with gold for military commanders. Dozens of journalists attended, among them the young Evelyn Waugh who immortalised the event in two books.

In 1974 Selassie was deposed (and secretly strangled, his body dumped in a cellar beside a latrine in the Grand Palace) by the communist Derg Party under their feared dictator, Haile Mariam Mengistu. For the next 17 years his hardline rule crippled the country. A Stasi-style police force silenced opposition and famine was used as a political tool: one million people, mostly those opposed to the Derg, died of starvation in 1985 alone. Communal farming and mass peasant resettlement programmes backfired, plunging the country into economic crisis. It's only in the decade since liberation that Ethiopia has got back on its feet.

After meandering through Addis traffic we eventually reached Rennie Orton's house. Our host lived just off the Bole Road in a kind of compound. Mike hooted and gates swung open to reveal a scruffy courtyard overlooked by a two-storey tiled house. A one-eyed dog called Lucy barked furiously at our tyres, but was all smiles and licking when we stepped from the vehicle. Rennie stood in the courtyard with hands on hips, his leather waistcoat unbuttoned, big knife holstered to his belt and Stetson pushed back on his head.

'What took you so long you fucking bastard?' he said, wrapping Mike in an affectionate hug. He was a big man and Mike almost disappeared.

Rennie had a worn face, but the boy was still there below a web of sunburnt lines. He'd known Mike at school in Cape Town and now worked for our Nairobi friend, Ed. He ran the Addis arm of the business, but his demeanour was more that of a sheriff in a lawless town.

'Come, let's go to my workshop and give your Landy a good clean,' he said after the greetings. 'Boetie, you drive with me, not in Mike's Christmas tree.'

He flattened the accelerator and Mike vanished in a puff of dust behind us. 'Hope that slowcoach remembers where my workshop is!' he shouted. 'I'm not waiting for him to find the bleddy handbrake.'

Trying to distract myself from the speedometer, I asked him about Addis. 'Eight years I've been here. Love it, love my job. I do mostly construction for Ed, but also a bit of security, some trucking.' He was loud, brash and likeable. A frontiersman using local opportunities and bureaucratic laxity to mould a comfortable place for himself in the highlands.

I tried to compose – and hold – an unfazed expression as we hurtled along, overtaking on blind rises, trying to intimidate oncoming traffic, driving up a closed section of highway and other forms of entertainment to whiten my knuckles. We skidded to a halt outside a compound filled with cranes, trucks and containers. After much hooting the gates flew open, scattering workers. Rennie leapt from the cab and hit the ground shouting, 'Come boys, when the Land Rover gets here let's give it a good clean, hey. Put the food in the fridge. Boetie, we'd better sort you out with a new tyre. Can't head north with only one spare.' I didn't feel I had a say in these matters; Rennie was like a tropical storm and I didn't mind being swept along.

Vikram, Rennie's Indian second-in-command, followed him about with papers to sign. He was clearly in awe of Rennie and had adopted a few of his mannerisms and his dress code. The leather jacket was there and some of the bravado. He managed to be both fawning and vaguely macho, carrying himself like an, albeit petite, body builder. Rennie raged about the yard in an amiable tirade punctuated with an endless stream of 'fucks', 'arseholes' and 'can't get a bloody job done around heres'. No one seemed fazed. I followed, just another acolyte. 'This scoop is for a gold mine in the south,' he said to me, 'that 50-metre crane we rent out, this truck is going to our bottling plant in the Sudan.'

He was the kind of man who likes to get his hands dirty, who 'knows his Africans and how to get the best out of them'. So it was surprising when he told me he was sponsoring a boy in Moyale and had agreed to put him through university as long as he came to work for the company after studying. Another disciple in the making.

That evening we met Marta, Rennie's girlfriend. She was 25 years his junior, a bird-like, fine-boned woman with soft, slow eyes. She moved with difficulty and Rennie explained she'd been seriously ill with a stomach ailment that required surgery. Mike told me he thought she had Aids.

Marta had made us soup and fresh injera. She spoke hardly at all and seldom looked up from her plate. The contrast between this big, boisterous South African and the frail Ethiopian could hardly have been greater. Meanwhile Mike and Rennie chatted animatedly about old times, the journey at hand and the nuts and bolts of vehicles: Pirelli versus Michelin, jacking points and snorkels, tyre and engine size. I let it wash over me.

The feeling in the house was oppressive, with the one-eyed dog eyeing me suspiciously, a subservient maid from a rural area who hadn't opened her mouth since we'd arrived, ailing Marta who could hardly lift the bowl of soup and Rennie trying to pretend all was well. Marta's eyes knew that Rennie had taken a new lover (Mike kept me in the picture), that his sudden interest in going to the gym and getting trim wasn't innocent. Then there was the side-kick, Vikram, who came and went at odd hours and had been ejected from his saggy bed in a windowless room to make way for me. Perhaps it was Mike's mention of Aids, or maybe it was Marta's resemblance to the young woman we'd seen on the bier, but the overwhelming aura in the house was one of foreboding.

Later Mike and I headed for the Sheraton, by far the grandest hotel in Ethiopia, to meet up with Margy Beves-Gibson, friend and *Getaway* editorial assistant, as well as Bridget Hilton-Barber, a regular contributor to the magazine. Both were spending a long weekend in town on a media trip organised to celebrate South African Airways' (SAA) introduction of direct flights from Jo'burg to Addis. After days on the road the luxury of the Sheraton was overwhelming: soft carpets, tinkling music, terraced gardens and not a morsel of injera in sight. Tables were weighed down with tasty nibbles, the wine was South African, the cocktails umbrella'd and the hall filled with journalists, VIPs and GGs (glamourous guests) from home. The *Sunday Times* journalist complained about the bad organisation and lack of press packs. One guest mopped his brow with a handkerchief and said, 'I can't bear the poverty here – it's just not like our poverty back home.' Another complained, 'I simply refuse to see another limbless child. Tomorrow I'm staying put on the pool deck and drinking pina coladas.'

Sipho Gumede and his band had been flown in from Jo'burg to provide the music and soon the South Africans were jiving, treading fallen canapés into the carpet. As I watched them dance, it struck me that they were a strange phenomenon, these new Africans from the deep south with their spanking democracy, their wealth and self-assurance. How far we had come in just ten years. Here were South Africa's movers and shakers, a new black elite whose backyard was the entire continent. They seemed to express in their attitudes and body language that same sense of ownership and confidence one often finds around American travellers. A kind of imperial 'world is my oyster' demeanour. But because it was new and (still) relatively benign, there was an innocence there, a sense of celebration at being wealthy, powerful, free and African. We'd grown up under isolationist apartheid and now it was wonderful to join a group of compatriots in darkest Commie Africa, at the seat of the old OAU, and feel pretty good about ourselves . . . more or less at home, so many miles from home.

Next day, while Rennie tinkered with the vehicle and Mike corresponded with Cape Town by Bushmail, I went into town with Margy and some of the journalists. It was to be our one day of unrestrained sightseeing. We hired a taxi to the cathedrals of St George and the Holy Trinity. A soft-spoken archdeacon with a goatie, prominent cheekbones and a broad brow led us through a church museum filled with relics, crowns, capes, holy umbrellas made of velvet, prayer sticks and a bell donated by the Russian Orthodox Church. There were paintings by 'many a famous Ethiopian artist' whose symbolism he explained in careful English sprinkled with archaisms. St George and his dragon featured everywhere, while Jesus got hardly a look in. In a country where wild animals were a real threat, a spear-wielding saint who could fell even the meanest beasties was always going to have an edge on a pacifist saviour, at least in the iconography.

Beggars stood with cupped hands on the church steps, others prayed Wailing Wall-style around the perimeter. We removed our shoes and entered the octagonal cathedral built to commemorate Menelik's defeat of the Italians at Adwa in 1896. The archdeacon led us through a cavernous interior glowing with the light of chandeliers, our nostrils prickling to the scent of incense. He showed us the spot in the church where Selassie was crowned, and talked us through murals featuring the emperor in various guises.

We each found a pew and he demonstrated the slow and fast chanting of religious ceremonies as well as a quaint skipping dance that went with each chant. Getting into the swing of his performance, he showed how tired priests would lean on their crutch-like prayer sticks during the long, 12 hour services. When he beat the big ceremonial drum, its booming seemed to shake the walls. This was a Christianity whose ceremonies packed a holy punch: even the rowdy journalists were silenced.

After a succession of churches, culminating in the Holy Trinity Cathedral, I'd had my fill of religious buildings for the day, so I broke away to visit the National Museum and pay my respects to Lucy. Like many African museums, it is a blend of eclectically collected and haphazardly categorised material: a jumble of palaeontology, ethnography, history and art. Hominid skulls and pre-Judaic fertility symbols were tossed in with guns, swords, bronze seals and paintings of famine victims. It was as though pre-historical periods formed an unbroken continuum with contemporary national history. As a categorising philosophy, albeit unintended, it was rather appealing.

In a dingy basement room I came upon the skeleton of Lucy – or Dinquinesh ('Thou art wonderful') to Ethiopians – lying in a glass coffin. Despite her advanced age of 3.2 million years I found her beautiful. Lucy was an early hominid, killed at age 20, whose skeleton was uncovered in a dried-up lake bed northeast of Addis. At the time of her discovery in 1974 Lucy proved that our ancestors were walking on their hind legs two and a half million years earlier than had been suspected. She was given the scientific name *Australopithecus afarensis.*

I rejoined the journalists, who'd been tucking into the 'Stolly' over lunch, and told them about my visit to Lucy. 'She's gone to pieces of late, hasn't she?' said one.

'Poor dear, she's just not holding up,' offered another.

'Let's face it, she's aged badly.'

'Now then, we must remember she *is* getting on a little,' Margy reasoned.

Bridget stepped to her defence. 'Whatever you say, I still think she's gorgeous. But then again, I suppose one does make allowances for family members.'

That night I joined the SAA contingent at the Crown Restaurant to experience traditional singing and dancing. The interiors were all of reed matting and we sat on low stools beside *mesobs* (tables woven like baskets). The orchestra played a range of curious instruments: lyres, one-string fiddles, bamboo flutes. The sound was cacophonic at first, then by parts more intriguing. After a couple of bottles of St George, I was quite captivated.

But really, the dancers were the thing. Their movements were acrobatic, shoulders jerking to the manic rhythm provided by the musicians. There were hops and leaps and all the while the music wailed, burped and cajoled the dancers into ever more daring feats. Now and again all hell broke loose and the troop would be released across the floor like balls whirling from a cannon. Each dance had a story which slowly revealed itself, and every one seemed to be about courtship. There were lads in farm clothes carrying hoes and hunters returning from a kill, there were maidens in their finery, bridal couples and warriors with spears.

One girl caught our attention. Her shoulders shrugged and wiggled coquettishly, her breasts flapped up and down to the rhythm and her eyes rolled in her head. You wouldn't think showing the whites of your eyes attractive. Indeed, this was unfamiliar erotic territory, made all the more alluring by its strangeness. Let's just say she had the attention of every South African man in the room.

Mike and I ended up later that night at the expat Dutch Milk Bar. There was a pool table, a few cruising Ethiopian women and a crowd of foreign men, mostly doing contract work in Addis. I got chatting to a handsome fellow at the bar who was staring down the barrel of his umpteenth whisky. His was one of those Blixenesque 'I had a security firm in Aaafrica' stories.

Peter, it turned out, worked for Ed and Rennie. Small world, Addis. His chin only just cleared the top of his glass and his eyes were far away – in Nairobi, actually, as I was to learn. Peter was an ex-British army officer who'd been employed by one of the biggest security companies in Kenya. The owner of the business, a former brigadier in the Kenyan army, had died in a freak accident while hunting in Uganda. The brigadier's beautiful wife, 20 years his junior, took Peter as her lover and made him managing director. He built her a house in Karen – Corinthian columns, pool, unbreachable security, complete with state-of-the-art video surveillance. But she kept him on a tight leash and a tight salary. And, he contends, at arm's length – albeit in her bed. 'She 'ad me under 'er thumb. 'Olding a candle for the brigadier, she was.'

This continued for many years, then the innocuous turned venomous. They decided to join the local polo club, but she refused to sign them in as a couple, insisting they join separately. He'd had enough, resigned immediately and left her to join Ed in setting up a rival security firm with branches in Nairobi and Addis. Peter's revenge would be to see Ed's company eclipse hers, he vowed. Rumour had it she was spitting mad.

That was his side of the story anyway. On the way home Mike put a different spin on things. 'Actually, she came home to find Peter naked with a teenage girl in her cupboard . . . booted him straight out.'

So white mischief, I'm pleased to report, is alive and well in these parts.

We left Margy and the journalists sipping post-breakfast margaritas and bade exaggerated farewells in the Sheraton lobby. 'How will you cope, you poor dear,' said the *Sunday Times* correspondent. 'You're such a sweet petal. Do you have moisturiser and conditioner? Oh please tell me that you do. You must take all the fruit from our complimentary baskets. We won't starve.'

Our Land Rover riveted the northbound towns to the map; high on bitumen dreams we flew. Blue mountains beckoned and we edged skyward over tall passes and Italian-made stone bridges. The earth opened in chasms, revealing hamlets surrounded by a patchwork of millet and wheat fields pimpled with haystacks tended by men with forks, like dwarfs at a giant meal. Cherubic girls suspended three metres above the ground in baskets on stilts acted as human scarecrows. The singing of sickle-wielding harvesters carried across the broken terrain.

The last 50 kilometres to Kombolcha was driven in a dusky gloom, a terrible ride through construction works and homebound herds – a tangle of 4x4s, trucks, cranes and seemingly blinkered pedestrians. A herdboy with a stick across his shoulders appeared, silhouetted in the lights of an oncoming bus. The beams refracted in the dust around him like a biblical painting. 'Jesus, brake!' I shouted. Horn blasts from two sides sent the Lord and his flock scampering for the ditch.

At Kombolcha we found a rough inn where a woman in a starched white coat assured us the rooms were 'self-contain-*ed* with hot *and* cold water.' Of course she was lying – about the hot water, not the cold – but we were too tired and irritable to look further. Food was perfunctory and sleep an almost immediate knock-out blow.

After the fall of Addis, the South African forces were ordered to advance along the road we'd been following all day. Their objective was the port of Massawa in Eritrea, where they'd be shipped to Egypt to help defend against the onslaught of Rommel's *Afrika Korps*. But the road north led over some of the continent's most awesome mountains. One pass, just outside Kombolcha, was defended by 10 000 troops, including two Blackshirt battalions, and 52 guns, some of which were built by the British in 1916 and were set in concrete on high ground. The South Africans ran into heavy fire as they tried to enter Kombolcha. So they dug in and a furious six-day artillery duel ensued.

Ethiopian patriots, many clad in lion's manes and plumes like medieval warriors, harried the enemy artillery positions and, working round to the rear, played havoc with the Italians' lines of communication. But it was the banana boys of the Natal Carbineers who swung the balance, with a daring night-time raid on a strategic hill in the midst of the Italian positions. About 300 men stole silently up the enemy's eastern flank and got within ten metres of the defences before the alarm was raised. In a cold and misty dawn the Natalians swooped on the Blackshirt battalion. Many were shot even before they could throw off their blankets. Machine-gun nests were silenced with hand-grenades and mortars. As the light improved, the Italians regained some composure and the South Africans came under air-burst attack from artillery. But the hill had fallen and the outcome of the battle was now inevitable. Fearing the massacre of Italian women and children in nearby Dese by shifta and patriot bands, the forces surrendered.

We eased through the bustling streets of Dese the next morning. The only signs of its former occupation were a few Italianate buildings lining the main street. But there was plenty of evidence of more recent fighting. Discarded T54 tanks guarded the road, their barrels facing the passes from where the invading Eritreans and liberation fighters had come. Some tanks were covered with foliage woven together into camouflage mats. The plants had died and were pealing away, revealing the menacing shape beneath. Although their turrets pointed north, all the tanks faced south, poised for flight if the enemy proved too formidable.

A short political digression is needed here. There have essentially been two major wars in Ethiopia over the past three decades. Mike and I would come across burnt-out tanks and sites of battle in the ensuing days, but it was hard to know which armies were represented by the military hardware. In the first struggle, Eritrean forces and Ethiopian guerrillas combined to rid Ethiopia of its hard-line Communist leader Mengistu and his Derg Party. This was finally achieved in 1991. Eritrea was granted complete independence, but border disputes with Ethiopia during the late 1990s escalated into skirmishes. When Eritrean planes dropped cluster bombs on civilian targets in Mekele and Adigrat in June 1998, it turned into another full-scale war. Nearly half a million soldiers were poured into the fray. Despite a ceasefire in 2000, and UN intervention on the ground, the region still simmers.

At Lake Hayk we left the main road and drove onto a peninsula across a narrow isthmus lined with pines. Here we found the lakeside monastery of Istafanos, established in 862 AD by an itinerant saint from Jerusalem. The region was formerly home to a pagan cult of python worshippers, but converted to Christianity when the saint worked his magic, using his cross to make the resident python disappear. Another curious legend concerning the Sisyphus-like saint suggests he spent his waking hours hauling around a stone cross, which he kissed 10 000 times a day.

Istafanos had an aura of absolute peace. The lake was ringed by green hills chequered with terraces, while the monastery had citrus orchards and plots of millet, sorghum and wheat. Colourful rowing boats oared by monks plied the shallows, and further out fishermen poled *tankwas* (papyrus-bundle boats like those of ancient Egypt).

A monk in purple robes and carrying a wooden cross blessed us, then led us past an octagonal church to the lake shore where water licked the edge of the lawn and marabou storks fished. Some of the clergy stood atop haystacks and forked them into shape, others wove baskets from grass. Our monk showed us into a straw-and-mud-walled chapel. There were no windows and he left the door open to throw light on the simple interior. We could just make out grinding stones and farm implements, but what caught our attention were the wooden shackles used to chain the feet of wayward clergy, and an engraved stone cross that looked to be centuries old. Could this be the much-kissed and much-lugged crucifix of the founding saint?

From Weldiya the road climbed 3 000 metres in tight switchbacks, traversing stone-terraced terrain dotted with mimosa and euphorbia trees that pointed their prickly arms at the sky. Trucks whose brakes had failed lay far below, impaled on the rocks. We stopped for lunch in a field. The sniping breeze was cold and the landscape almost devoid of vegetation. Our bread, cheese and tomato rations had become dislodged and had slipped to the bottom of the fridge where they'd mingled freely with spilt Coke and the blood of old mincemeat. We salvaged what we could, only to find a circle of villagers watching our meal with eyes that said 'decadent feast'. Women with amphorae of water on their backs stood behind the elders; beyond them were inquisitive sheep and goats. They were like a group of poor man's paparazzi.

Mike gave the leader a packet of biscuits and he distributed them carefully among the group. There was much curious smiling, smacking of lips and murmurs of *ameseghinallehu* (thank you).

The road climbed again through wildly beautiful country towards the holy town of Lalibela, tucked into a corner of Drakensberg-like peaks. But the place was proving hard to find, particularly given that we were taking a more scenic route than intended. All three of our maps of the area contradicted one another, and the GPS gave an even more creative interpretation of our whereabouts. It suggested we were pioneering a new route, heading into *terra incognita*, lost in the Mountains of Lasta.

After a few frustrating hours we happened upon the outskirts of Lalibela and drove along steep lanes lined with two-storey circular stone houses. Plonkers ran beside the vehicle shouting welcoming 'you-you-you's as well as the names of secret *pensions* whose location only they knew. Unfortunately for them we found a perfectly nice one under our own steam.

I left Mike with his Bushmail correspondence and hit the town's famous rock-hewn churches, considered the unofficial eighth wonder of the world. The subterranean precinct is cut into pink tufa and connected by tunnels, trenches and bridges more suited to a children's fairytale. These 800-year-old monoliths are not ancient relics preserved as museums, but living shrines with pilgrims arriving every day to pray. On saints' holy days they're packed with worshippers wrapped in gossamer-fine shammas, leaning on prayer sticks or prostrating themselves before the altar, the priests resplendent in red-and-gold robes. Services last through the night, accompanied by hypnotic drumming and chanting, clouds of incense and tolling bells.

This is a Christianity far removed from sanitised Western incarnations. For the better part of 1 500 years the Ethiopian Church was cut off from Europe's ecclesiastical adaptations and modernisations. It's like stepping into the pages of the Bible and experiencing a faith with its ancient fundamentalism and trappings still intact. Here the pagan origins of those rites seem to shimmer just below the surface, like a mysterious presence in the religion's subconscious, and find expression in fertility dances, animal sacrifices and sacred monthly feasts.

The churches' construction is attributed to the 13th-century King Lalibela, around whom many legends have been spun. As he emerged from his mother's womb, it is said, a swarm of bees surrounded him and she immediately named him Lalibela – 'the bee recognises his sovereignty'. His brother, the reigning king, tried twice to have him poisoned, then abdicated in favour of the charmed brother. After a period in the wilderness (compulsory in these tales) and a business-class tour of the Holy Land (courtesy of an angel), the new king poured his energy into fulfilling God's command to build a series of churches. Their design was made clear to the young king during a dream in which he was taken to heaven by an angel for a virtual site-meeting and given the specs. Back on earth, he mobilised a huge workforce – some say 40 000 would have been needed. The labourers toiled by day, then angels took over for the night-shift.

A more prosaic explanation for the building of the churches is increased Muslim control of the Holy Land, which created the need for an 'alternative Jerusalem' for Ethiopian pilgrims to visit. Indeed, the stream flowing through the church complex was named Jordan, symbolic graves for Abraham, Isaac and Jacob were dug, and tombs for Christ and Adam built.

As I descended the stairs into a great pit cut by countless masons I ran my hand along walls whose red, lichen-patched rock had been chipped, grooved and worn like a labyrinthine sculpture. In the perimeter were hermit cells: tiny caves where elderly worshippers now prayed and slept. Occasionally begging hands – some leprous and without fingers – would emerge from these caverns as I passed.

The largest monolith is Bet Medhane Alem. With its own mighty colonnade of 36 square pillars, each carved to represent a stone pier surmounted by a wooden capital, Medhane Alem makes the boldest statement. Inside it was cool and dark. A lad read from an illuminated Bible bound in a cover of richly worked silver. Bearded priests stood over him, correcting his mispronunciations. His teenage voice, chanting in Ge'ez – the Semitic language of church litany – cracked every now and then. Deeper among the forest of columns a service had begun. Three monks in red vestments swung censers and recited verses, their voices bouncing sweetly off the living rock. I marvelled at the precise carving of these interiors. There had to have been detailed plans and architectural models; what's more, the ornamentation in the dark recesses could only have been done by torchlight . . . or by angels.

A child who bore a remarkable resemblance to a very old man, offered in halting English to be my guide. He had an irresistible smile, wore clothes far too big for him and broken sandals tied together with string. His name was Zelalem and he didn't seem at all like a plonker. I handed him my tripod and sandals (visitors are only allowed in the churches with bare feet) and let him lead the way. Even with its legs compressed, the Manfrotto reached to his shoulder, but I was happy to be free of the weight.

Zelalem first showed me round Bet Maryam, one of Ethiopia's most beautiful churches, where worshippers had gathered for a service in the courtyard, while others circled the church kissing its walls. I couldn't get over the fact that this was all taking place many metres below ground level. We emerged into the next courtyard and a blind woman stepped out of a cavern, arms outstretched like a zombie, moaning for alms. We skirted round her, but she moved like a cat, trying to cut us off. I sidestepped her and broke into a discreet jog, my pint-sized tripod-bearer beside me. She seemed supernaturally quick over the uneven ground as she followed our footfalls, and soon we made an unholy pair running helter-skelter to the next church.

Later Zelelam pointed into a tunnel. 'You have torch?' he asked. I shook my head.

'Hold onto the sticks, *eshi* (okay)?' he said. I grabbed the tripod's feet and he led me into the pit.

'You there mistah? *Awo*, keep acoming, it is tall for your head.'

The ground was rough and I steadied myself with one hand against the rock. Zelalem had no such trouble and could obviously see in the dark. A saint in the making? We inched along for about 50 metres before emerging into the bottom of a sheer-sided hole which held a square chapel. The Abyssinian ancients certainly knew how to play the chiaroscuro game to maximum spiritual effect.

And so it went, from church to church. Monks in robes and turbans drew back curtains to reveal vellum books and the intricate silver fretwork of Lalibela crosses. The wall paintings, triptychs and icons depicted biblical stories and it was interesting how much information about secular life one could glean from them. Donors who'd paid for the picture were often shown prostrate at the bottom of the image, *à la* Quattrocento Florentine art.

The last church on Zelalem's tour was Bet Giorgis. The story goes that St George was so offended that none of the 12 churches was dedicated to him that he paid King Lalibela a visit. Words were exchanged. Maybe a dragon was mentioned. Next day the plans had changed: one more church needed to be dug. Pronto. The result was the most magnificent monolith of all.

Bet Giorgis lies apart from the others and has no protective scaffolding over it, heightening its dramatic impact. I stood at the rim of a square crater, awed by a church in the shape of a Greek cross below, its ogival windows decorated with carved arabesques. The building was 'constructed' on a three-tiered plinth and stands a few storeys high, but, like the others, its roof is flush with ground level. Down in the moat Zelalem took me to a cave in which lay a skeleton, dried skin still attached to the bone. They were no doubt the remains of a pilgrim who'd wanted to die beside the house of St George, hoping to be spirited to heaven on the celestial steed (whose hoof prints were discernible near the entrance to the church).

Back at the backpackers' joint I found Mike settling down to lunch from a menu that boasted 'oatsporriage, vegitable soap, steake sandiwich and beaverages'. We ordered a bottle of *tej*. It's a bright yellow and potent mead made from honey or sugar and can sink an afternoon, much as chat can.

We resisted the temptation to polish off the potion and headed for the market, Mike with video camera and me with my Nikons. Strolling down the alleys, we glanced through open doorways to see women pounding peppers for wot or cooking injera over wood fires. One mother with two children invited us in to watch the process. She poured the fermented batter from an earthenware jar onto an iron skillet placed over a fire. In a few minutes it was cooked. Injera jars are never cleaned, so the old scraps of dough help speed the fermentation process when the new batch is added. The woman tore off a piece from her pile for us to try and smiled expectantly. It was very good in an injera sort of way.

At Lalibela market the ground was a kaleidoscope of coffees, nuts and grains. Wind lifted spices into the air and shoppers went about coughing and sneezing, particularly around the chilli-sorting area where dark-red carpets of the spice covered the earth. Stalls offered everything from cheap plastic sandals to beautiful fabrics and jewellery – including Ethiopian crosses in silver, brass and steel. Children sold handfuls of *kolo*, a snack of roasted grains, for peckish shoppers. Bargain goats were tethered to each other by their legs. Like markets everywhere in Africa, it was a social event, a piece of theatre with bobbing black sun umbrellas, children weaving and dodging, women gossiping at the tops of their voices and animals braying, bleating and barking.

The road from Lalibela twisted through some of the highest terrain I'd ever seen. It was a landscape in the vertical. Each of a succession of mountain passes soared on spindly tracks, then plummeted into gorges sliced by boulder-strewn streams. The Land Rover was having a hard time of it, but more astonishing were the women, often burdened with bundles of wood or large amphorae, trudging up these passes. Their industrious menfolk were no doubt at home discussing things of a philosophical or political nature over a sprig of chat.

In Sekota a policeman blew his whistle and stopped us, asking whether the governor had given us permission to be in his town. No, unfortunately Mike had to admit we had no letter of introduction. We were obviously not welcome and left in a hurry. A couple of hours later, near Maychew (pronounced 'Macho'), a herdboy threw a stone at us which bounced off the bonnet. It was the second stoning incident that day and I slammed on the brakes. We both leapt out. I was incandescent with rage – in retrospect unnecessarily so. Mike grabbed the boy's stick and I poked him in the ribs. His cattle scattered down the hill.

'You little shit!' I shouted. 'If you ever do that again I'll fucking kill you.' What was the use? He understood no English and was transfixed with fright. I quickly gave up trying to get through to him and climbed back in the vehicle feeling rotten.

Xenophobia and a distrust of faranjis are part of the psyche here and I shouldn't have taken it personally. Children grow up on stories of foreign barbarians and their atrocities. This mountain fastness has been surrounded by enemies for millennia. Abyssinia clung on as a Christian enclave in a state of siege, suffering at the hands of various invaders and continual slave raiding. Many men still carry weapons and these northern parts had suffered attacks and bombing raids by Eritreans as recently as the previous year. The boy was acting in a way that would have made his forebears proud. First cast a stone, then ask questions.

Indeed, once I had calmed down and got to thinking, I realised that the history of this part of Ethiopia in particular had informed the reflex of that child's throwing arm. The very road we were on was the scene of heavy fighting as the Derg attempted to halt the advance of liberating forces in 1990. Similarly, the area around Maychew had witnessed the final and decisive defeat of Ethiopian forces by the Italians back in 1936. It was also just outside Maychew, at the village of Korem, that the Natal Carbineers, advancing on the defences at Amba Alagi, liberated 161 Greeks and an Englishwoman, Violet Mazzarini, who'd been imprisoned by the Italians on a diet of lentils and beans for 11 months.

North of Maychew the country grew drier and the peak of Amba Alagi rose out of the plain. For the South African troops, this was the last major stronghold preventing them reaching the port of Massawa. The fortress mountain was a warren of seemingly impregnable positions where the Italian Duke of Aosta, nephew of the Italian king, was to make his final stand. The defences were built around the 10 000-foot Toselli Pass, which switchbacked up Amba Alagi between cliffs honeycombed with artillery positions and machine-gun posts hewn out of the rock. A vast Allied force, including Sudanese and Indian divisions, completed the encirclement of Amba Alagi. The South Africans were to spearhead the attack from the south. The road ahead of us was deserted, but in April 1941 the view that greeted the troops would have revealed an unbroken, 12-kilometre column of vehicles abandoned by the Italians as they retreated on foot to their last-ditch-stand positions.

Radio Roma broadcast somewhat extravagantly that '30 000 brave Italian troops, under the heroic leadership of the Duke of Aosta, are holding at bay 300 000 enemy troops, representing the best fighting forces of the British Empire.' After incessant artillery and aerial bombardment, which sapped the defenders' resistance, the Allies began simultaneous assaults on all sides. The South Africans were joined by Ethiopian patriots and shiftas who surged ahead in their white robes, shooting and mutilating their victims or flinging them screaming from the cliffs. The ghosts of the Addis massacres were being avenged.

Uncle Uys used Amba Alagi as the inspiration for his poem 'The Taking of the Koppie' in *Hart Sonder Hawe*, where he describes how a young soldier is brutalised by combat, transforming the child with 'innocent eyes' into an emotional cripple able to kill mercilessly:

> Then I put my bayonet through each of them in turn,
> just in the right place, and they did not even grunt
> or murmur . . .

The Duke of Aosta surrendered on 19 May 1941. Allied troops turned out as immaculately as if on parade and formed a guard of honour with fixed bayonets beside the road to Asmara. Then, in a straggling line, the Italians poured down from their defences. The guard of honour presented arms as the 5 000 exhausted survivors, led by their generals, marched past and into captivity, their feet finding it difficult to keep step to the unaccustomed sound from the pipers of the Transvaal Scottish.

Tigray is Ethiopia's northern province and the cradle of its ancient civilisation. Traditionally a politically volatile region, it was from here that combined Eritrean and Tigrayan freedom fighters launched the attacks that finally saw the demise of the Derg.

Outside Mekele we passed a caravan of more than a hundred camels, loping out of the wheat fields on big padded feet. Their humps were loaded with bricks of rock salt cut from surface deposits in the Danakil Depression, one of the lowest and hottest places on earth. In town the camel drivers told us they'd been trekking for nearly three weeks. The camels' backs bore salt-encrusted wounds where the bricks had chafed them. These salt ingots, called *amoles*, have served as currency for centuries and are standardised by size and weight. Their value is determined by the distance they've travelled to market – price equals camel mileage. The dirty bricks stood in piles beside the beasts like Lego buildings. Men and unloaded camels rested in the shade while traders haggled over the precious commodity in a manner little changed in a millennium. The animals, their faces in need of a shave, watched the goings-on sagely.

This was as far as camels got before turning back to the eastern lowlands. In the tableland they don't survive long. Perhaps it's the thin alpine air, steep tracks and chill rainy season, or maybe it's the herbs and grasses that lethally inflame their stomachs. Whatever the case, their aversion to the highlands has saved Ethiopia from the kind of (Islamic) camel-borne invasions that befell most other North African regions.

Deciding to treat ourselves to a bit of luxury, we spent that night in Mekele's Italianate castle with turrets and faux crenellations. For $20 – our most expensive night of the trip to date – we'd hoped for something more salubrious than a dungeon with cold water, a toilet that refused to flush and a door that wouldn't lock, but accommodation in the highlands is a hit-and-miss affair, the cheapest hovels often proving the most homely and welcoming.

The medieval rock-hewn and cave churches of Tigray make for great off-the-beaten-track exploring. Had there been time we could easily have based ourselves in Mekele and dedicated a fortnight to the dozens of isolated chapels and monasteries, many of which have been visited by only a handful of faranjis. Our route took in only those easily accessible from the main road, but even they seemed pretty remote, offering steep climbs to cliff-face cave chapels or hilltop settlements.

North of Wikro is the charming Tekle Tesfai cluster of churches surrounded by fields dotted with dry-stone hamlets. We bounced down the access road – prickly pears scraping the vehicle's sides – escorted by a key-clutching monk and a group of boys running beside us shouting directions. When the stony track became too steep for the vehicle, we continued on foot. By now the panting monk and his entourage had caught up and he pointed aloft with a toothless smile. Worn hand-holds were cut into the sandstone and he indicated that we should start climbing.

The 'steps' made the ascent relatively simple, although dodgy for anyone lacking a head for heights. We scrambled onto a ledge halfway up the cliff and stood before the small whitewashed chapel of Petros and Paulos. It commanded prime views of the plain below and a sinuous landscape dividing itself towards the horizon into segments cordoned with stone walls. Although Petros and Paulos appeared derelict with part of its roof caved in, there were some fine murals of angels and saints, now exposed to the elements and fading fast. 'This holy water,' said the key-bearer pointing to a pond. Beside it lay a skeleton and a few disembodied skulls. My shoe scuffed the remains of a pilgrim's spine. Okay, time to go, I thought, and declined the sacred water.

Heading for the more celebrated 10th-century church of Medhane Alem Adi Kasho on the next hill, we walked for half an hour through fields along a path that in places had been worn two metres deep by the feet of worshippers. Our thinning entourage mounted a rocky incline where the priest pointed out moon-shaped grooves in the rock. 'These cuts they Giorgis horse hoofs,' he said. It was only later that we discovered what he meant. St George had apparently ridden up here, no doubt stalking another dragon, and his steed's hooves had left their imprint in the sandstone. Had he roughed up the local monks to get this church built the way he had in Lalibela?

On reaching the summit we had to wait an hour in a grove of juniper and olive trees loud with the chatter of babblers while the keeper of the key was summoned. Beyond a stone wall lay Medhane Alem, a cave church whose white-and-green façade decorated with angels filled an opening in the cliff. We removed our shoes in an ornate portico and stepped through a red door into darkness. The priest lit a wick and attached it to the end of a pole. With this he traced the coffered ceiling's geometric decorations and crucifixes. The columns were fat rectangles of monolithic rock, cold to the touch and grooved with a myriad of tiny chisel bites. Behind a partially drawn curtain we could make out icons and silver crosses . . . and beyond them the curtains of the inner sanctum, housing a replica of the Ark of the Covenant, where no faranji could ever set foot. I was itching to peek. Mike told me in a gruff whisper to put such foolishness out of my mind.

Adigrat was the northern-most town on our highland circuit and the last big settlement before the Eritrean border. We found a *pension* and pulled the vehicle into a courtyard criss-crossed at different heights with laden washing lines. I set off immediately to photograph Adigrat's colourful stalls and shop-fronts. There were bedmakers, shoeshine lads, music shops issuing wailing Tigrayan tunes and 'barbery' shops (barbers). Horse traps cantered up and down along a line of inns and drinking halls with names like Bar

Hollywood, the Titi Pub (its logo featured the Lion of Judah with a mischievous grin) and the Semen Hotel whose night-time entertainment Briggs remarks upon in his guidebook: 'Amongst the usual dizzying selection of knock-shop-cum-budget-dives, the Semen Hotel merits recognition for its unintentional honesty!'

Trucks were pulling into town for their overnight stops and women in the flimsiest of evening wear called to the drivers from doorways. A group of giggling girls passed me, herded by a madame resplendent in traditional garb – white robes, gold ornaments in her hair, hands and feet painted with henna and Cleopatra-like eyes outlined with heavy kohl.

That evening the hosts at our *pension* cooked us a typical Tigrayan dinner of *tholoh*. Two comely waitresses rolled balls of cooked barley which we were instructed to impale on the end of a stick and dip first into a spicy meat sauce, then into yoghurt to temper the kick. The balls were extremely filling, but when Mike indicated we'd had enough, our waitresses looked shocked. Their expressions made it clear that scrawny fellows like us needed nourishing. They took over the feeding process, forking balls into our mouths and mopping the sauce dribbling down our chins. It was like being a toddler again, or trapped in a very pleasant dentist's chair. When we could consume no more the women scolded us playfully, then went to fetch a man they wanted us to meet. Maxwell was from a village near Umtata. 'Gosh, you're a long way from home!' said Mike.

Maxwell was a major in the South African National Defence Force serving as an observer with the UN. So, after 61 years the South African army was still here! Maxwell had initially spent six months on the Eritrean side of the border monitoring the ceasefire. These days he was based in Adigrat. After the glamorous SAA crowd in Addis, Maxwell provided a different take on South Africans in the highlands. 'I used to be with the old Transkei Defence Force based in Port St Johns. Now I'm at Tigray's Central Sector HQ,' he said. 'It's quite a change, but hell, I miss my kids, man.'

Homesickness was written all over his face as he went on prosaically: 'We negotiate with villages on both sides, get the warlords together, hear the grievances. It's pretty quiet right now. I've had to learn some Amharic and some Tigrinya, just to get by, you know.' Part of his Ethiopian stint involved patrolling the frontier and trying to stop armed cattle rustlers moving between the two countries. 'Ag, I'm used to this sort of thing from the Lesotho border. Those Basotho guys were always trying to steal livestock and get it quickly back over the Berg. It's just the same thing here.' His distant look seemed to take in rondavel villages, cattle kraals and the green hills of Intabamnyama, Matatiele and Moshesh's Ford.

The morning road led west towards Adwa, an early sun baking the sandstone passes. Guards with semi-automatic weapons rode shotgun on top of Fiat trucks that crawled in front of us, covering the Land Rover in dust. Men crouched on their haunches harvesting golden tef (the grain used to make injera) in terraced fields beside the road. Like an ebbing tide, their sickles nibbled bites in a flaxen sea.

A turning to the right led to Debre Damo. This sixth-century monastic enclave sits on an impregnable flat-topped *amba* (koppie). It was once a prison for princes – where emperors kept the many possible heirs to the throne in cold storage . . . and out of trouble. Punishment for trying to escape was mutilation or death. During some purges all the princes were murdered. Ambas like Debre Damo have played a crucial part in Ethiopian history. In times of strife, when the country was overrun by invaders, it was often the ambas that acted as final strongholds where a handful of men were able to keep attacking armies at bay. Many served as monasteries preserving the Christian faith, others as royal treasure houses. When the invaders retreated, these ambas formed the seeds from which highland culture could again flower.

Surrounded by cliffs of spongy volcanic rock, Debre Damo can only be reached by way of a 20-metre plaited leather rope which, when we arrived, was being used to pull up firewood. Getting an ox aloft meant inspanning a troop of monks to haul it up on the same rope. Mike shouted in the direction of a doorway. After the protracted negotiation of a fee with unhelpful boys and a mongoloid teenager, the rope was lowered. The teenager kept shouting, 'Mistah, you, 50 birr!' and then cackling. 'Money, money, you, you, you.' It got to the point where I felt that if I ever reached the top I was going to hurl him over the edge.

The teenager disappeared and our fate was left in the hands of a bunch of boys. One lad tied a length of inexpertly laced cowhide around my waist as a 'safety harness'. Slipknot instead of a bowline, I noted ruefully. He thrust the rope into my hands and said. 'You climb mistah, *eshi?*'

'*Chigger yellum* (no problem),' I said, unconvinced by the whole set-up.

With the aid of hand-holds in the rock I shimmied up the worn leather, grazing elbows and knees. A lammergeier, that giant of vulturine raptors, swooped by. I could hear the rush of its wings and felt like Prometheus about to be clawed by the Caucasian eagle. But the bird had no interest in me and sailed on down the valley. I eased myself over the lip to find that the eight-year-old taking up the slack on my safety line had not put a turn round the bollard provided. If I'd fallen it could have been tickets for both of us.

The settlement on top looked Tuscan, a dry-stone-walled maze of enclosures accommodating 150 monks. There were cisterns cut in the rock with steps leading down to water covered in floating algae. 'Here only boy-sheeps and cattles, no kinds of girls,' said our young priest-guide.

'Debre Damo was being built by Abuna Aragavi in six century,' explained the priest as he directed us to the main church. 'Aragavi was saint from Syria. The Lord sent him a big snake to climb up the amba, like a rope. He made this church on top. There were 6 000 monks on the amba, and 3 000 nuns down in the valley.'

The church, considered the oldest surviving in Ethiopia, exhibited the characteristic Axumite style – a layered 'cake' of wood and whitewashed stone. Wind chimes tinkling on the roof lent an appropriately mystical atmosphere. The man with the key wasn't topside so we couldn't gain access, but the narthex with its thick carpets, icons and intricate wood carvings gave us a taste of what we were missing.

Upset about the key, we took a walk along a cliff-edge path that was unfortunately being used as a toilet. Below us in the amba's wall were caves where hermits resided. Bread and water were lowered to them by rope. Beside the path we noticed hollows cut in the rock where pilgrims found their final resting places. Peering into one of the caverns, we saw yet another body, partly decomposed, flesh still hanging from the bones.

Heading west for Axum, we passed inselbergs and extinct volcanoes jutting from the plain in all manner of improbable shapes. At one point we were entirely surrounded by them. Looming from their own black shadows, they looked like clubs, weapons, severed heads, fists – all sprouting from the earth. Here was a Lalibela church for giants, the stele of a pagan deity or a bishop's mitre cut from towering granite. There could be no better setting for a battle between men, or gods. Perhaps my mind was playing games with me on the road to Adwa – or Adowa, as my high-school history textbook called it – the setting of the greatest defeat of a modern European power in Africa.

In the 19th century the Italians arrived late at the colonial table and scrambled for leftover crumbs of the African cake. They advanced their claims in Eritrea and then Tigray province, looking for a pretext to annex the only sizeable chunk of the continent not accounted for by a European nation. Emperor Menelik II, wanting to avoid war at almost any cost, was cornered into signing a treacherous treaty in which the Italian version was worded differently to the Amharic. The offending document had Menelik reducing his country to an Italian protectorate. When trouble brewed, the Italians used a border incident as pretext to march into Adigrat.

Menelik could see no alternative to confrontation and issued a mobilisation proclamation in Addis Ababa: 'Assemble the army, beat the drum. God in his bounty has struck down my enemies and enlarged my empire and preserved me to this day . . . Enemies have come who would ruin our country and change our religion . . . These enemies have advanced, burrowing into the country like moles. With God's help I will get rid of them.'

Messengers galloped to all corners of Ethiopia and war drums sounded from hill to hill. The capital's great banqueting hall was made ready and 2 000 leaders gathered for a feast of raw meat to toast the coming battle. For days the war bands kept arriving in Addis. It was a medieval pageant, with leaders wearing red-and-gold brocade and lion's mane headdresses. Soldiers carried modern rifles, but also swords and buffalo-hide shields. Accompanying priests marched under processional crosses and striped silk umbrellas. Women and slaves followed the columns to do the menial work and prepare food for the army.

Menelik decided against attacking the Italians at Adigrat and marched along the route Mike and I were driving to a plateau just east of Adwa. The emperor deployed 100 000 men on rolling ground between the mountains and waited for the advance of an Italian force comprising nearly 20 000 well-armed soldiers, backed by 52 cannons. At 4 a.m. on 1 March 1896 the imperial couple and the chief ras took Holy Communion at the Church of Enda Giorgis on a ridge above Adwa and prayed to St George that they would slay the Italian dragon. At dawn the first shots rang out and battle was joined.

Almost everything went wrong for the Italians. Faulty maps, poor reconnaissance and communications failures created confusion among the attackers, who'd fatefully chosen to advance under the cover of darkness. When sunrise came they found they'd lost their way. Even so, it took 25 000 Ethiopians to break their centre and at noon the Italian commander, Baratieri, ordered a retreat which soon turned into a rout. The enemy was driven headlong from Ethiopian soil.

A year later, the former British vice-consul for the Red Sea,

Augustus Wylde, was sent to Adwa to report on the causes of the Italian defeat. Describing the retreat, he wrote sympathetically of the European invaders and, with thinly veiled racism, equated the Ethiopians with a force of nature or natural disaster: 'The survivors from the Italian centre were then attacked by the Agamé population and many cruel massacres took place, the bodies of the slain being mutilated and their heads cut off and put on the rocks that lined the sides of the road . . . At many points on the line of retreat, officers and men turned and attempted to hold the road, freely sacrificing themselves with splendid courage in the attempt to cover the retreat of their comrades. On these human barriers the Abyssinians came down like the spates in their own mountain rivers, sweeping all before them.'

The Italian army was annihilated and the pursuing Ethiopians captured much equipment and all the enemy's artillery. It was a great day for Africa. Ethiopia remained the only jigsaw piece in the African puzzle to escape the scramble.

Adwa inspired Marcus Garvey's Back to Africa Movement, known as Ethiopianism, as well as the various forms of Pan-African consciousness that were to corrode Europe's possessions from within. Those with the knack of predicting the future might have seen Adwa as the beginning of Europe's colonial demise. Three years later a bunch of Boers inflicted humiliating defeats on British imperial forces in the far south of the continent; 15 years later an escalation of greed over African colonies would help spawn the First World War. From then on, African countries began a steady march to liberation.

Wylde concluded his report saying that his battlefield visits were 'perhaps the most disagreeable task I ever had to perform in my life, one position being more foul smelling and disgusting than another. A burying party of Italian engineers had been allowed by the Ethiopians to come and inter the dead, but the condition of the corpses prevented them from being moved, and a few loose stones were their only covering which, instead of facilitating the decomposition, only retarded it; not half of the bodies had been attended to, and in some places, putrescent masses held together by ragged clothes marked the details of the fight . . . Bird and animal life was absent, they even could not face the horrible Golgotha, and the hyenas had long ago left the district to procure something more tempting than what the battlefield offered them.'

Adwa's main road was lined with patriotic billboards celebrating the Ethiopian armed forces. My mind still in a different century, I thought they might refer to the rout of the Italians, but on closer examination I noticed modern fighter jets in the roadside murals. Being so close to the Eritrean border, this district had seen plenty of military action in recent years. But apart from battlefield ghosts, there was nothing to hold us in Adwa and, with Axum only 20 kilometres down the road, we pushed on.

Axum had existed as an urban centre as early as 600 BC and from the first to the sixth centuries AD it became the nub of an empire that stretched from the Nile River across the Red Sea to Yemen. It was here, in the fourth century AD, that Christianity was first adopted by an Axumite emperor.

This remarkable empire was well known to the Greeks, Romans and Persians, and even the Chinese. However, during the Middle Ages it was all but forgotten, save for the persistence of the legend of Prester John, which spoke about a mysterious Christian king living somewhere in the African highlands. Rumours of his existence were given credibility in 1165 when a letter allegedly arrived at the court of Emperor Comnenus. In this missive, Prester John described his kingdom and all the creatures to be found in it, including the fire-dwelling salamander. His palace was built according to the designs of St Thomas and contained a miraculous mirror in whose reflection the prester could see his entire kingdom. He went to war with a vanguard of 13 gold crosses, each followed by 10 000 horsemen and 100 000 foot soldiers, and it was his life's ambition to march on Jerusalem and annihilate the infidel.

For a Europe under constant threat from the east, this promise of a Christian ally who could take the Muslims from the rear proved most compelling. However, although Axum remained a place of religious importance, its political significance had declined. In the words of Edward Gibbon in his *The Decline and Fall of the Roman Empire*: 'Encompassed on all sides by the enemies of their religion, the Aethiopians slept near a thousand years, forgetful of the world, by whom they were forgotten.'

The first comprehensive description of Axum by a European was produced by Father Alvarez, an intrepid Portuguese traveller who visited during the 1520s. He writes: 'This town was the city, court, and residence of the Queen of Saba [Sheba] . . . who took the camels laden with gold to Solomon, when he was building the temple of Jerusalem . . . The town is situated at the head of a beautiful plain, and almost between two hills, and the rest of this plain is almost all full of these old buildings, and among them many of these chairs, and high pillars with inscriptions. Above the town there are many stones standing up and others on the ground, very large and beautiful and worked with beautiful designs.'

We are fortunate indeed to have Alvarez's account of early 16th-century Ethiopia. Immediately after his visit the country was invaded by Gragn the Left-handed, an Islamic warrior who swept into the highlands from Harar and laid waste to much of the empire's literary, architectural and cultural heritage. His goal was to stamp out the infidel's religion and he set about burning churches and manuscripts, and forcibly converting Christians. Gragn looted the famous monasteries at Lake Hayk and Lalibela, then pushed on to Axum, where he destroyed the old church of St Mary Zion.

When all seemed lost, it was the Portuguese who tipped the scales in favour of the Ethiopians. The arrival of 400 musketeers under the command of Christovão da Gama, son of Vasco, along with cannons and gunpowder, managed to halt Gragn's advance. The Islamic leader in turn appealed to the Turks in Yemen for help and received 900 matchlock men who swung the tide back in his favour. All but 120 Portuguese were killed in battle and Da Gama's severed head was displayed to boost morale. The fighting continued back and forth for two years until eventually the remainder of the Portuguese, accompanied by the king's forces, made a last-ditch attack, during which Gragn was killed. Seeing their leader dead, the warriors broke rank and fled. Still today, highland peasants speak of the horror of Gragn's invasion and how close Ethiopia came to succumbing to Islam.

Despite its sacking by Gragn, Axum is still layered with millennia of architectural history. Most striking is a field of 75 stelae noted by all early travellers. These are the largest examples of monolithic obelisks in the ancient world. Many questions remain unanswered. How were these obelisks erected? Were elephants used to haul them to this site?

Hewn from single blocks of granite, the tallest of these monuments to the dead – erected by King Ezana in the third century AD – stands 23 metres high. It resembles a modern skyscraper and is decorated with carved doors and windows and crowned by a crescent and disc capital. Beside it, shattered into megaton blocks, is a far larger stele, which toppled soon after erection and crushed a tomb complex. The monoliths and vaulted tombs have a haunting aura, emphasised by the apparent modernity of their design, the precise interlocking of giant blocks of masonry. There is a preoccupation with symmetry, and all ornamentation is minimalist. It's a level of sophistication you normally only expect from Pharaohs and Hellenes. The craftsmanship puts most other highland architecture of the ensuing millennium in the shade.

Further up the hill lie the remains of King Kaleb's residence, which greatly impressed a Byzantine traveller named Cosmos who visited Axum in 525 AD. He described it as being adorned with brass statues of unicorns, and sporting a tame elephant and giraffe wandering about the grounds. Impressive too were the Axumite king's lavish garments embroidered with gold and pearls, and his chariot drawn by four elephants.

Today there's not much left of the palace at ground level, but the gatekeeper directed Mike and I down perfectly cut granite stairs to a series of underground chambers. He lit a flaming torch and led us along passages, our progress monitored by bats hanging from the ceiling just above our heads. 'This was treasury for gold and silver and pearls. Much riches,' he said, showing us an empty room. 'This was tomb.' He pointed to a stone sarcophagus with a crucifix and elephant engraved on the wall behind. 'There is secret tunnel from palace all the way to Eritrea. I don't know where.'

Back down the hill and opposite the stelae field is Axum's museum complex. To reach the entrance we parted a sea of trinket sellers who offered ancient Axumite coins, necklaces and crudely painted icons. An ageing museum guide with a holed jacket and long beard guided us among the exhibits. He had an exaggerated stoop and didn't smell too good, but his knowledge was extensive as he led us through the ages from Sheba's time to the Christian era. There were glass bowls and Axumite artefacts, coins and crosses, as well as a 700-year-old leather Bible. The Amharic language and its antecedents have changed so little over the millennia that he could easily read the Sabaen inscription on pre-Christian tablets. Just try that with English.

Next door is Tsion Maryam, the holiest precinct in the country. Ethiopian culture and identity are inextricably linked to their archaic brand of Christianity. The rituals have many Jewish influences and Ethiopians recognise both the Christian Sabbath of Sunday and the Jewish Saturday. Central to their beliefs are the Ark of the Convenant and the tale of its mysterious disappearance from Jerusalem during the reign of Solomon. Ethiopians believe the ark was brought to the highlands, where it still resides today.

Few historians take the ark legend seriously, but the fact remains that there *was* considerable contact between Axum and Palestine, and ancient Jewish practices are still found in the Ethiopian church. Indeed, there are more than 30 Old Testament references to Cush (as Ethiopia was known to the Hebrews). Even the Ghion River – or Blue Nile – which 'compasseth the whole land of Ethiopia' is referred to in the book of Genesis. And Moses, of course, married an Ethiopian beauty.

The Ark of the Covenant purportedly resides in a humble building beside the ruins of a fourth-century church – the oldest in Africa – and is the symbolic home of the Ethiopian Orthodox Church. Only the keeper of the key is allowed in. Only he knows the truth. Could it be that the holy of holies, crafted from shittim wood and plated in gold – the home of Moses's tablets, lies behind the locked door? Whatever one may think, its symbolism is of immeasurable importance and the Ethiopians' belief in their direct link to the royal house of Judah has been a unifying and defining myth down the ages.

A laid-back monk in sunglasses unlocked a cabinet to show us the gold and silver crowns of a succession of kings, each studded with precious stones and topped with tiny replicas of the Ark of the Covenant. I slipped him a few extra birr and he began hauling out religious books. These illuminated manuscripts were centuries-old. Written on goatskin and bound with leather thongs, the texts were adorned with patterns of interlaced foliage and geometrical decorations. Many pages were filled with religious paintings. Again it was a mounted St George, riding a stallion in a halo of light, that seemed to dominate. The medieval snapshot-takers invariably caught him, spear raised, at the moment of impaling some unfortunate creature.

You trip over the ancients wherever you go in Axum. Beside the stelae field is Queen of Sheba's Swimming Pool where modern Shebas come to collect water; nearby are the alleged ruins of the queen's residence. They lie a short drive out of town and we reached her palace and adjacent stelae field just as the sun was setting. There was not a soul about. A 50-room structure rose from a stone podium with a monumental entrance. Ascending the grand stairway, we picked our way through the foundations: passages, kitchens and steps leading to a non-existent second storey. Did the legendary African queen really climb these stairs and wander these halls trailed by a boy king who would found a dynasty that lasted 237 generations, only to be snuffed out in our time? Research was patchy and the archaeological record is nowhere near comprehensive.

Ethiopians will tell you that Sheba ruled from Axum with a fleet of 73 ships and a royal caravan of 520 camels. She travelled widely, even as far as King Solomon in Jerusalem. The two developed relations that were more than just diplomatic (Solomon is said to have conned the queen into losing her virginity). She arrived back in Axum a convert to Judaism and carrying the future King Menelik in her womb. At the age of 22 Menelik undertook the long journey to visit his father in Jerusalem, where he resided for three years and learned the Law of Moses. Menelik returned to Axum accompanied by the eldest son of each of Solomon's high commissioners and 1 000 people from each of the 12 tribes of Israel. But here's the tricky part. Menelik also stole the holiest Judaic artefact, the Ark of the Covenant. When Solomon discovered the theft he was furious and led his soldiers in a chase to catch up with Menelik's entourage, but then he had a dream that God had ordained the theft . . . and the Ark has remained in Ethiopia ever since.

Sheba's massive fallen tombstone was decorated with human faces and tef stood tall around its base. Phallic shadows grew from the forest of stelae. Unlike Stonehenge, where you're kept at a distance on roped-off walkways, we were in a farmer's field that just happened to be the last resting place of the Queen of Sheba. Goats milled between the monoliths and herdboys used the fallen tombstones as toilets.

Early one morning we joined a procession of hundreds of worshippers clad in white robes. Priests rang hand bells, clinked sistra or held out their crosses to be kissed; icon sellers offered their wares and beggars mingled with the throng, pleading for alms. We were walking through pages of the Bible and the pagan, pre-Christian stelae in the background seemed to put the spanking new faith into perspective. Tigrayans are strikingly good looking with delicate features, aquiline noses and large eyes. The men were dressed in jackets draped with homespun shammas and white turbans. The women wore long cotton dresses; some had wooden or silver crosses around their necks, others necklaces of triangular or half-moon charms to ward off the ill effects of the evil eye or crescent moon.

Then I spied a woman, who looked like Moses's mom, bearing a bundle of bulrushes. Well, grass actually, but she looked the biblical part in her white attire. And she was beautiful. Feeling a bit awkward, I sidled up and asked to take her picture. She offered a radiant smile and agreed in halting English. My legs jellied a little as I snapped, thanked her and retreated.

A few minutes later there was a tap on my shoulder. The cousin of Trahas (her real name) had been dispatched to invite us to a *buna* (coffee) ceremony. 'My cousin she is expecting you in one hour.' It felt like a regal summons. Mike had told me about the coffee tradition and we jumped at the chance.

Coffee originates in Ethiopia and still grows wild in the Kaffa region. Highland soldiers of old used to make cakes from the beans, which they chewed during long marches to give them energy, just as the Incas did with coca leaves. Coffee drinking was initially frowned upon by the clergy and had to be carried out in secret. But over time it became more acceptable (monks no doubt enjoyed a bit of dark tipple), acquiring many social customs and developing into a tradition with almost as many nuances as that of the Japanese tea ceremony.

Exactly an hour later we presented ourselves at a humble semi-detached building where Trahas lived with her entire extended family. The main room had a bed, couch and a few chairs and was dimly lit with candles. There were no windows and the main source of light was the doorway. The floor was strewn with grass. There were pictures of Trahas on the walls which may have been put up in the last hour. She had changed and looked lovely in a traditional Tigrayan dress, full length with a green pattern, her light dreadlocks wrapped in a white scarf.

Trahas asked us to sit, then sprinkled blocks of frankincense and myrrh on a charcoal brazier. The room soon clouded with their fragrance. She offered white honey with warm bread. When I spilt a drop of honey on my trousers she scooped it up with a finger and popped it in her mouth. The nails on her left hand were immaculately groomed, but those on her right were short. 'For food,' she said and smiled a smile to disarm an Eritrean battalion.

Trahas then roasted the green coffee beans in a pan, wafting their aroma over us with a fan, before grinding them with pestle and mortar. The powder was tipped into a pot and we waited for the coffee to brew. Each move seemed rehearsed. The pouring – a glide of the pot through the air high above the cups, sending a long black spout – the cleaning and repouring, all followed prescribed steps. The coffee was strong, sweet and delicious. After drinking we handed back the china demitasse cups for washing and awaited the next round.

Conversation was sparse. The cousin spoke the best English and acted as intermediary. I asked him about the war with Eritrea. 'The leaders of Ethiopia and Eritrea, they are cousins. They all fought together against the communists. I don't know why they hate each other so much now. It takes many, many lives.'

'Did you fight?' I asked.

'Yes, a little. Some of my friends they do not come back. My country is always war, war, war.'

He grew silent and talk dried up. Then Mike tried his limited Amharic and Trahas translated into Tigrinya: *eshi* was *tsebuk* in Tigrinya; *tenayistillign* (how are you?) was *selam*; *awo* (yes) was *harray*. It was slow going. From the halting conversation we discovered that Trahas did not want to become a nurse or a nun. She wanted to learn languages and find out more about the world outside Axum.

Then the cousin, as though impatient with the speed of proceedings I was not aware of, interjected. Was I married? No. Then was there someone in my life? No. Well, Trahas was single too . . . and *konjo*, beautiful (as though we hadn't noticed). When would I be returning to Axum?

I could see the conversation's trend. Her eyes caught mine with deadly playfulness. This was not coffee: this was wedding talk. Suddenly I had an image of Trahas and 23 relatives turning up unannounced at my two-room apartment in Cape Town. Or maybe I should pack in the travel-writing lark and shack up in Axum. Buy myself a little field of tef, and a hut, and take Trahas to be my... The coffee was making me light-headed.

After two hours and three blow-your-head-off bunas we floated out into the dazzling sunlight. Trahas and I walked arm in arm back to the Land Rover and Mike distracted the family by giving the cousin one of his Bob Marley CDs. If I haven't mentioned it before, Mike's a good fellow. Trahas and I kissed fleetingly behind the vehicle and she said, 'God go with you.' Then I reversed inexpertly down the lane with shaking hands, trying to wave at Trahas and nearly taking out a pole and then a camel.

The road bent southwestward through a land in the mellow glow of harvest. No sign of the predicted famine to come. A man winnowing his crop tossed bundles into the air with a wooden fork and was enveloped in chaff and grain. Against the light it looked like a shower of gold leaf. It struck me suddenly that this was Africa's ancient bread-basket, one of the first places our nomadic ancestors put to the plough so many thousands of years ago.

Over a rise we came upon the remains of a battlefield. Mangled armoured cars, artillery pieces and burnt-out T55 tanks dotted the fields. A Rüppell's robin-chat perched on the barrel of a mounted ack-ack gun sang a lovely ditty to the morning. Local farmers continued to plough, simply taking a detour round the military hardware. Further down the road we reached a bridge which created a bottleneck, perfect for ambush. Lined up as if in a shooting gallery were rows of tanks, all shattered. Other vehicles had been reduced to indecipherable tangles of metal. We inched past, watched by farmers carrying Kalashnikovs.

The Land Rover approached the Simien Mountains climbing into a landscape contorted and diced into grotesque shapes. It seemed that only yesterday white-hot lava had spewed from the earth to form these massifs. The jagged horizon looked like a sentence written in Amharic script. As one British soldier campaigning in Ethiopia in the 1860s commented: 'They tell us this is a tableland. If it is, they have turned the table upside down and we are scrambling up and down the legs.'

Down we plunged along one of those 'legs' into a canyon a mere 800 metres above sea-level where a fallen bridge dammed the stream in broken bits and a fort stood peppered with bullet holes round the gun slits. Then up and up to 3 000 metres again, switchbacking around the basalt buttresses.

We sat behind a truck piled with wood, on which a terrified black sheep stood tethered by one leg. Perpendicular views offered toy villages. Even up here on the cliffs there were people everywhere, many carrying old bolt-action rifles, others bearing haystacks on their heads. The road itself was the most dramatic of the journey, a series of arabesques that reached for the clouds. Mussolini's engineers had outdone themselves; there was even a drinking fountain halfway up the pass, sculpted in a fascist Baroque style with allegorical figures representing the union of Italy and Africa.

The Land Rover topped out into alpine scenery: pine, juniper and giant lobelia, cattle grazing in meadows and bubbling brooks. We passed horses decorated with red tassels, their saddlebags bearing the Lion of Judah. It was Sunday and the riders were out on show, sporting their steeds for the local maidens to admire. Horsemanship is prized in the highlands, especially here, and Ethiopian cavalry was often lauded by visitors to the country. Gondar's royal cavalry wore coats of mail and carried five-metre lances. Plates of brass studded with iron spikes covered the horses' heads and riders wore copper helmets.

We spent a night in the flea-pit of Debark at a truckers' stop doss-house. Plonkers appeared from every doorway with grandiose offers of negligible substance. Children called out 'Give me plastic!' – which I assumed meant pens, of which we had brought a pile of spares to hand out. But they also shouted the more cryptic, and all-encompassing, 'Give me!' which sounded like a mantra for Third World need and was not as easy to respond to. Our rooms were dirty, the communal squat-toilets rancid – sewage arrangements throughout the town were still in an experimental phase – and Ethiopian music in the courtyard competed with hip-hop pounding from the bar which only just edged out the bickering of a television set.

We cleared out early the next morning, eager to put some distance between us and the delights of Debark, now nicknamed Debacle. Our destination was Gondar. The Land Rover passed through lovely countryside: a pattern of wheat, barley and tef fields. Everywhere were horses, fat-tailed sheep, long-horned cattle and flocks of sprightly piebald goats. Stands of shimmering eucalyptus hid settlements of stone tukuls.

Just before the outskirts of Gondar we pulled off at the remains of a Falasha (Ethiopian Jewish) village. There were a few clay trinkets for sale, supposedly crafted in the Falasha tradition, but any sense of this being a Jewish settlement was gone. The origins of highland Jews are confusing. One theory has it that the original Jewish emigrants accompanied Menelik I and Sheba, while a second major wave came after the Roman conquest of Palestine. Many historians believe that the Falasha are a more recent arrival, having emigrated from Yemen in the first century AD. However, this does not take into account the archaic nature of Falasha rituals, which appear to date from before the reforms of Josiah, around 640 BC. Perhaps this early Jewish presence in the highlands accounts for Ethiopian Christianity being more Old Testament than New. After all, the king of Ethiopia and his people were, in a Solomonic sense, the children of Israel.

In 1991, during the violent last days of Mengistu's Derg, almost the entire Falasha population of 25 000 was airlifted to Israel under the Law of Return. An ancient and valuable component of the Ethiopian population had been surgically removed.

Resembling Camelot, Gondar was home to a series of 17th- and 18th-century kings who built fabulous palaces and churches. Some royals were enthusiastic patrons of the arts, creating an African Florence. Throughout the medieval period Ethiopia had no permanent capital. Emperors ruled from vast tented encampments which frequently changed location, particularly when firewood became depleted. Founded in 1635 by King Fasilidas, Gondar marked a change: the establishment of a fixed centre, which it remained for more than two centuries.

The new town has an Italianate feel, with a wide piazza and art deco buildings. We devoted two days to exploring. At Debre Birhan Selassie Church a monk in canary-coloured robes led us through a perimeter wall studded with 12 domed towers (denoting the 12 apostles, while the gatehouse represented Christ) into a precinct thick with juniper trees which twitched with flocks of vultures. The church houses the finest religious paintings we encountered in Ethiopia: its ceiling was decorated with a pattern of winged cherubic faces and the walls sported a delightful blue devil licked by flames and munching on an unfortunate soul, ubiquitous St George atop a white horse looking smug about his exploits, St Samuel riding a lion and St Tekle Haymanot standing patiently on one leg (which he did for seven years, receiving just one annual meal in the form of a seed fed to him by a bird).

The nearby Royal Enclosure had recently been restored and is a jumble of ramparts, turrets, balconies and defensive walls. There are sauna rooms, concert halls and cages where royal black-maned lions were kept, while the interiors were once decorated with ivory, gold leaf and precious stones. It's a place where you can while away many hours, or even days, marvelling at this strange Arcadian Africa. The architectural styles are eclectic, featuring European, Axumite and Asian elements. Participation in the defeat of Gragn was only the beginning of Portuguese involvement in Ethiopia, which lasted another 100 years, and features of Renaissance Portuguese architecture are clearly evident in the Gondar castles.

King Fasilidas gave the town its initial impetus as a commercial centre and began attracting Jewish and Muslim craftsmen. His palace appropriately dominates the compound and is a four-storey structure of golden limestone punctuated with round-headed windows encased in blocks of red tufa. We wandered through reception and banqueting halls, then climbed to the first-floor roof, used for religious ceremonies. Higher still we reached the king's tower quarters – a fairytale bedroom with oversize chairs, candle holders and bed, all sporting flared legs like bell-bottom trousers ... or camels' feet.

A French doctor, Charles Poncet, was the first European to set eyes on Gondar and his descriptions give us a vivid impression of the 17th-century court: 'After having conducted me thro' more than twenty apartments, I enter'd into a hall, where the Emperour was seated upon his throne. It was a sort of couch, cover'd with a carpet of red damask flower'd with gold. There were round about great cushions wrought with gold. This throne, of which the feet were of massy silver, was plac'd at the bottom of a hall, in an alcove cover'd with a dome all shining with gold and azure. The Emperour was cloath'd with a vest of silk, embroider'd with gold and with very long sleeves. The scarf with which he was girt was embroider'd after the same manner. He was bare-headed and his hair braided very neatly. A great emerald glitter'd on his forehead and added majesty to him...

'Two princes of the blood, richly cloath'd, waited for him at the palace gate with a magnificent canopy, under which the Emperour march'd, with his trumpets, kettle-drums, flutes, hautboys, and other instruments going before him, which made a good agreeable harmony... Then came the musketeers, in their closebody'd coats of different colours; and were followed by the archers, carrying their bows and arrows. Last of all, this procession was closed by the Emperour's led horses, richly harness'd and cover'd with costly stuffs of gold hanging down to the ground, over which were the skins of tigers, extremely beautiful.'

Later kings added smaller palaces to the Royal Enclosure, making their particular contributions to the highland Renaissance. King Iyasu, for instance, encouraged religious studies and sponsored the study and refinement of *zema* (chanting), *qene* (poetry) and *tergum* (interpretation). Eighteenth-century Queen Mentaub was also a great patron of the arts. She was allegedly chosen to be Emperor Bakaffa's bride by courtiers who'd been sent to find the most beautiful girl in the region. A more romantic version suggests that the emperor became ill while travelling in a remote area and was nursed back to health by a farmer's beautiful daughter. After Bakaffa's death, Mentaub continued to play an active part in political and cultural life and eventually built for herself a palace on a hill overlooking Gondar.

Near the imperial compound are good King Fasilidas's baths – an enormous stone 'swimming pool' set in an enclosed precinct. Strangler figs clamber over the basalt walls and turrets, their muscular roots choking the structure. The pool has probably always been used for religious ceremonies rather than serving as the Gondarine municipal baths. It's still the main stage for the annual *Timkat* (Epiphany) celebrations in which thousands of white-robed worshippers gather to be blessed with the holy water. There's the smell of incense, the boom of kettle drums, the tinkling of rattles and the chanting of priests in brocade vestments bearing replica arks and *tabots* (representing Moses's tablets) from each of their churches. Early descriptions of the ceremony, however, make it sound like a slow degeneration into municipal-bath mayhem, with hundreds of lithe-limbed deacons leaping headlong into the pool and trying to splash all the worshippers with muddy water.

Armoured cars lined the road to Lake Tana. We'd got caught up in a convoy of buses, their dust trails making driving unpleasant. Army units were encamped on the hills and a military Land Cruiser mounted with a heavy-calibre machine-gun sped past, leading a line of UN vehicles. A South African overlander had recently been killed by shiftas at a roadblock on this stretch of road and no one seemed to be taking any chances. Which was reassuring, I guess.

It was muggy and marshy round the eastern shores of Ethiopia's largest lake. We crossed a bridge over the spot where Tana's smooth waters funnel into the Blue Nile. Villagers washed their clothes, vehicles and even large trucks along the banks. To all intents and purposes, this is the source of the mighty river. The fertile lowlands of Egypt and the consequent flowering of its civilisation were thanks to the rich Ethiopian soil that the highland rain carried downstream over millennia.

The Landy grumbled through palm-lined Bahir Dar and onward to the Tis Isat Falls ('water that smokes') where we walked into a gorge and crossed an arched stone bridge built by the Portuguese in 1620. Here the chocolate-coloured water boiled through a cleft with enough power to propel it all the way to the Mediterranean, more than 4 000 kilometres away. We attracted a crowd of teenage trinket and cold-drink sellers who accompanied us along the track as the whispering of distant water grew to a roar. The path took us to a spot where the trees opened up to reveal a view of the falls across a valley green with ferns. In front of us the Blue Nile toppled over a lip that stretched a few hundred metres to left and right – a stationary tidal wave caught in the act of breaking. Mike and I wanted to get closer so we let the children lead us on a half-hour walk down the valley, through maize fields and across a stream.

'This is holy water,' explained one of the girls. I filled my cap from the river and tipped it over my head to cool off. Suddenly I realised this might be disrespectful, but figured that there was so much more water here than an average baptismal font no one could really take offence.

On a ridge directly below the falls our group entered the Nile's 'smoke'. Drenched in moments, we stood staring skywards as tons of water poured over the edge. Cattle grazed unconcerned beside us, enjoying the spray's coolness.

Our last night on the road was spent at another insalubrious truckers' stop in the village of Dejen. There were pop videos in the bar and country girls wrapped in muslin shammas drank Cokes and watched Shakira and Kylie with open-mouthed incredulity. We figured the raunchy Western videos were laid on to help stoke the truckers' trousers for later.

There were complimentary condoms next to the bed and lasses milling about downstairs – the HIV-exchange system in full swing. Trucker routes are the Aids arteries of Africa. Later I listened to the scream of wood on lino floor, and moaning interspersed with childlike giggling. Throughout the night there was the banging of doors and the sound of great comings and goings. When I went to the communal toilet in the early hours, I found a man carefully washing his penis in the sink.

I woke to find the trucks gone and a vulture outside my window. Women were sweeping out the rooms and bundling mattresses and bedding over the balustrade to air.

The run to Addis was a breeze on roads whose tar became more silky as we approached the capital. We crossed the Blue Nile at a modern bridge with tight security. Here the river had swollen in width from the few boiling metres below Tis Isat to a flood that had sliced a canyon 29 kilometres across and more than a kilometre deep. The walls of rock looked like marble cake – layers of creamy limestone and red sandstone topped with black basalt icing.

The taxi-donkey-pedestrian turmoil of downtown Addis embraced us. A legless beggar moved on his knees between the 18 lanes of traffic on Meskal Square – he mustn't misjudge the robots, I thought, or he'll be street pizza. In Mengistu's day this imitation of Red Square was decorated with images of Marx, Engels and Lenin and signs announcing that 'The Victory of Socialism is Inevitable!' It was hard to imagine all that was only a decade ago.

We returned to Rennie's house, me to pack for my flight and Mike to prepare for Don Pinnock's arrival and to gear up the vehicle for a long drive across the Sahara. Ethiopian thoughts spooled anarchically through my head as though needing organisation, or an anchor of some sort. I knew it would take months to digest. My idea of the continent had been transformed by this Old Testament land. Ethiopia simply didn't fit. Centuries before Christ, when my own forebears were shivering in their northern European hovels, there was a sub-Saharan African culture with a written language building multi-storeyed palaces in stone. Christianity was thriving here hundreds of years before it reached my ancestors. Lalibela's monoliths are some of the most startling religious structures on earth. When the first Europeans arrived in Gondar they found Oxbridge façades, Lisboan manor houses and visions from Kublai Khan... they found Camelot.

Today in Ethiopia very little works. It's dirty, the roads are buggered, hot water is cause for celebration, the food wears heavily on your palate and the people are desperately poor. But the place is like a drug. It's got all the elements that are so compelling and challenging about Africa, with a twist. I knew I'd have to come back. Mike had already planned his return for the following year.

At Rennie's place Marta looked even more frail, but seemed pleased to see us. Her eyes were friendly but it was like looking down a tunnel. She sat in the courtyard for hours, basking in the warmth of the winter sun and nibbling on chat to numb the pain. Within a month she would be dead.

I'd seen more bodies in Ethiopia than in my whole life. The spectre of death hung over the country like a pall... and a new famine was on the way. But the people had grown used to the ubiquitous shadow, even seemed to smile in the face of it. Perhaps this *sol y sombra* – sun and shadow, a marriage of joy and sorrow, sensuous creativity and ever-present death – were part of what made rummaging through Africa's attic so compelling.

It was almost midnight when Mike dropped me outside Addis International. Don and I would pass in the air, him flying in to join Mike on the last big push to Cairo, me heading for a soft pillow and food I could recognise... and pronounce.

ADDIS ABABA TO CAIRO

The desert road north

Don Pinnock

I As usual before travelling, I got ready to die. Nothing dramatic: I tidied up my will, neatened my desk so nobody could say I'd left a mess, said farewells with a sense of nostalgia. Because I do this often and then don't die, I looked for signs and portents. Why did my friend Marian suddenly ask me out for coffee, talk about nothing special, then hug me like it was for the last time when we parted? Why did my motorbike blow its top a week before leaving?

To ease my mind I e-mailed Roger Arsenant of the United Nations in Khartoum to see if it was safe in Sudan. It wasn't a good idea to go, he said, and directed me to a website which noted that around two million people have died in the region's civil war during the past 15 years. After that I had feelings towards the trip I imagine soldiers have before a battle – a strange mix of excitement tempered by trepidation. But the tickets were booked and the trip needed a resolution, so I just busied myself with arrangements and tried to forget about bandits and body bags. I'd had a good life so far . . .

As the departure date approached I fell to brooding. Travel in Africa evokes in me complex emotions. The numbing inefficiency and the officials with their overdeveloped sense of importance make me weary just thinking about it. They and their befogged systems are what I despise about the continent. The pitiless poverty that generally results is distressing, but the simplicity and surprising gentility of the poor is so often a delight. Why does Africa have such wonderful, warm, hospitable people and so many autocratic swamp crocodiles for rulers? It's a puzzle I've never worked out.

I sat waiting for the connecting flight from Johannesburg to Addis feeling sad and not quite knowing why. Travel on this continent requires so much energy, something I realised I was low on just then. About that time Justin phoned – he'd just landed in Johannesburg and was delighted to be home.

'It's okay,' he assured me. 'Long, hard, but okay. And Mike's easygoing.'

<u>II</u> Addis Ababa trickled under the Boeing's wings and the officials, when we landed, were friendly and efficient. I get a sinking feeling of imminent arrest whenever I see men with uniforms and guns – a hangover from my political past – so my ease of entry was a relief. Mike was at the barrier outside, waving cheerfully among the sweating, bargaining crowd.

'Glad you made it,' he said.

'You don't know what a relief it was to see you in that crowd,' I told him. 'Those porters are the nearest I've seen to human wolves.'

We dropped my bags at the house of his friend, Rennie, and headed for the Dutch Milk Bar which, it turned out, wasn't Dutch, didn't serve milk but did good beer and pizzas.

It's one of those expat places you find all over Africa: middle-aged to older white men with local young consorts at their sides. We did the 'Hi, this is Don from Cape Town' thing for a bit then settled down to a pizza. We were soon approached by two dark-eyed girls who made it quite clear we could include them on our Milk Bar menu. On the way from the airport Mike, a complete enthusiast for anything Ethiopian, had explained that the young Ethiopians in these places, or anywhere, were not on the make when they approached you, they were just naturally friendly. I looked at the brown breasts being wiggled at me from a low-cut dress and didn't believe a word of it. We were probably moments away from discussing the price when we sidled out, leaving the two girls pouting about the time they had wasted on us. Bed, after the long flight, felt good.

In Addis the next day I had to get a visa for Sudan and pick up two new tyres. To get the visa I first required a letter – very formal it was – from the South African embassy to prove they approved of me. The only promotional stuff in the South African embassy was a glossy fold-out touting pink Cape Town. There was even an advert for a gay laundromat. I wondered what impression Ethiopians got from that rather one-sided depiction of my country.

In return for $60 and two mug shots the Sudanese visa was promised for the next day, but it was Ramadan so anything was possible. Between the bureaucracy and hunting for tyres we found ourselves jammed for much of the day in anarchic traffic and the worst city smog I'd ever seen. The horizon was an evil brown fug, obscured from time to time by blue smoke from teetering buses and dangerous-looking, dented lorries. Mike had developed a hacking cough and I understood why.

That evening we zigzagged through dark streets devoid of traffic lights, stop streets or any perceivable order to the Finfine Adanagh Hotel. It's an old, all-wood place with rooms that include an en-suite thermal-spring bath and wide colonial verandas. The upstairs dining room is all railings, rafters and room dividers. The waiter spoke only Amharic and we hand-signed our way to a traditional dish that Mike recommended. It was, he said, delicious.

I need to digress for a moment. Religious penance takes many forms. Some sinners wear hair shirts, some beat themselves with ropes, there are those who pierce their bodies with hooks and spikes, and devout Muslims can develop a permanent bump on their foreheads from thumping the ground in prayer. Ethiopians, I've decided, use trial by wot. It's a subtle but searing reminder of the frailty of the flesh. The ceremony involves a round basket table, a large dish of injera and a dish of wot – chicken or meat, it doesn't matter. Wot is a dark sauce made from heaven-knows-what plus way too much red chilli.

You break bits off the soggy bread, scrape up some *wot* and begin the ritual by stuffing it into your mouth. The pain of penance begins at your lips, then it involves a fearsome sting on your tongue, then your gullet. From there, over the course of the next few hours, you can feel the passage of the wot through your stomach, experience shocked peristalsis as it's shoved through your intestines, and yelp in agony the next day as it exits. The ritual at the Finfine was accompanied by wailing women and howling men interrupted by glottal stops and jerking bodies otherwise known as local music. I repented, I swear, of all junk food I'd ever eaten and promised evermore to eat lightly boiled vegetables, yoghurt and goat's cheese. I also promised myself never again to accept Mike's recommendation on a meal.

On the way home we dropped in at a smart place named My Pub which contained a dangerously high percentage of beautiful girls. Ethiopian women are certainly among the more startling beauties of the world. They have deep-set eyes, thick black hair, long, graceful bodies and smooth, coffee-coloured skin. The ones in My Pub, unlike the women of the Muslim world we were about to enter, were also assertive. We escaped them too, but only just.

'They're just being friendly,' Mike insisted.

In the deep, dark silence of the night before we left Addis I was awakened by a spine-chilling scream. It was short, terrified and ended abruptly in a high-pitched shriek. Shortly afterwards there was hammering on the high steel gate of Rennie's yard and his dog, Lucy, began to whine. I shivered and pulled the blanket to my chin: it was no business of mine.

|III| We left Addis early on a Saturday morning. The air was already a nose-searing brown. Mike has an umbilical attachment to the place, but to me it's a pile of inchoate villas, shops, factories and high-rises; with its head in the smog and its feet in a slum. It felt good to be moving out.

The roads in Ethiopia, one soon realises, were constructed for people on foot. Motorised vehicles seem to come as a complete surprise – even though the first 100 kilometres north is fast blacktop highway. Everything and everyone moved slowly and, when we hooted, looked at us in complete puzzlement. What was a vehicle doing on the highway? If you look at a map of Ethiopia it's easy to understand why. Considering the size of the place, there are remarkably few roads. One gets the impression that roads are unusual, recent things that cut across ancient peopleways – though if roads are there, they are walked upon.

Beyond the village of Fische we ran out of tar and thumped down onto what was undoubtedly the strong undergirding of an old Italian-built road. Many bumpy kilometres later the road descended into a vast gorge sliced by the river that would be our guide through valley and desert to Cairo. The trip down the Blue Nile had begun. Just before we crossed the bridge at the bottom, three armed soldiers flagged us down.

'Oh shit,' said Mike. 'This looks like trouble.'

Not a bit of it. They wanted to show us the remains of a crocodile someone had hauled out the river and dispatched. I took their photo – at their insistence – with their hands bravely jammed down its throat. Trial by crocodile, obviously.

We bounded our way to Debre Markos where we lunched on egg sandwiches and strong tea at a roadside restaurant, then hit deviations. For maybe the next 50 kilometres we crawled beside the makings of a fine road that ran tantalisingly smooth and straight beside us. An abrupt rainstorm scrubbed the dusty air and then the afternoon sun set ablaze fields of bright yellow *aday abeba*. Dusk turned to darkness and we still hadn't reached our destination, Bahir Dar, on the shores of Lake Tana. Some trucks and buses had lights; donkeys and cows had none. It was dusty, dangerous and stressful driving. Mike stopped talking, probably working on will-power to help me drive.

Twelve hours after leaving Addis we ground into Bahir Dar and found the good but inexpensive Papyrus Hotel. Hot showers, soft beds, beer and a good meal. We slept perhaps 300 metres from the source of the Blue Nile.

That first day was long and hard, so I expected no more of the second. Early, terribly early, the muezzins began singing competitive songs to Allah – it was Ramadan and their fervour was obvious. As we picked our way out of Bahir Dar, white-girded men and women were drifting through the soft pre-dawn towards their places of worship. Dressed that way, they appeared to my untrained eye to be Muslims, but when we reached the large church they were gathering round, it had a cross on top. Lining the wall on either side of the church gate, they were kissing it as they worked their way towards the gate.

The road out of town skirted Lake Tana and we were soon in peasant country. Fields of green tef, golden wheat, white cotton and yellow flowers stretched away on all sides into the rippling hills. The scene was rustic and beautiful.

'Hey Mike,' I said. 'This seems better than yesterday.'

'Yeah,' he agreed, dodging donkeys and trudging humans. 'Less dust.'

Nearing Gondar, we rolled along below the turrets of what seemed to be an ancient stone castle. Though we searched, we could not find a way up. At the village of Azezo, some 12 kilometres south of Gondar, we filled up with diesel for the trip down the escarpment into Sudan. I wandered through the market. Other than bright bowls and plastic buckets, I could have been in any century. The children were curious about the faranjis in their midst, but adults just went about their conversations and trade.

We expected bad roads from here to the border but encountered a new and fast dirt road. Beyond Azezo it tipped us down the Ethiopian Escarpment. In *The Decline and Fall of the Roman Empire* Gibbon writes how Ethiopia was forgotten by the world. The reason was made palpably clear to us: no army could get up the escarpment we were heading down.

When the all-conquering Turkish army rampaged up the Nile

through Sudan in the 1820s, looting and enslaving, they stopped short when they saw the great mountains from the flat desert plain. Even if their leader, Ismael, had wanted to go on, it was discovered that the Blue Nile they had followed south vanished into an enormous gorge that was impassable to men, even on foot. For those who had lived all their lives in the desert, these mountains had a sinister quality that repelled them. In 1862 the adventurer Samuel Baker and his wife saw the escarpment and described it as 'a confused mass of peaks of great altitude'. Daunted, they too turned back north.

'Spectacular' hardly describes the escarpment, unless you throw in 'weird' as well. The ramparts are studded with great domed inselbergs and sliced through by deep gorges. Green fields cling to impossible places, as do ancient cedar trees. We dropped 1 500 metres, gear-braking down hairpin bends, until the lowland bushveld rose up and swallowed us in acacias, baobabs and hot, stifling air. Our road, I was later to discover, followed the homebound route taken by James Bruce in 1771. That he was there at all is extraordinary, and his journey is worth recalling.

Even the briefest glance at Bruce's life reveals the great gulf that divides us from the privileged classes of 18th-century England. He was a man with ancestral arms, an entailed estate, a classical education with an emphasis on manners, titled patronage and violent prejudices. He hated the Papists as some people hate snakes. Unlike the Victorian explorers who followed him, he took no moral stance on such matters as slavery or the abject poverty of Africa's poor. He was by all accounts a formidable man – tall with red hair and a loud voice. He studied Arabic and fought a duel in Brussels. When his young wife died of consumption, the tragedy drove him south, to Spain, then Algiers, then Cairo.

The year 1768 found him travelling up the Nile dressed as a dervish, his mind set on Ethiopia about which nothing was then known. Blocked by tribal wars, he made his way to the Red Sea, then trekked inland to Gondar from the port of Massawa. His writings about Ethiopia were to shock the English. He told of people with rings in their lips instead of in their ears, people who wore the warm entrails of devoured cattle, men who ate the living flesh off their beasts, debauchery and ten-year-old mothers – horror upon horror and a welter of brutality and bloodshed. The country seemed to thrive on constant raiding and war. Oddly, amid all this, Bruce was honoured by the young king, Tecla Haimanout, who was busy putting out the eyes of a dozen captives when Bruce first met him.

Bruce explored Lake Tana, stood at the source of the Blue Nile and ventured to the Tis Isat Falls. After two turbulent years in Gondar, he picked his way down the escarpment to Metemma and the deserts of Sudan. On the way down he nearly died of fever and in the desert some of his party expired of thirst. Two months after leaving Gondar he struggled into Sennar on the Nile. He finally reached Europe ten years after leaving it.

Shehedi was unmarked on any map we had but turned out to be a bustling and friendly town all the same. We stopped at an eating place which had rooms out the back with comfortable beds and mosquito nets. But the lure of the border was strong, so we bought some egg rolls and tea and pushed on to the Sudanese border where we planned to sleep. It proved to be little more than a cluster of huts with no inn. So we backtracked to Sak Besak Hotel in Shehedi (its name means 'laugh and laugh') and booked two rooms. The owner's name was Solomon, and he looked the biblical part.

The serendipity of travel is amazing – you throw yourself at the unpredictability of the road and it treats you kindly. At Shehedi we met a Russian advertising executive, his lawyer buddy and two South African cyclists who were hitching a ride with the Russians. The cyclists had pedalled through the Middle East and were heading for Johannesburg. The foursome had just come south through Egypt and Sudan, and they could thus provide us with information of the road – down to GPS points. We toasted to adventure.

IV The Sudanese border was straight out of some Evelyn Waugh novel about a forgotten African outpost. The first official puzzled over our passports for an almost obscenely long time, entering everything into a dirty textbook. After that he dragged his chair over and asked us, confidentially, what country we were from. Eventually, only a map solved the problem.

African border posts are a tough test of character. There were plenty of guns about and Mike seemed the sort of person who would take only so much crap, then blow. That would be a really bad thing to do here. I knew he'd travelled Cape to Cairo on public transport, so he must have had plenty of experience with such matters. But he had an unpredictable edge that made me think he could lose his rag quite easily. Mike, though, just sighed, smiled and waited. Perhaps he was waiting to see if I would lose it.

Eventually a man with shoulder pips was ready. He went through the usual procedure again, then checked the vehicle papers, serial numbers on everything mechanical and electronic and asked for 325 dinars. We handed him a D1000 note. He didn't recognise it and tried to give it back. When we protested he held it up to the light, opened a safe and checked it against a wad of other identical notes, worried over the watermark then finally, reluctantly, gave us D700 change.

All the while the fan rattled dangerously overhead. With nothing better to do, I studied the office – cracked tile floor, ceiling stained with watermarks, walls about a metre thick and built to withstand a siege. There were dusty rolls of probably confiscated linoleum, four badly battered desks, countless spider webs, a steel box from some previous Turkish invasion and four chipped antique safes, one of whose handle seemed to have been blown off.

Pips, ensconced behind what looked like a farm gate, kept diving into the safes, coming out empty-handed, fiddling in another one then sitting down with a thump, looking puzzled. He seemed to have constantly misplaced things and scratched in his drawers between safe forays, getting frustrated. Then the form in triplicate with addendums and additions wouldn't tear, so he scrabbled on the floor for a used staple, bent it straight and ripped it down the edge of the page. The hours dragged by. The fan rattled. Spiders extended their webs. The safes sagged under the irresistible force of gravity. Pips suddenly stood up, handed us our passports, shook our hands and said, 'Welcome to Sudan.' We shot out and roared off before he could change his mind.

Along the road to Al Gedarif the trees thinned out, the land flattened and, occasionally, we'd pass a camel and rider. The contrast with Ethiopia was visually shocking; the endless flatness, after the cool mountains, was intimidating. Al Gedarif was bustling almost beyond belief. Thousands of people, cars, donkeys and sheep flooded the streets. We'd read that it was necessary to register as aliens so we found our way to a door in a wall where a man sat at a desk with the television blaring. We handed him our passports. He stared at them, closed, for a while and then began a surreal exchange:

'Your father's name?'

'Copeland.'

'Your name?'

'Michael.'

He turned to me and said, 'Michael, where is your passport number?'

'No, no, he's Michael. I'm Don.'

'Ah yes, Don.'

Then he turned to Mike and said, 'Don, where is your number?'

'No, I'm Michael.'

'Where do you come from?'

'South Africa.'

'You American?'

'No, South African.'

'England?'

If anyone was going to lose his rag it would be about now. But Mike grinned and rolled his eyes. This was a man I could travel with.

The official duly transcribed all this misinformation into Arabic on a scrap of paper, then disappeared out the door with our passports. Much later – as we watched an over-acted soapy in Arabic – he returned, handed us our passports and shooed us out the door. Did we have proof of registration? Did he? What the hell...

We headed out of town along a fine tar road towards Wad Medani and our next encounter with the Nile.

|V| Wad Medani had the air of a place that had once been a holiday destination, with locked and deserted shady parks lining the Nile like forgotten dreams, and some faded-looking hotels. We tried one inn, but it looked as if nobody had stayed there for years. The man at the desk seemed surprised as we walked in. The next one was the Nile Hotel and, though deserted, appeared somewhat more functional so we checked in. As the muezzin began to call at sunset we were invited to break the fast with the hotel staff. We sat round a mat under the rising moon and stuffed ourselves with bean *fuul*, lentil patties, tomato salad, fresh bread and sweet orange juice. Nobody could speak English so a Dinka schoolboy was fetched who could.

Between translations of the many questions and answers, he told us all was not well with his people. When we arrived in Sudan the fragile cease-fire that had interrupted the oldest civil war in the world seemed to be holding – after 19 uninterrupted years of ruinous conflict. More people had died in the country's civil war than in Rwanda, the Gulf War, the Balkans, Afghanistan and Iraq combined. All of this seems to have passed by the rest of the world unnoticed – an apocalypse in a vacuum.

Sudan is really two countries: the north – drier, wealthier and largely Muslim Arab; the south – underdeveloped and populated by Christian and animistic Dinkas, Nuers, Azanders and many other ethnic groups of African descent. The south – once known as Equatoria under British rule – has oil, the north has power. An unhealthy situation.

The Sudan People's Liberation Army, a ragtag outfit led by John

Garang, who has a doctorate from Iowa State University, is contesting Arab rule of the south. He claims to be fighting for a non-secular, united Sudan, but in truth this is a war rooted in the old toxic relationship between Arab master and African servant. In 1989 a democratically elected government in Khartoum was toppled in a coup by the radical National Islamic Front, ushering in a new dark age. Unions and independent newspapers were suppressed, political moderates fled the country and the war escalated to the drumbeat of jihad against infidels. Outlaws like Osama bin Laden and Carlos the Jackal settled in mansions around Khartoum.

In the south people died in their thousands, killed by war, drought, epidemics, mass starvation and slaving raids. Oil was discovered right in the middle of the war zone and in 1999 engineers in Khartoum opened the tap on a 2 000-kilometre oil pipeline from the lowlands of the Muglad Basin to a tanker terminal on the shores of the Red Sea. Every metre has to be defended.

That evening we made an awful discovery: amid the hassle at the border we'd left the laptop computer behind – 370 kilometres back down the flat, hot road. Fervently hoping Pips was an honest man, we left Wad Medani well before dawn. The streets were deserted but for a dying cat, recently run over and with its guts on the road.

'That's not a good omen,' was all I could get out of a sleepy Mike.

As the sun lightened the sky we began to encounter the desert buses, most of them battered 1960s Bedfords. They seemed to have no restrictions about where you could sit. Passengers were packed inside, on the roof and latecomers hung off the sides. From the front they were an awesome sight – like giant hedgehogs. Passengers travelled this way on grain and charcoal trucks, hanging onto loads sometimes twice as high as the truck. On the dirt road to the border we came upon the downside of the high ride. A bright blue Bedford had toppled with its load of charcoal and passengers. Bags, smashed watermelons, charcoal and people were everywhere. We stopped to ask what we could do to help. Four passengers were dead, we were told, but no, we were going the wrong way to be of use.

A bit further along the road a line appeared which resolved, through the heat shimmer, into a camel caravan. Sword-armed and cloaked men on huge bull camels were shepherding dozens of other camels and long-tailed sheep. On some mounts were colourful canopies, probably for women and children. We stopped and watched, mesmerised, as the caravan swung out across the scrub until it was swallowed by mirage. An ancient and inexplicable memory stirred.

Some way before the border we came upon a waterhole surrounded by hundreds of cattle and camels. They were strung out beside the water, their awkward necks bobbing and swaying like ostriches. I hauled out my camera and wandered among the animals. A wild yell made me look up from the viewfinder. An utterly black man, wearing only gaudy pantaloons, was bounding in my direction whirling a wicked long-sword above his head. It was such a magnificent sight I just stood and watched his advance, my mind quite blank. With a howl he leapt into the air in front of me and went into a crouch, his sword flashing. Then his face split into a smile as white as the circling egrets and he greeted me: 'Salaam aleikom.' We shook hands and I asked to see his sword. It was no toy: a long, beautifully beaten blade with a Turkish-style flared pommel. I handed it back and he slid it into a scabbard made from the body of a tin torch and two strips of leather held together by yellow insulation tape.

He wanted to look through my camera which, just then, had a 200-millimetre lens attached. He peered then leapt back, laughing, and called to his herders to share the experience. When we parted the warrior put his hand on my shoulder, then on his heart.

It turned out Pips was an honest man. He hauled our laptop out of one of his safes, apologised for our inconvenience, shook hands and wished us well on our journey. That border would give us more problems in the future, but for the moment we were relieved and headed back to Wad Medani. When we passed the felled Bedford there were some people trying to right it with a tractor, but nobody else was around. How had they and four corpses departed? Well, there was nothing we could do. We popped *The Best of the Eagles* into the CD player, sucked on a bottle of cold water and headed north into the Sahara. What more could one want of life?

That evening, at the Nile Hotel, we were again invited to break fast. It suddenly struck me there were no women around, so unlike Ethiopia. We had seen one or two in the market at Al Gedarif but they were clearly off the masculine social map. Where exactly did half the population hide? It was a little creepy.

VI We left Wad Medani with the sense that the deeper we drove into Sudan, the further back we moved into the country's turbulent history. Because of the Nile, that umbilical cord which connects Egypt to both Ethiopia and Central Africa, the history of Sudan has been tied to developments in Egypt for thousands of years. The great civilisation of Pharaonic Egypt had a southern echo at Meroe in Nubia and the remains of pyramids, palaces and temples still litter the Sudanese desert along the Nile. For centuries caravans from Alexandria trailed south along the river, branching west at the meeting place of the Blue and White Niles to Lake Chad and Timbuktu, or east to Massawa on the Red Sea.

In Europe, the great southern lands of sand and pitiless heat remained a mystery to all but a few brave travellers. That all ended in 1798 when Napoleon Bonaparte landed an army at Alexandria and fought his way to Cairo, dragging a slumbering Egypt out of the Middle Ages. It was to be the first real integration of West and East in that country since the departure of the Roman garrisons one and a half millennia earlier.

With Bonaparte came learned men who followed the French soldiers upstream past Luxor and Aswan, marvelling at the ruined structures along the riverbanks. The French did not hold onto Egypt for long. British warships barricaded the coast and Turkish armies massed on the border. Bonaparte slipped back to France to wage war across Europe, and in 1801 the French marched out of Cairo. In the vacuum they left Muhammad Ali, a Turk who rose to power by violence and cunning. When the British landed on the beaches of Alexandria in an attempt to emulate Bonaparte, he raised a force and drove them back. Ali then set himself up as ruler of all Egypt.

This was to impact on Sudan in a particular way. Before the French, the rulers of Egypt were a wild band of eunuchs from Georgia and the Caucasus known as the Mamelukes. They opposed Ali's rule, but he pushed them south up the Nile. Aided by Bedouin marauders, they continued to pose a threat, so Ali sent his son, Ismail, and an army of several thousand to eliminate them. He offered the troops whatever they could loot and, furthermore, 50 piastres for every human ear they could obtain in battle. In return he demanded slaves – at least 40 000 of them – and any gold they could lay their hands on. The army drove south of Aswan, through Nubia, past the confluence of the Niles and to the foot of the Ethiopian escarpment.

At Sennar, however, Ismail was killed by Sudanese tribesmen. The revenge of the Turks was to be terrible. They thrust back down the Blue Nile, emasculating all men they found and cutting off the breasts of women, the wounds being filled with boiling pitch. By 1823 Sudan had been subdued at terrible cost. Of some nine million people in the country before Muhammad Ali's campaign, about 75 per cent had either been killed or enslaved. It was the peace of death along the river.

In 1824 the Turks moved their capital from Omdurman to a fishing village on the promontory of land formed by the confluence of the two Niles, an area known to local Arabs as El Khartoum. Vile, squalid and filthy were the usual epithets bestowed on it by early travellers, but it was at least an outpost of civilisation where both European and Eastern wares could be bought. Samuel Baker and his wife loathed it on sight. 'A more miserable, filthy and unhealthy place,' he said, 'can hardly be imagined.' But then, this was the man who had described the African mind as being less interesting than that of his dog.

The road to Khartoum along the Blue Nile has long since been repopulated and is now punctuated by hundreds of mosques and squat dwellings with flat roofs built without rain in mind. Everywhere I was struck by the power of Islam. It would seem there is little enough to thank God for in this nightmarish desert or in the history of its despoilment, and yet the poorest and most wretched inhabitants prostrated themselves upon the sand five times a day with a simple concentrated fervour that we would not see in Nilotic Egypt. No village lacked a minaret and its attendant muezzin calling the faithful to prayer. Perhaps it is the very austerity of life in these arid wastes that predisposes the people to worship. It was after all in just such a place that the Prophet Mohammed lived and received his inspiration.

We stopped for a breakfast of tomatoes and unleavened bread under the only tree we'd seen in ages. As the engine died an immense silence possessed the surrounding desert. The heat induced a feeling of trance-like detachment in which monotony dissolved into a natural timelessness. In such a place visions must take on the appearance of reality and asceticism could itself become a religious object. Suddenly, all round us, was the sound of creaking doors and a strange chatter. I looked up to see the sky filled with thousands of migrating cranes, seeking thermals and drifting southwards – a grey-white blizzard in the sun-bleached sky.

Central Khartoum is no longer either a miserable or dirty place, though Baker would find little changed in the huge squatter camps surrounding the city. We threaded our way through the busy city traffic to the Khartoum Yacht Club where we'd been advised to camp. I was soon sitting on the banks of the Nile near its confluence watching black-shouldered kites wheeling over the water. The river is immense at this point, more spectacular for having flowed through the dry nothingness of Sudan. Small yachts were gliding upriver and, moored on the opposite bank, were huge, squat floating hotels. The most interesting craft, though, was almost at my elbow, marooned some 30 metres up the bank, listing slightly and now surrounded by lawn. It was the *Malak*, a welded iron gunboat that had blasted its way up the Nile under the command of Lord Herbert Kitchener to avenge the death of General Charles Gordon. It now serves as the yacht club's office and a storeroom for assorted nautical junk.

Khartoum is indelibly linked to the history of these two men, so different, yet both so British. At the age of 41 Gordon was already famous, having served with great bravery in the Crimean War and having led the Ever Victorious Army through hazardous adventures in China. He was a mystic who had no time for women, but was apparently not homosexual. A pious man who liked his brandy and soda for breakfast and dinner, he sometimes retired to his tent for days in fits of melancholy. Nonetheless, he was a brave man of action, generous and kind, an erratic sort of saint and definitely a little mad.

In 1872 the Egyptian prime minister met him in Cairo and offered him the job of governor of Equatoria. Gordon accepted. With a ragtag bunch of adventurers he headed up the White Nile, establishing forts all the way to the present-day border of Uganda. Within two and a half years Equatoria was firmly under Egyptian rule. Gordon, however, grew tired of the pressures of controlling the far-flung empire and resigned. Before he could get too far, he was offered the governorship of Sudan and accepted.

The country was a mess, wracked by slavery and graft. Gordon moved into the palace in Khartoum, but was soon on the move, criss-crossing Sudan on camelback, making deals, meting out punishments and winning respect. Within months trade began to flow, banditry decreased and Khartoum began to look like a modern city. The country was better governed than it had ever been. But Gordon's enthusiasm again began to evaporate. He flew into rages, drank too much and fired off telegrams that enraged his superiors in both Cairo and London. In 1879 he resigned and left Africa.

In his absence arose one of those strange, magnetic characters whom only deserts seem to spawn: a warrior-priest named Mohammed Ahmed Ibn el-Sayyid Abdullah, the Mahdi. According to one report, 'There was a strange splendour in his presence, an overwhelming passion in the torrent of his speech.' The Mahdi was a man possessed. He demanded absolute adherence to Islam, tortured blasphemers and declared jihad against Sudan's Egyptian rulers. It was as if a dam had burst. By 1883 thousands of warriors had rallied to his call. Khartoum was in a panic. Only one person seemed able to stem the crisis: General Gordon.

He was not a man who could stay out of Africa for long and, with promises of a free hand from both the British and Egyptian governments, he sailed up the Nile to Khartoum in 1884. But he had underestimated the force of the Mahdi. Before long the city was surrounded and Gordon and his troops were trapped. The telegraph lines were cut and Khartoum and Gordon vanished from Western sight. After far too long, and only at the insistence of Queen Victoria, a force was assembled to save Gordon. But it arrived too late: Khartoum had fallen. Gordon's head had been lopped off and paraded round the streets of a city now under the Mahdi's control. The expedition sent to save him fell back down the Nile in disorder.

In England, by then, Gordon had become a household name. When news of his death reached London there was an outpouring of grief equalled only by the death of David Livingstone. The Mahdi outlived Gordon by only five months. Following his success he became very fat, spending most of his time in his harem. According to one story he was poisoned, according to another he died of smallpox, months of debauchery having left him with little strength. A tomb was erected over the Mahdi's grave and, for a time, this shrine was deemed by some more sacred than Mecca. Khalifa Abdullah replaced him and, if anything, was even more authoritarian. Khartoum was razed and the old city of Omdurman, across the Nile, was made his capital. Slaving became a primary source of income.

In Britain the public bayed for revenge and, eventually, the government responded. The man chosen to exact that revenge was Lord Kitchener. In 1896 he sailed up the Nile with a well-trained force and gunboats of the Royal Navy. In his retinue was a young journalist named Winston Churchill. He watched as the British closed in on Omdurman: 'At dawn the soldiers saw the great dome of the Mahdi's tomb rising in the sky and, beneath it, a long shadowy line that looked like a *zeriba*, a defence-work made of thorns and tree branches. Suddenly the black line of the *zeriba* began to move. It was made of men, not bushes. Behind it other immense masses and lines of men appeared over the crest; and while we watched, amazed by the wonder of the sight, the whole face of the slope beneath became black with swarming savages. Four miles from end to end, this mighty army advanced swiftly. The whole side of the hill seemed to move. Behind the masses horsemen galloped continually; before them many patrols dotted the plain; above them waved hundreds of banners and the sun, glinting on many thousand hostile spear points, spread a sparkling cloud.'

The Mahdist forces, however, were no match for British artillery and, several hours later, some 10 000 bodies were lying on the slopes, with many thousands more injured. Kitchener reportedly shut his spyglass as the last shots echoed and remarked that the enemy had been given 'a good dusting'. Gordon's death, he declared as he raised the Union Jack at Khartoum Palace, had been avenged.

The body of the Mahdi was dug up and flung into the Nile. Khalifa Abdullah, who had escaped upriver, was pursued and killed, his head being sent by Kitchener to Cairo with a suggestion that it be made into a drinking cup. Queen Victoria was revolted by the gesture and the Khalifa's head was returned and quietly buried at Wadi Halfa.

VII With around five million people, modern Khartoum is noisy, busy, dirty and, in that way, a rather standard African capital. But along the Corniche – the road beside the Nile – are some beautiful old buildings with the palace as their centrepiece. The museum, though rather neglected, has some breathtaking ancient Nubian carvings, huge Coptic artworks and you can trace, in tools and statues, a history going back thousands of years.

As it was Ramadan, Khartoum's citizens broke fast at sundown, feasted and partied into the night. We were awoken at around half past three by strident muezzins and were subsequently pretty dozy all day. On our first morning the Catholic cathedral, not to be outdone, began ringing its bells at four-thirty just over the road from the Yacht Club where we vainly chased sleep. Finally we gave up the fight and headed out to visit the Mahdi's tomb, photograph the bustle of the market, then hang out in the boat-building yard at Omdurman. That evening we threaded our way through dark streets to an outdoor restaurant where good food was served on dirty plates and cost us next to nothing. Men in hooded galabiyyas sat around, deep in conversation, drinking mint tea and spitting at the floor.

Travelling is a strange business. To have been in Khartoum is somehow more poignant than actually being in Khartoum. Being there involves dust, suspect water and feeling displaced and homesick. To have been there is amazing. Memory and learning weave altogether more fabulous cloth. As already mentioned, claiming and holding this city had been the goal of Napoleon, Muhammad Ali, Gordon and Kitchener. It was the centre of one of the cruellest slave markets in the world, the southern-most entrepôt of the caravan routes, the site of lascivious harem life under the Mahdi and the grave of tens of thousands of his soldiers. It was a city with strange ghosts.

On my last night in Khartoum a cat peed on the tent right near my head. In the opal light of dawn the kites were patrolling the river – they fly so deftly – and wagtails were quartering the lawn. Most of the city was sleeping off its excesses and the air was cool. It was a good time to leave. Yes, to have been in Khartoum felt good.

An excellent tar road leads from the capital almost straight through the desert to Abu Dom on the Nile. We contemplated going via Berber and Meroe, but that would have resulted in a 500-kilometre leg through empty desert between the Third and Fourth Cataracts. Taking a single vehicle across hundreds of kilometres of roadless Sahara would have been a foolish thing, and we'd heard tales of bandits along that route.

We pulled off at a truck stop for lunch – bean fuul, unleavened bread and sweet tea. The place was squat and made of brown mud with a reed-roofed veranda. Great, pointy-bottomed urns of cool, precious water were propped in the shade – gifts, as all such urns are in Sudan, in memory of some dead ancestor. Later, in a featureless piece of the Nubian Desert, we again came upon an old blue Bedford in trouble, this one with its guts spewed all over the road. It had a broken crankshaft and had been there with its crew for three days under the pitiless sun. When we stopped a man came over and proffered his wrist to shake – the rest of him was covered in oil and brown grease. Somehow he'd secured a new crank and the engine was being reassembled. The three men had a load of dates in the truck so they hadn't gone hungry, though they must have grown weary of the fare. We gave them some water and took to the road again. Eventually we hit a T-junction and the Nile.

There is no road from Abu Dom to Dongola, just vague tracks in the desert. To the east was a low tree-line along the river, to the west just peach-coloured sand rippling off to the horizon, on and on for thousands of kilometres to the empty dunefields of southern Libya. We slipped JJ Cale into the CD player and ploughed through the sand, dust billowing out behind, not really sure where we were going.

'Cocaine, all around my brain,' sang JJ Cale. It was somehow appropriate in this land of nothing. I was missing my wife and children. If the Land Rover broke down we'd be in deep trouble. Nobody could speak English. Our Arabic was zero. There were no garages or shops or even people. What the hell was I doing there anyway? I remembered some lines from *Pensées* by the French philosopher Blaise Pascal and made a note to myself to look them up. They matched my mood exactly. 'When I consider the small space I occupy and which I see swallowed up in the infinite immensity of spaces of which I know nothing and which know nothing of me, I take fright and am amazed to see myself here rather than there. There is no reason for me to be here rather than there, now rather than then. Who put me here?' On looking up the lines I found another which put it more bluntly: 'The sole cause of man's unhappiness is that he does not know how to stay quietly in his room.'

For a while we followed a Toyota bakkie overloaded with white-hooded passengers. The driver seemed to know where he was going. It eventually stopped and we asked the way to Dongola. A man, speaking perfect English, assured us we were on the road, then asked us if we could take him and two others to the next village. Half lost, we were only too happy for the company. Our new guide had worked for Saudi Airlines and was heading for El Goled Bahri. After several hours we entered the village, a rambling clutter of squat brick houses and high-walled yards along dusty thoroughfares. We inquired our way to the *souk* – the marketplace – and caused a sensation when we rolled into it in a cloud of yellow dust. People gathered round the Landy, then shook our hands, smiling in delight at the strange visitors.

As the muezzin called the end of the fast we were directed to a mat with our fellow travellers and offered a large tray of fried felafels with squeezed lime, fuul, tomato-and-onion salad with guavas and bananas. After about an hour we bade our fellow travellers farewell and headed for the Nile, pitching our tents beside some palms under a brilliant desert sky. That night I tucked into my sleeping bag to the sound of toads in the irrigation canals, crickets under the palms and a muezzin in the distant village. Occasionally a donkey brayed. But the immense silence of the desert seemed to drown them out. There wasn't a breath of wind and, close by, the Nile slid silkily towards Cairo.

|VIII| Early next morning we broke camp and set off on the non-road to Dongola. Camel caravans crossed our path – heading for the river, maybe, or on their way to Egypt. The wind-varnished gravel was criss-crossed with tracks, many going nowhere; they simply ended and we'd track across the gravel until we picked up another set. Eventually, by accident and almost with a shock, we came upon a tar road that led into Dongola.

Our guidebook – an old *Lonely Planet* and the only one we could find on Sudan – said it was a boring town with little to recommend it. Either the writer was in a bad mood when she arrived – and the road might explain that – or it had changed a good deal in seven years since she'd visited. It's a busy place with big shade trees and a bustling souk offering an extraordinary variety of fresh vegetables, fruit, beans, lentils, shoes, clothes and the usual blur of plastic and packaging.

In 1814 the traveller John Lewis Burckhardt came upon just such a souk there, but the wares then were more exotic. 'It was a fabulous market for so small a place,' he wrote. 'In an open space in the centre of town, a thousand miles away from any part of the world that one could call civilised, you could buy such things as spices and sandalwood from India, antimony that blacked the eyelids, medicines, German swords and razors, saddles and leather goods from Kordofan, writing paper and beads from Genoa and Venice, cloth, pottery and basketware of every kind, soap from Egypt, cotton, salt and Ethiopian gold. There was a lively sale in monkeys that were trained to do tricks, and Sudan's wooden dishes, battered and blackened by being held over the fire, were famous. The market was also renowned for its sale of Dongola horses, and for camels and other beasts to carry these goods across the desert, and, of course, for its slaves.'

We bought fresh felafels, onions, shiny red tomatoes, tiny limes, bananas and freshly-baked bread, then headed for the Ola Hotel. But no, we could not book in, we were told, until we had a letter from the police. Why? No answer. Where were they? Just round the corner. Some 15 minutes and many meandering kilometres later we were shown the police station by a man on a bicycle who pedalled ahead, beckoning all the while. The officer seemed at a loss about how to treat our request. Eventually six uniformed men had our passports under intense scrutiny. After nearly half an hour of this nonsense one scribbled something on a scrap of paper (with no stamp), gave us our passports and shooed us out.

The hotel man was near frantic to get at the bit of paper and wouldn't show us our room without it in his hands. What that was all about I'll never know. The room had a neon light, a fan, two beds, a table and no window, just a high slot into the foyer. It would have made a good prison cell. The cost – a couple of dollars.

While doing some washing at the tap in the courtyard, I met the hotel skivvy, an utterly black Dinka named Kuon, who was washing the hotel sheets. He spoke some English and told me a bit about his history. The Dinka are the menial class of northern Sudan, working for virtually nothing to escape the war-wracked south and living, often, in appalling conditions. When I mentioned the name John Garang (the southern rebel leader) Kuon's eyes shone with sudden hope. 'Do you know him?' he whispered, looking round to see if we were being overheard. 'Is he well?' There was little news I could give him, but he was happy that someone from the outside world knew about Garang.

That evening I was travel weary and rather down. My notebook recorded it: 'Why do I travel through countries like Sudan? I can list the reasons not to. The ground is steeped in sadness, and warfare of some sort or another has been going on here for hundreds of years. The cell I'm sitting in has filthy walls and an unswept floor. There is a sheet on the bed but no blankets – there never are – and the shower merely trickles. The WC is a hole in the ground with no toilet paper and it stinks.

'Outside there is just dust and piles of rubbish. The road here was also just dust. Actually it wasn't even a road and it seemed interminable. I don't speak this language and almost nobody speaks mine. The souk is full of hagglers and rotting heaps of old vegetables and camel shit. It's hot. So hot that if you walk outside without a hat you get a headache. And at night it doesn't cool down. Yet this is winter. This is the middle of absolutely nowhere.'

I guess every trip has its nadir and this was it. Too much difference can be exhausting. In our ancient past we might have been nomad hunters, but we sure as hell had our families and friends near at hand. Pastoralism made us even more home-birdy. The sort of travelling we were doing is a new thing undertaken in the past by the very few – the Marco Polos of this world. It's stimulating and inspiring until it gets uncomfortable and lonely.

We sliced the bread and filled it with felafel, tomatoes and onions, then squeezed limejuice into it and munched. It was delicious. We burped luxuriously and I picked up my notebook; perhaps I had merely been hungry:

'Maybe we travel for the contrast with our normal lives; maybe we forever seek that which we do not yet have or know. Perhaps some of us are simply travellers by nature, seekers of horizons and far, exotic places. The contrast between the highs and lows of rough travel is extreme, but I wouldn't describe such travel as pleasure. Maybe travel settles best in the memory, is merely the raw material of memory, and we travel to be able to say, in retrospect: "I once crossed the Nubian Desert, lingered in the souk of the ancient capital of Dongola and followed the Nile to the sea." Right now, in this cell, there is nothing but stifling heat and the chop chop of the overhead fan.'

After dark Dongola changed mood. Shops opened, twinkling lights came on and shopkeepers touted for trade: 'Hello meester, *tamam* (I greet you).' Strolling down a busy street, we met a young man, Ahmed, keen to practise his English and he invited us to share some tea and sweet cakes. His story added to that of Kuon.

There was a time, he said, when English was the second language in all the schools of Sudan and some subjects, like science, were taught in that language. Teachers came from Britain and those Sudanese able to speak English found overseas travel easy. But the new fundamentalist government arabised Sudanese life and English was dropped. Today war, poverty and language locks up the Sudanese in their country.

'We are poor because we spend all the money on war – and no tourists come,' Ahmed complained. 'Also every man must go to the army after school. Many come back from the south with bad malaria or without limbs or in a coffin. I want to leave. I want to go to London to study. So I listen to the BBC and CNN and I talk English when I can.'

There are many Dinkas in central and northern Sudan and most are probably political or economic refugees. They are virtually slaves and are unable to travel home for fear of being branded as spies or terrorists. The problems between the north and south were many, said Ahmed, but the spark was the imposition of Islamic Sharia law across the whole of Sudan – severe and an anathema to the animistic or Catholic southerners. Garang united the southerners in a battle for an independent Equatoria, but the south has gold and oil and the Arabs won't let it go. As in Congo, Rwanda and elsewhere, Africa forever bleeds.

|IX| We crossed to the east bank of the Nile at Dongola on a thudding old ferry, then motored northwards through villages completely different to those further south. We passed yards with cheerfully painted gates and patterned walls. There were large trees, well-watered fields, no litter and – strange for Sudan – women in bright cloth. We stocked up with our usual bread-and-tomato fare at a souk in Argo, then parked beside the river at Kerma en Nuzl a bit further north.

Breaking Ramadan rules, we ate sandwiches under a large fig tree and only into my second sandwich did I realise the cloth spread on some grass right in front of me had a human under it. He eventually bestirred himself, picked up a small green water jug and squatted beside the river. Then he wiped his bum with his left hand and washed it from the jug.

As the sun dipped we bumped into the small village of Majaziep in the Abu Sara region. On the way there we'd ended up looping back south – which gave us some concern – to negotiate our way around a series of large mountains. It was hard to tell whether they were granite or sandstone – all rock in Nubia seems to be burnt black. The village appeared when we needed it and when we drove in, the locals looked at us as though we'd beamed down from outer space. But, as usual, the children broke the ice and I ended up surrounded by them. One little girl hung over my shoulder, watching me write my diary, a boy sat next to me with a beautiful infant on his lap. They watched every movement, commenting and laughing at the pen's progress across the page. Had they never seen anyone write?

We were asked to break fast with the villagers, as travellers always seem to be. They prayed briefly and shared their food with us, delighted at the tinned offerings we contributed. Mike headed for bed in the rooftop tent, but I joined the villagers in their second evening prayers – a thanksgiving to Allah for the bounty of life.

The men chanted their prayers on a mat in the courtyard, while the women followed the ritual inside the house a metre or two away. Light from within the room rippled across the faces of the men as they knelt, then bowed on the mat, their backs to the Nile and their faces to the stars of the Pleiades. They touched their foreheads to the ground and softly chanted 'Allaaahu Akbar' (God is great) beneath the glittering arch of the heavens. It was a ritual so old, so simple, so intense. I sat on the mat beside them, transported and brought nearly to tears by the beauty and sincerity of these humble, generous people.

After about 20 minutes they simply stopped, got up and walked back to their houses while their women filed out, giggling shyly at the stranger who had appeared so suddenly in their midst. We left at dawn, long after their morning prayers.

Further north, in Abru, we decided to stock up for lunch. We found our way to the souk, then asked a man where we could buy tomatoes. He led us through a door into the security police offices and demanded our passports and travel documents. We explained we'd tried to get travel documents in Wad Medani but they didn't give us any, and had been to the security police in Dongola and they merely gave us a slip of paper.

They puzzled over our passports, then asked us to show them our entrance stamp to Sudan. There was none. Way back there at the Sudanese border, after taking an hour over our passports, the ponderous man with the many safes had failed to stamp them. Problem. A country in the throes of a civil war is not the sort of place you want to arouse suspicion. After much more discussion and waiting they planted a fresh-faced young man named Muhammad in our van and told us he had to ride with us to Wadi Halfa, our exit point from Sudan. And no, we couldn't have our passports back, they were firmly in Muhammad's pocket. He spoke a bit of English and said he was at university in Khartoum, studying Islamic history. So he needed a ride? Yes, his girlfriend was in Wadi Halfa.

The way north – still merely a direction rather than a defined road – was impossibly rutted, but the countryside was breathtaking. Fields to the west and desert to the east. Trucks had left hideous corrugations that banged us around until our teeth chattered. Mike was driving.

'Mike, you have to drive faster on corrugations,' I said, 'There's a speed where you just hit the tops and it's not bumpy.'

'Bullshit,' he replied. 'If I go faster we'll shake to pieces.'

So we continued to rattle along. I expected bits to start falling off the Landy. At one point we were forced away from the river by black mountains dusted with yellow sand. On a gravel plain we stopped for lunch under a solitary acacia tree.

'Danger,' pronounced Muhammad, hauling an Uzzi sub-machine-gun out of his briefcase and leaping from the van. I had visions of two shallow graves and Muhammad with a new Land Rover, but he began stalking the tree.

'What's up?' Mike shouted.

'Snakes,' was the reply, pointing at holes near the base of the tree. If a serpent had stuck its head out just then, it would have been blown into the arms of Allah. So why is a student carrying a sub-machine-gun? I inquired. Well, actually, he was also security.

A captain? Yes, a captain – during his holidays. We ate a snake-free lunch while our minder looked the other way.

I took the wheel and we were back on the roadless road. I gunned the Landy until it smoothed out over the corrugations, hurtling along but comfortable.

'Hmm,' said Mike. 'The road seems to have improved.' I held my peace.

Later, when Mike was back at the wheel, we tried to pass a bus but it kept weaving dangerously to prevent us from doing so. Eventually we raced across the desert and managed to get ahead. Muhammad was furious about the bus. 'Stop in front of it,' he ordered. The bus slewed to a halt and our man, Uzzi in hand, stalked up to the driver, shouted a lot, then returned and packed away his gun.

'What did you tell him?' asked Mike.

'He must report to security tomorrow. He in big trouble now.'

You clearly don't mess with the security police in Sudan. It reminded me of South Africa in the 1980s.

'Hey, the surface has become corrugated again,' grumbled Mike as we juddered painfully towards Wadi Halfa.

X Wadi Halfa is a squat, featureless town strung out along the shore of the High Aswan Dam. There are some attractive hills dotted about but not much else to recommend it to the traveller. We spent a few minutes at the security-police office – an anonymous door in a wall and a room with a battered desk, tatty chairs and a blaring television set. They promised us our passports the following morning, early, so we took Muhammad and his Uzzi to his girlfriend's house and booked in at The Nile Hotel. It was interestingly minimalist: bare rooms, beds, a hole in the ground for a toilet and a shower consisting of some drums of water, a sawn-off plastic oil can and a cut-off plastic cooldrink bottle. The shower trick was to fill the oil can, take it into the shower cubicle and use the cooldrink bottle to throw cold water over you. Well, it got the dust off.

Afterwards I sat on the bed and located a dull fear inside me. Because of my anti-apartheid activities in the 1980s, I loathe security policemen and fear the worst in their hands. They embody for me the mindless evil in a society – young men with big egos, weapons and a licence to kill. Would the Sudanese variety surprise me? I feared not.

Well, we were sure done over the next morning. The Landy was pawed through by a number of eager searchers and one important stern-faced fellow with prerequisite reflective sunglasses. He wagged his finger at us, struck a bad B-grade movie pose and growled: 'You never going to leave Sudan.' He was doing the bad cop bit. The good cop was his second, who kept telling us everything would be all right. Then Dark Glasses started pointing at things.

'What's this?'
'Radio.'
'What?'
'BBC.'
'Oh. This?'
'Fridge.'
'Open it. And this?'
'Rooftop tent.'
'What?'
'Sleeping. Camping.'
'Oh. This?'
'Video.'
'Show me film.'
'It doesn't play back.'
'Give it me.'
'Okay, you try.'

A long comedy of button pushing and knob twisting followed. Finally they confiscated the tapes. Then gave them back.

'Where are your cameras?'
'Hotel.'
'Okay, we go fetch.'

Accompanied by an armed teenager, we headed for the hotel and returned with the required items. Spread out on the desk they looked impressive – long lenses, two cameras, a flash unit . . . all black and threatening. My film, I suddenly realised, was in a round, flat tin that looks like a Claymore mine. That didn't interest them, but the flash did. I flashed it for Dark Glasses. He felt the warmth of the flash, holding the unit thoughtfully for a while. The lens filters caused even more interest.

'What these?'

'Filters.'

'Why?'

'You want me to give you a lesson in photography?'

Eventually they eased up and began to smile a bit. Then the letter writing began. Ballpoint in one hand and our passports in the other, a scribe questioned Mike.

'Name?'

'Address?'

'Number of children?'

'Age?'

Slowly the letters grew. After about half an hour Mike's was done and my trial began. There were many diversions, random conversations, much boasting. Flies exploited the stillness when the office emptied, then headed for the ceiling when it filled again. Failing to get an entry stamp, it seemed, was a serious matter. But, hopefully, the long letter would explain the problem to immigration. Eventually, we sensed that we might– if we were infinitely patient – clear customs, buy ferry tickets and head for Egypt. We tried to make conversation: 'Can we swim in the Aswan Dam?' Mike asked.

'No, ten-metre crocodiles. But no hyenas.'

Finally a security man accompanied us to the passport office where a large man in uniform read the letters. Slowly. But he, it seemed, was just the clearing clerk. Off we went to his superior who questioned us. Then he called an underling who took dictation on two more long letters about us. A man with two pips on his shoulder watched the whole performance of about an hour without moving. Was he alive? We were given forms to fill in, one an entrance form *to* Sudan, the other allowing us to travel *in* Sudan. But we were attempting to leave Sudan and did not wish to travel, we told him. No matter, the form had to be filled in. Then off to another office to pay (dearly) for travel permits we didn't need, and then to the passport office.

Oops, they needed a photocopy of our passports and visas. But they didn't have a photocopier. That was in what appeared to be a telegraph office down the road. But, unfortunately, there was an electricity failure. Maybe power would be back after one o'clock. We sat down. There was a pair of crutches in the corner. Not a good omen. At least it was cool in the office, so we did what everyone in Sudan seemed to be doing: we waited. The décor in the office was interesting. A calendar a year out of date with a picture of yachts and apples, two pictures of very European-looking babies, three hanging objects which, on closer inspection, turned out to be very dead-looking plastic flowers, an ornate gold-rimmed wall clock only an hour behind.

Suddenly the neon tube flickered and the power was back. The photocopies were duly made and cost around $5. Back at the office, a man stamped our passports into Sudan for a few more dollars, then a clerk asked for $10 for a file to put our documents into 'because the captain won't look at papers without covers'. We refused and won a small victory. The captain did look at them. We were now allowed to be in Sudan. The following day we would go through the process again to be able to leave.

By then it was too late to deal with customs, so we retreated to The Nile Hotel to celebrate. It was a strange place – a collection of dark rooms, each with four beds, and surrounded by verandas made of stout poles supporting palm-frond stalks overlaid with papyrus matting held down by packed mud. The floors were all sand. The first night we were the only guests and had a room to ourselves. The next night the ferry from Aswan arrived and the price of our room was more than doubled so we elected to sleep on the veranda. A cot and a mattress, nothing more.

As evening fell, ancient Land Rovers piled with people and goods began arriving: Nubians with satin-black skin returning from Egypt; an Egyptian with trade goods waiting for the desert bus to Khartoum; old Sudanese men in sweat-stained galabiyyas dragging their camel-leather slippers and mumbling the rosary; the inevitable German; a gangster from Burkina Faso washed up against Sudan's northern border and trying to hustle cash for a visa to Cairo; a couple of Japanese, one of whom peered into the toilet, stepped back with a look of horror, then plunged in; Dinkas heading south; lighter-skinned Bantu, a long way from home, in long-sleeved cotton shirts and cheap trousers with turn-ups, who haggled deep into the night over what I knew not; and an American backpacker who said it was all so cool.

They all filed past my bed on the way to the toilets, which gradually grew smellier. With nothing particular to do I had turned in at 7.30 p.m. Way past midnight I hadn't slept a wink as the shouting, spitting, debating and trading continued. At 2.30 a.m. the devout lined up just beyond my veranda and offered their praises to Allah. Far-from-tame cats zigzagged through the people, meowing continuously. The toilet stench grew.

Then, suddenly, it all stopped. The lights went out, everyone settled down and even the cats fell silent and I slept. At five-thirty the devout were at it again, praising Allah, then tucking into a meal before the sun could catch them at it. By that time the romance of being at one of Africa's great crossroads had long worn off. I lay there fervently wishing they'd all bugger off so I could get some more sleep. I realised one thing, though. During Ramadan all those men slouched in chairs looking dopey or dead are actually catching up on the rest Ramadan denies them every night for a month. This is hot, desert country, but during the day the devout neither eat nor drink. They are not even allowed to swallow their own spit, which leads to a good deal of spitting. Did Allah decree it evil to swallow your own saliva?

There are travellers in Africa and there are African travellers. There's a difference. The former pass through it, the latter seem to get swallowed by it. Joseph Conrad would understand. Wadi Halfa seemed to be a clearing house for the latter sort and Stephan was definitely one. When we met him the next day he was having familiar troubles with officials and paperwork. 'If God ever wanted to stick an enema into this planet,' he grumbled over mint tea, 'He'd stick it right in Wadi Halfa.'

Stephan had bought an old Volkswagen Syncro with a bed and a kitchen in Germany and set off to travel Africa four years previously. He got stuck in the Sahara: Syncro campers are not exactly Land Rovers. Then he was robbed by Tuareg and the only reason they didn't steal his vehicle was that, right then, it had broken down. He fixed it and got to Kinshasa. Actually he fixed it all the way to Brazzaville – springs, shocks, clutch, wheel bearings, prop shafts, tyres, exhaust. It was a tough lesson in mechanics. But Stephan persisted.

There was no way he could get through the jungles of the Congo, but he wanted to visit Angola. So he found a boatman who planned to take logs down the coast from Brazzaville to Luanda. First, though, he had to build up a load. Stephan waited. There was only one small crane attached to a tractor so the boat could only be loaded when the tractor was being used (by someone else) to cut and haul trees. Three weeks, four weeks in the sweaty, malarial jungle. Then it was loaded. But no, the engine was faulty so it had to be disembowelled on the dock. Another week. Finally Stephan left for Luanda, his Syncro tied precariously atop the pile of logs.

Angola, he said, was wonderful except it was hard to get spare parts and there were landmines. He fixed the Syncro through Angola to Namibia, where he left it and went home to earn some more money for necessary repairs – and a new engine. Then he was back and off again – around Namibia and South Africa, then up through Zimbabwe, Zambia, Malawi, Tanzania and Kenya, rebuilding his beloved red bus all the way. The Ethiopian roads trashed his springs and he couldn't find replacements so he had to fit oversize ones. That stressed his shocks and prop shafts. By the time he entered Sudan, only the front wheels were attached to the engine.

Somewhere along the line he heard you could drive around the Aswan Dam to Egypt. You can't: the road is permanently closed. Misinformed, he drove through the desert for six days and arrived at a huge fence going as far as he could see in either direction. No border. So he turned round and headed back. There were no villages out there. He ran out of food and water. Finally he reached the Nile opposite the village of Abri. There was no ferry, so he convinced a boatman to take the Syncro across. The boat listed dangerously and he nearly lost the vehicle.

We met him looking for a ferry to Aswan. But he was running low on cash and had to wait around for a cargo pontoon. We sat in the tatty hotel with him. He was happy. Travelling was wonderful.

'Have you written a diary or taken photographs?' I asked. No, he hadn't.

'What would my diary say? Fixed car today, fixed car the day before...'

'Why don't you get a decent overland vehicle?' I inquired.

'No, I love my Syncro. It's my home, I can sleep in it.'

For all I know, he's still in Wadi Halfa.

XI   Trying to leave Sudan reminded me of a line from the Eagles' song, *Hotel California*: 'You can check out but you can never leave.' Well, you can, but it takes ingenuity, for the officials will find 'errors' and insist that you bleed money. The whole thing was a muddle. We had to get our passports stamped to leave, but after queuing for some time to do this, we were told we had to queue at another office to pay to leave, then return to show a receipt. There were no signs, just people crowding at windows. It was not clear what we were paying for. Port tax? Immigration tax? Officials would get up at any moment and wander away, chat to friends, maybe take a cup of tea. The queues grew. Then we were given exit forms and had to pay for them too – at a third window. Could we get our passport stamped? No, this was just where you paid, passports were stamped at the port, three kilometres away.

But wait, what about customs? They were in a building about a ten-minute walk away. Fortunately they proved rather efficient, and only took half an hour. Then it was back in the opposite direction to get ferry tickets to Aswan – which cost around $700 for the Landy and us. Then back to the port where we were stopped by a whistle from a smart uniformed fellow who checked all our bits of paper. And, yep, another charge: port duty, to be paid to a man who didn't have an office. We had to shove through an irritable throng to find him. Oh yes, there was customs clearance next.

'I thought we cleared customs,' I protested. But no: three more signatures and another $10, then we were in the passport queue. Unfortunately they had to deal with the Sudanese first, then the Egyptians. Europeans were told to 'sit and wait'.

Well, we got out in the end. It took three more security checks before they finally stamped our goddamn passports and we loaded the Land Rover onto a pontoon strapped to the side of the ferry. We sat on deck, dazed. Was this really it? The ferry hooted and pulled away from Sudan. Mike and I stared at each other and began to laugh hysterically.

There was a downside: Dark Glasses was on board. Well screw him. We had a passable meal and, as evening fell, we dropped over the side onto the pontoon, swung up the rooftop tent and figured we were the most comfortable passengers on the trip. The rest slept on the juddering steel decks. We passed the evening in the vehicle going backwards to Aswan at a steady ten knots. When Allah required praising, the throb of the ferry's engines ensured we didn't hear a thing.

On board we met Martyn. He'd set off from Amsterdam in a little Opel Corsa. Things were fine, he said, until he got to Mauritania. The sand was not good for the Corsa, so he sold it and hitched a ride to Mali. Martyn's an environmental urban planner and he hoped to work there, but the projects were small-scale and he couldn't get a job. He pushed on. Ghana, Nigeria, Cameroon, Gabon, Angola. He bought a bicycle in Zambia and began his return trip. Somewhere along the way he met the beautiful Yvette. By Kenya Yvette was going strong but Martyn's bike gave up. They took public transport, slept rough: Ethiopia, Sudan, Egypt, heading home.

Martyn was depressed. 'I do not like to say this, but I think there is no hope for Africa,' he said. 'In 20 years if I come back it will be much worse than now, a terrible place with drought and people dying. But the West is consuming the planet even faster. It's depressing. I need to go back to Amsterdam, which I love, and think about all this.'

Martyn badly needed a rest.

Jude Thaddeus, whom I met hanging over the rail with his gaze fixed northwards, was on a different mission: hope kept him going. His desire was not to travel, but to be in Canada. He was a qualified nurse from Cameroon. Quiet, intelligent and keen to further his studies, he had formulated a plan. He had Canadian friends in Albania and, he figured, if he could get to them he could travel with them to Canada when they returned. But the only place in northern Africa where he could get an Albanian visa was Cairo. So he set off overland: through northern Cameroon to N'Djamena and into Chad, heading for Khartoum.

Jude began with enough money to get all the way to Toronto. But Chad was a nightmare. First it cost him money to get across the border. Then, every 50 kilometres or so he came to a checkpoint set up, he reckoned, expressly to fleece travellers. There would be a security officer, then a police officer, then a customs check, then another officer whose function he never discerned. They had no uniforms, their offices were generally just lean-tos for shade and they had no form of identity.

'They took everything out of my bag. They said they were looking for drugs. They put all my things in a pile and my money they put in another pile. They divided my money – so much for us, so much for you. I asked them what the money was for. They said it was tax. Then I would go to the next office and they would do the same: so much for us, so much for you. All the way across Chad.

'When I got to the Sudanese border I had no money left. The Sudanese immigration official paid for my stamp and gave me bus fare to the nearest town. There I contacted my family and they sent me money to continue.'

At Wadi Halfa Jude began losing money to officials again. But he wasn't too worried about that.

'After Chad, nothing else is a problem. That's a hell place.'

When I met him he had been on the road for nearly two months. He still had three countries to go. 'I have to get to Canada,' he said. 'It is my goal and I will get there.' I believed him.

XII You don't want to know the next bit of this story. Really, Kafka be my witness, it's too miserable to recount. The ferry docked in Aswan, we got the Landy off the pontoon and returned to the ferry. There our passports were stamped, no problem. Then we waited. Everyone waited. Why? Nobody could tell. Two hours. Three hours. Tempers frayed, people crowded round the exit door and passages leading to it.

At the door was Sergeant Terrier, small, noisy and threatening. People tried to get out but he beat them back. Porters tried to get in and he beat them out. One man holding back the Siege of Tobruk. He screamed and lost his beret from time to time in scuffles. It began to look nasty. Mike and I backed out of the passages and found a section of deck that was close to the roof of the docking barge. We climbed out and down, then sneaked to the Landy.

When we started it three policemen (without uniforms – they said they were police) tried to stop us moving. Sergeant Terrier arrived and screamed. We cut a deal. The Landy had to be cleared but, to prevent us escaping, a policeman would ride with us to customs. Face saved all round.

This was all merely a prelude, the less stressful stuff – simply a near riot and near arrest. The customs man looked at our carnet.

'Whose name is this?' he asked.

'Kotze, the owner, the head of my company.'

'It's not yours?'

'No, but we have the licence forms – originals – and a letter from Mr Kotze allowing us to drive it.'

'No! Impossible,' he thundered. 'You are not on the carnet. I cannot let you drive one metre!'

We argued, we suggested a change of dollars. He was offended: 'I am an honest man and this is the law!' Ramadan was clearly not being kind to this man.

'So what do we do?' I asked.

'You go to Cairo and get the Automobile Club of Egypt to add your name to the carnet. You get their stamp and you come back here.'

'What? Cairo is a thousand kilometres from here.'

'Yes. You take train. But remember, tomorrow AA closed because Friday.'

He wouldn't budge. His parting shot was: 'We keep car here. It cost £20 a day and £10 for police guard.' Well, at least he arranged a lift to Aswan in the customs bus because we had no Egyptian pounds for a taxi. The ATM, when I slipped my credit card into it, said I had the wrong pin number – then it told me it had retained the card and requested me to inquire within (the bank was closed). After a nerve-wracking pause, it spat out the card. But no money followed.

We walked to the station, a kilometre away, lugging inappropriate bags, a heavy backpack of cameras and a satellite phone with directional dish. There we were met by Kariem. He deserves careful description. Kariem was squat, fat, jovial and effusively helpful. His headscarf kept slipping over one eye, giving him a piratical air. He intuited our situation in its entirety: 'You come from Wadi Halfa. Yes? You need ticket to Cairo? Machine no give you money so maybe you want me change money? You hungry? Maybe you need food for train?'

Yes, yes and yes. It was done in a flash – pounds at a good rate considering it was Ramadan, two first-class tickets, then he puffed his way to platform two under most of our luggage, refusing to let us help. He sweated, he limped, he rolled his eyes – if anyone wants to make a film about Egypt, Kariem simply has to be in it.

'You need food. Give me £20 each I get you.' We were bemused by his performance and handed over the money, only coming to our senses as he limped out of sight. We realised we'd just lost 40 Egyptian pounds to a first-class scam. But we were wrong. Just before the train was due to roll, Kariem returned, now bathed in sweat, with the finest meal we'd seen in weeks: grilled chicken, meat, kosheri rice, spicy salads, stewed vegetables, mint sauce in a sachet, four fresh loaves of unleavened bread and a bag of oranges.

'You no trust Kariem?' he asked, knowing full well we thought he'd made off with our money. Then he carried our bags onto the train, settled us into our seats and demanded £50 baksheesh. I gave him £20 and thanked him profusely. He looked horrified and did a perfect, theatre-trained shock number, complete with hyperventilation and a convincing stagger. He ran through all the wonderful things he had done for us. He kissed Mike on both cheeks, pumped my hand and started all over again. We were firm. He helped a Japanese traveller find his seat for £1, then returned to explain his worth. Could he serve us our meal? Could he take out the arm-rest tables? Had he done anything wrong? No, we said. He was wonderful and £20 was the extent of our gratitude. He looked at us hard and long for a while, in silence, figured that was it, and said goodbye happily, an absolute gentleman to the last.

As the luxurious overnight express pulled out, dead on time, the incongruity of the situation hit me. We were completing the Cape to Cairo quest, but without the Land Rover. After the desert sands and scruffy hotels, though, the train was a wonder of comfort and efficiency. We ate Kariem's delicious meal, eased the seats back to sleeping position and let the countryside roll by.

There was one event on that long train ride, however, that

caused me to extend the meditation I'd had back in Sudan about certain personal habits in Arab countries. There is a rule I have never seen stated in guidebooks, but essential for your well-being: hang onto your loo roll and expect surprises. Planning a trip off the tourist circuit, you need to calculate roll usage like a Tuareg estimates waterholes when crossing the Sahara.

Finding toilet paper in say, Cairo, is not an insurmountable problem, but in some desert souks they look at the depleted roll you wave before them with real interest.

'What is this?' they will ask. 'For what you use it?' You mime a wiping motion in the appropriate place and they look shocked. 'You no use water? You use this?'

The ultimate answer is by then a foregone conclusion: they wouldn't be seen dead with the offensive stuff in their shop. In the desert, different cultural approaches to the activity pose no real problem, only mutual amazement, and Western-style hotels have Western-style conveniences. But between those extremes falls the shadow.

The train was one of those places. People obviously weren't expected to carry little green plastic pots of water into first-class carriages, but paper was way off the radar screen. Instead they had a sit-down loo with no green pot, no plastic seat, no flusher and no paper. The only way to use this object was to stand on the bowl, which by then was a grimy footplate. Even an express takes a long time to travel 1 000 kilometres, however, and one has to be resolute.

I duly stood on the seat then used my precious paper. I pondered what to do next. Then I noticed a tap and thought: 'Okay, that's it, you flush by tap. So I stood in front of the loo and spun open the tap for a good, strong flush. A fire-hose-strength jet of water shot out of the pan and hit me about waist level. I dodged without success and scrambled for the tap as water sprayed off the wall, drenching the whole place. Heaven help anyone actually sitting on the pan. It would blow off their nethers.

I emerged from the loo dripping in all the wrong places and hoping nobody would look up as I walked through the elegant carriage. They all did. Anyone who invents a workable solution to this cultural cross-over problem will make a fortune. But in the meantime, dear traveller, hang onto your loo roll and anticipate problems.

XIII The train ride gave me time to reflect rather bitterly on bureaucracy, particularly the form of bureaucracy British colonisation brought to Sudan and Egypt. Because reasoning with Africans and Arabs was initially unthinkable, the British merely taught them how to administer systems without explaining the reason for doing so. Of course, Africans and Arabs are well able to understand reasons, but unfortunately colonial bureaucratic currents were hard-wired into the system before the locals got round to doing much reasoning about it.

Today thousands of officials, big and small, are besieged – in their opinion – by unscrupulous corruption, thievery, political conniving (not to mention suspect foreigners) and they use their stamps, receipts, forms, queues, gates, whistles and guns as both shields and swords in defence of all that is correct, proper and moral. These tools give you power, and if you have power you wield it without compassion or compunction, irrespective of any suffering it may cause. That what they do – in the greater scheme of things – is incorrect, improper and immoral never seems to enter their heads. And if power affords you a little extra lucre on the side, well and good. I'm generalising, of course, but little of what we experienced in Sudan and Egypt – and in many other places in Africa for that matter – contradicts this argument.

We got our stamp in Cairo and my name was duly typed into the carnet – 15 times, one for each page – on a manual typewriter. It took several days (one being Friday and a holiday), several expensive cellphone calls to South Africa, several faxes . . . but we got it in the end. Then we spent six hours at Cairo Railway Station, in a beautiful Art Deco tearoom marred by a large-screen television blaring Egyptian soapies, followed by another

13 hours on the train back to Aswan. There we took another train – which should have been condemned back in 1890 – to the customs building at the High Dam.

We were not allowed to enter the customs area, however. Four soldiers with fixed bayonets told us, in relays, to 'Sit down!' Half an hour crept by. It was fiendishly hot. Eventually a guard said: 'Go in.' Why? Don't ask. Mr Customs also told us to sit down. He finished penning a letter that required four copies, created by battered carbon paper. He finished the letter, filed each copy separately, tidied the carbon paper and placed it in a drawer. Then he began tidying his desk, storing great ledgers in drawers, pens in a neat row. A junior came in with a glass of water and an electric plunger which he put in the glass, then jammed two raw wires into a dicey-looking electric plug. They both waited for the water to boil. Junior placed a tea-bag in the glass and squeezed it while Mr Customs watched to see he got it just right. Then he sipped the tea, leaned forward and said, 'You see, for you I even put aside my other work.'

He checked our papers, filled in forms. A policeman came in to demand money for guarding the Land Rover – £31. Mr Customs wrote a letter for him, in triplicate, with the battered carbon paper, which both signed. A while later the policeman returned with a receipt, in duplicate, which I had to sign. Then Mr Customs made a calculation and informed us we had to pay £1200. Mike asked whether we could pay in US dollars? No, only pounds. Now who comes into a country, having travelled half way round the planet, with their pockets stuffed with local currency? We would have to go back to Aswan to change money – by train. Aah, a special concession was offered. We could take Mr Customs home to Aswan, he would keep the carnet, and we could meet him the next morning at nine at the customs house with the money.

About then he began hinting that a present would be in order. We acted dumb. 'You want a pen? A cap?' No, no, he didn't want these. But he reminded us how easy he had made things for us. He had helped us, stopped work to do our papers (stopped work entirely, we reflected as we dropped him home at two-thirty). Oh yes, he offered as his parting shot, we needed to go to the traffic police to get new licence plates and new driver's licences.

That evening in Aswan – a pleasant-enough town with a pretty corniche along the Nile – we met four other overlanders who were heading out of Egypt. They were of the opinion that in Egypt almost everyone you meet sees you as a money-bloated tourist upon whom it is both their duty and desire to feed. There were, they said, undoubtedly millions of intelligent and interesting Egyptians with whom you could have a fascinating conversation. But you never see them, because tightly packed round you and the places foreign travellers go, are the pedigree tourist leeches. They were happy to be leaving the country, which gave us very mixed feelings about entering it.

Later that evening we cruised Aswan's huge souk. Among the tat were some wonderful Egyptian cotton shirts, doves that refused to fly away even when prodded, the largest cabbages I'd ever seen, turkeys wandering round waiting to be eaten at Eid, aromatic tamarind, saffron, sun-dried tomatoes and substances the purveyors knew only by their Arabic names.

Next morning we went to pay the customs fee and retrieve our carnet. Mr Customs was half an hour late; he said he had a headache. He took our money but retained our carnet. First we must go to the traffic police. No problem, he said, just half an hour more. We tracked down the place across town. It was filled with hundreds of yelling, pushing locals. Eventually an intelligent-looking man – a Copt named Thomas – took our letter, asked us to pay £33 . . . and then we waited. It seemed they needed the chief to sign something, but he wasn't in. So we waited some more. Eventually I went round the back of the counters and got our man to explain the delay. He sympathised. Maybe he could do something. But first we needed the vehicle checked by the engineering division. Where was that? Across town. I did a little hysterical number and he agreed to give us a guide. The place wasn't across town, it was way outside it.

When we got there a crab-like little man in dirty overalls went looking for numbers: the chassis number was easy, but where was the engine number? He ended up virtually standing on his head in the engine compartment with an audience of seven others offering advice. Nearly an hour later he was still looking. Eventually his superior got bored and filled in the engine number from the logbook. Now his chief needed to sign the form. But he was out. We waited. After a bit of yelling on my part the sub-chief agreed to sign it, but on the way back to town we passed the real chief heading the other way and our guide insisted we return so he could also sign.

We didn't go right back to the traffic department. No, indicated our guide, somewhere else. He got lost, he asked many uniformed men, then finally found the most mysterious office of all. There a man looked deeply into a great ledger filled with red numbers, demanded £38.25 and asked if the Land Rover was made in Japan. No, England, I said. Okay, fine, *tamam*. He signed and off we went to find Thomas the Copt. He was refreshingly efficient, clearly not suffering the effects of Ramadan. We soon had our licence plates, new drivers' licences and were heading back towards Mr Customs to get our carnet. He released it reluctantly, his power over us slipping from his grasp. His parting shot was to demand why the new licence plates weren't mounted. 'Because we just got them, fuckhead,' I said. It was amazing how powerful I felt with the carnet in my clutches.

It had taken us five days but now we were free to enter Egypt. We gunned the Landy out of town. But we might have known it wasn't going to be that easy. At the edge of Aswan we were pulled over by a brace of uniformed men. Because of terrorist activity in the past, tourists had to drive in a guarded convoy.

'What's that?' demanded a man with a galaxy of stars on his shoulders, pointing at our spare cans.

'Diesel.'

'Dangerous. Pour it out.'

'Why?'

'Very dangerous. Hot sun in Egypt. Can explode.'
'But we've carried it right through the Nubian Desert.'
'Dangerous. Empty them.'

Okay, so messily we poured the diesel into the Landy, watched by nine uniformed men standing in a circle around us.

'What's this?' He was peering into the back.
'Cooking gas bottles.'
'Dangerous. Empty!'
'But how do we cook? And it's dangerous just to open them.'
'Empty!' he barked.

So we opened the bottles and they were carried to a nearby wall by a three-star, hissing threateningly. A man with a mirror on a stick, meanwhile, was going over the underside of the Landy. Just who did they think the terrorists were? The hissing continued. The convoy needed to go. They brought the half-empty bottles back.

'Close!'

Then we were off, at breakneck speed, sirens blaring, passing on solid white lines, scattering people and donkeys, forcing other vehicles off the road. Suddenly, about 80 kilometres from Luxor (where the terrorist attack had occurred), they seemed to lose interest in us and disappeared. We cruised into the historic town at a leisurely pace and found, deep in alleyways, the Happylands Hotel – positively the most spotless place in all Egypt. All four floors and the roof veranda were constantly being cleaned by a pack of happy, pretty maidens who also did our washing. From their wide, hello smiles it seemed they might also have scrubbed our backs if we'd asked. That evening we scored another first: at the Sultana à la Carte Restaurant on Television Street we had what was to be the finest meal of the trip. Aish with tahini and hummus dips, freshly blended guava juice and wonderful moussaka. Next night we were back for more.

Any traveller will almost certainly be irritated by the insatiable bureaucracy of Egypt, worn down by incessant tat sellers shoving tourist trash in your face, infuriated by everyone showing you what you already know and demanding baksheesh for it. It's an overpowering sensation this, being constantly leeched! But when you stand in front of the Temple of Karnak, stare down the half-kilometre avenue of sphinxes to the Temple of Luxor, or gaze, dumbstruck, at the illuminated artwork in the tunnels of the Valley of the Kings, you know why you came to Egypt.

We did the tourist thing along with thousands of others. Busload upon busload of them, and this was not yet the high season. But the temples, palaces and tombs are so huge, dramatic and beautiful that the tourists somehow didn't matter. They were simply sidelined by the grandeur of it all.

Later we cruised the Nile on a tugboat towing feluccas (there was no wind) and enjoyed the free ride, helping a bit with the lines. One felucca skipper was boasting to his tourists and neglecting his course... and smacked into a stationary boat. There were almost wet, pink foreigners swimming along with the Nile perch.

XIV If you want to take the desert road to Dakhla and Farafara you have to be crafty. The convoy police do not like you slipping from their grasp. We tried crossing the Nile bridge to the Valley of the Kings with the intention of heading south towards Isna, then veering west. But we were immediately stopped when we did the unexpected, un-tourist thing of turning away from the resting places of the kings. No tourists this way, said a man at a roadblock. We retreated across the bridge and met an accommodating security man to whom we put our desire. He ticked off the ways we weren't going to get through, then thought for a bit.

'The desert road is very beautiful,' I tried.

'Yes,' he nodded. Maybe we had passed some kind of test because he suddenly offered us manna: 'Go south, cross the barrage at Isna, then north out on the desert road. You will make it.' We thanked him and did just that. And it worked. We were stopped briefly as we turned onto the western road, had our licence plates checked, but were mercifully shooed on.

The road was a new one. The green of the Nile soon fell behind and we were in the Sahara. The desert pavement alternated between black, white and gold as the road arrowed to the horizon. Eventually a sign appeared, a black dot on the horizon. When we reached it the directions were surprising: 'Bagdad 280'. Bagdad? We never found it, but we did discover the road to Paris. It's part of the old camel trail from Asyut to Nubia, and we saw the sign just before turning north to El Kharga. It's real name is Baris, but the sign writers obviously weren't too deft with Western script.

Near Kharga giant orange barchan dunes were prowling the desert. West of the oasis the scenery changed dramatically. Dunes gave way to what seemed like a kingdom of monstrous moles – conical piles of heat-smashed rocks dotting a gravel plain stretching for hundreds of kilometres. They only served to emphasise the depth of the emptiness, like Cepheid stars in the vastness of space.

All through the desert there were roadblocks in the oddest places. A few unfortunate soldiers would be stationed in the middle of nowhere in a concrete box with guns, some nasty tyre-ripping road spikes and barrels or traffic cones. No radio, no visible means of transport, no shade. The routine was always the same. We'd stop at an obstruction, a man with a weapon slung over his shoulder would saunter up, say 'Salaam aleikom' and shake our hands. He'd take down the details of our Egyptian licence plate, peer into the Landy at the two of us and ask, 'Two people?'

'Yes,' we'd nod.

'Country?'

'South Africa.'

He'd look puzzled and ask again, 'Country?'

At that point Mike would invariably raise his voice and indignantly repeat, 'South Africa!' I'd eye the gun and try the soft approach, grabbing the map for a brief lesson in geography. No soldier we met had ever heard of South Africa. The fellow would nod vaguely at my attempt to enlighten him, then ask where we were coming from and where we were heading, noting all this down on a scrap of paper, using a pen he'd borrow from us. When this was over he'd start again: 'Country?' or suggest one that he knew. 'Germania? Anglasia?'

Mike and I had several arguments about this process. I said it was useless and even dangerous to get cross with these guys. He said my efforts with a map were stupid because they probably didn't know what a map was. Finally we compromised and agreed we'd be from wherever the soldier suggested. After that it was easy. We'd nod at his suggestion, he'd smile, happy to have been so perceptive of our origins and then wish us a pleasant journey. He'd roll back the obstruction and we'd be off again, strangers in a strange land. Behind us, on many scraps of paper across Egypt, it was duly noted that a Land Rover from Germany, France, Holland, England or some other country had passed through. What they were going to do with them, heaven only knew.

To the north, eventually, a huge escarpment insinuated itself, growing ever closer and higher in the setting sun, which sank like a boiling ball into the road. The escarpment led us all the way to Dakhla Oasis and the village of Mût.

XV   All Egypt was redeemed by Mût. Surrounded by well-watered green fields and newer constructions, its heart is an ancient, crumbling citadel, some of it abandoned, but much of it very much alive. Its mud-packed buildings lean on one another, connect and turn lanes into cool tunnels. Mud-slap walls billow and ripple like the slow winds of time, the aromas of cooking and incense drift from doorways and mingle with the sounds of women singing and children playing.

The evening we arrived, old men – Nubians, Berbers, Libyans and Sudanese – sat sucking hookahs in the square and watching a video of Robin Williams playing Patch Adams (subtitled in Arabic) with the alert, puzzled look of desert fennec foxes. A young girl with a smile somehow wider than her face tended a stall selling dates – dried brown ones, some the orange of old Oregon pine and nearly as hard, and others slightly fermented, gooey and delicious. We bought a bagful, sat at a table, ordered mint tea, refused a proffered hookah and settled down amid amicable company to watch the night deepen. Nobody hassled us, offered us anything we didn't want to buy, or asked for baksheesh. The old men glanced at us with their dark, sun-wrinkled eyes, assessed us, nodded and accepted us in the old desert tradition of Moad Dib: strangers were guests and it was impolite to pry.

Next morning was the end of Ramadan and the first day of Eid. At 4.45 a.m. the muezzins let us know. There was a pause of about an hour, then they let loose again. What a cacophony! We had seen only two mosques in Mût but it sounded as though a hundred were greeting the sun. They sang, chanted, howled and, eventually, merely croaked. It was a stirring performance.

I got up, dressed and strolled through the alleyways of the old city. Men were hurrying to mosque, women in beautiful dresses were standing in doorways and the dust of devout feet hung in the shafts of dawn light like golden curtains. Mût was waking to the end of the fast and the beginning of days of feast and abandon.

XVI The bone-dry heat of the Sahara has a particular quality: it preserves. It is generally believed that this aided Pharaonic embalmers to preserve their masters by mummifying them, but there is a counter-theory that I rather like. It throws an interesting new light on the mummification process.

The failure of bodies to rot in the dryness of Egypt, so the thinking goes, drove the Pharaohs crazy: they were headed for the glory of the afterlife but their corpses wouldn't rot. So they designed elaborate rituals to ensure they were not trapped in this life. Elaborate tombs separated them from the moisture-sapping sands, and speeded rot. But, this theory suggests, they went even further. Noble bodies were filled with corrosive, caustic fluids and their orifices plugged. A few days later the plugs were removed and the putrid muck that resulted removed. Then the heart and kidneys were hauled out and the brain sucked out through the nostrils. All this goo was stored in Canopic jars and the body was filled with natron, a natural salt found at Wadi Natron.

After 40 days (the time required, according to the *Egyptian Book of the Dead*, for the soul to leave) the salt was removed and oils, frankincense and spices added, all of which combined to form a black, pitch-like stuff which gives mummies their name (*moumiya* is Arabic for pitch). What was left stayed intact for thousands of years.

There is, of course, another theory. The noble ones could only inhabit the afterlife, so it goes, as long as their bodies remained intact in this one. If they crumbled, pouf! No afterlife. I guess you can pick your theory.

Near Al Kasr we came upon some Romans who, by the first theory, obviously never made the afterlife. There's a Roman fort and, nearby, a hill pitted with tombs more than 2 000 years old. There they all lie, maybe ten or 20 to a hole, surprisingly small and shrivelled but intact, down to the ring on one soldier's claw-like finger. It was a strange mountain.

Much of Al Kasr is, like the hapless Romans, preserved by the desert. It's a beautiful oasis about 30 kilometres from Mût with an old quarter dating back to well before the time of the Ottoman Empire. A knowledgeable guide, Magdi Alia, showed us around. We climbed the dusty stairs of the mosque's mudpack tower, wandered through cool lanes, into low-ceilinged houses and around an ancient mill, forge and olive press. The last was made of hard olive logs with a central wooden screw that was cranked down into a hole in the log. Carving the male screw in that hard wood must have been task enough thousands of years ago, but how did they carve the screw thread into the log?

The courtroom spoke of the harsh hand by which the Ottoman Turks ruled the oasis community. It's a grand building in its own cramped way. There's a platform for the judge, a dungeon for the condemned and, outside in a small courtyard, a garrotte of ingenious construction to ensure a gradual death by hanging from a hook driven through your jaw into the roof of your mouth.

From El Kasr we drove 290 kilometres to the oasis of Farafara and dived into hot water – which may seem an odd thing to do in the desert, but it was thundering from a thermal spring into an oasis pool. We spent that night in style in the Al Badawiya Hotel and left at sunrise to explore the White Desert. Its strange limestone forms began showing up about 25 kilometres beyond Farafara. Some looked like gigantic sugar cubes on the golden desert sand, others like madly teased cotton wool. Soon there were thousands of blocks, spires and cloud-shaped mounds. The further we travelled, the more they littered the desert, eventually clustering into a high, white, badly eroded escarpment.

The glaring white limestone was sprinkled with black volcanic pebbles, some so angular they'd have sliced the Landy's tyres to shreds if we rode over them. Later the whole desert turned black, as though a giant tarring machine had disgorged its contents from horizon to horizon. Beyond this came the oasis of Bawiti, then the desert flattened to featureless nothing. Occasional road signs provided the only relief. It was difficult not to be lulled to sleep. Finally one sign read 'Cairo 276'. Beside it lay the skeleton of a camel. I guess he read it and gave up.

XVII Cairo appeared at the edge of all that nothingness in the form of uninhabited high-rise apartments, hundreds of them plonked in the desert. It was spooky. After nearly 40 kilometres of this empty and unexplained suburbia we came to inhabited Cairo with its power-lines, mad traffic and families celebrating Eid beside the highway on grassy verges.

Suddenly and startlingly the pyramids were in front of us, far more massive than I had imagined, their perfect geometry severe against the urban clutter. They were so big they stayed with us for a long time as we nosed our way through the traffic towards the Nile – like mountains which it takes an age to pass.

Exactly 205 years earlier Napoleon Bonaparte had taken this

road with a good deal more hardware than we had. His reason for advancing on Cairo, though, was about as obscure as ours. He was 29 at the time and keen to show his mettle to a Europe still waking up to his impact on the civilised world. Success was infectious and he needed more of it. Perhaps, too, he wanted to avoid confronting his wild, Martiniquan wife, Josephine, about her incessant love affairs.

In 1798 his assembled fleet carrying 13 000 men slipped past the prowling British and landed in Alexandria. The French took the town with little effort and marched up the Nile towards Cairo. Within sight of the pyramids they faced the massed Mameluke cavalry. Here was the oddest of armies. The word Mameluke means male slave, more especially a white male slave, but they were slaves of an unusual sort. They had been bought as children from impoverished peasant families in Georgia and the Caucasus and imported to Egypt by their masters, who had also been slaves in their time. Here they were castrated and trained in warfare with the express purpose of ruling the country on the lines of a military oligarchy. War was their trade, and they preferred to buy children to keep the caste intact.

By 1798 there were 100 000 in Cairo alone, flamboyantly dressed supermen with magnificent Arab horses – and they ruled all Egypt. The strange contradiction of their existence is captured by an early English traveller, Edward Lane: 'A band of lawless adventurers, slaves in origin, butchers by choice, turbulent, bloodthirsty and too often treacherous, these slave-kings had a keen appreciation of the arts, a taste and refinement which would have been hard to parallel in western countries.'

As Napoleon's troops came within sight of the pyramids he spied the Mameluke camp, which he estimated at about 20 000 infantry. Displaying his brilliance as a tactician, the French general created a pincer movement that flushed the Mamelukes onto an open plain. In the heat of the midday sun, 6 000 horsemen charged, Muslim pennants flying above their horses, robes flowing behind, each man leaning forward with a sabre in his right hand.

The French waited in defensive squares until the leading horsemen were within 50 paces, then fired. The battle was lost before it had begun. Napoleon, commanding one of the squares, was upon the Mameluke camp before they could ready their guns. 'From this point onwards,' wrote one of Napoleon's generals, 'it was no longer a battle: it was a massacre.' Those who survived fled into the desert. As the French marched past the pyramids towards Cairo, mobs began sacking the Mameluke palaces.

Napoleon did more than restore order. After his Italian campaigns he was an old hand at dealing with captured cities. He imposed law, insisted that shops reopen, sent for the leaders of the frightened community and demanded they restore order and all food production. He appointed a military governor and assigned Egyptian executives to the provinces. Many of those who had fled into the desert returned.

Canals were cleared, roads rebuilt, bridges thrown across the Nile, beautiful buildings designed, a university established, a census carried out and the city was accurately mapped. A force was sent out to catalogue the country's antiquities. Egypt began to reveal itself to the world. Modern Cairo is still the product of the massive public works set in motion by the French.

XVIII After the silence of the desert, I was prepared to detest Cairo. By the time we reached the heart of the city I was in love with it. More than 26 centuries ago the Pharaohs of the Old Kingdom established Memphis (now Cairo) as their capital. Later it was named al-Qahira, the Conqueror. More often, though, it has been conquered – by Persian and Byzantine empires, Arabs, Ottomans, Napoleon, Muhammad Ali and Britain.

I was glad Mike was driving so I could stare at the architecture, the people and the crazy traffic. Ancient buildings were decaying gracefully beside the tat and squalor of a city obviously way beyond the control of its cleansing department. The skyline was brown with pollution and wind-blown sand. The traffic hooted constantly and seemed to obey no rules. Cars and buses were weaving between lanes as pedestrians dodged across wide roads between vehicles. The city seemed wired for sound, with great klaxon loudspeakers attached to walls and under parapets from which imams cajoled citizens into prayer and remembrance. The sound emanating from the streets was almost visceral. It was the noisiest place I'd ever been in, other than a steel foundry. Yet for no reason I could figure, it was wonderful.

There is a tale in *A Thousand and One Nights* which begins with a circle of men in a mosque in Mosul talking about foreign lands and the marvels of cities.

'Baghdad is Paradise,' says one, to which the eldest sagely counters: 'He who has not seen Cairo has not seen the world. Its dust is gold, its Nile is a wonder, its women are like the black-eyed virgins of Paradise; and how could it be otherwise, when she is Umm al-Dunya, Mother of the World?'

Using every available device and aid – GPS, maps and guidebooks – we picked our way gingerly to Tahrir Square where Mike remembered a hotel from a previous trip. We spotted the sign for Ismalia House and parked in an alleyway behind. Then we threaded into a gloomy passage, hunting for the entrance. Eventually we found it and were confronted by two lifts. They were vaguely Art Deco, though they could have been an ironsmith's version of Pharaonic. The lift shaft was not enclosed, just a rising tower of steel mesh within a stairwell ascending into the gloom. As we opened the door and stepped in, the lift bounced disconcertingly. The electrics were exposed and rudimentary; dangerous-looking wires connected to copper plungers which acted as cut-outs when you opened the lift's wooden batwing doors. A woman got in with us, closed the door and pressed the up button. The steel mesh flashed downwards past holes created by the lift's broken windowpanes. If you stuck your arm out it would be sliced off. When the woman got to her floor she yanked the doors open and the lift bounced to a halt. At least we now knew how to stop it.

Ismalia House was quite unlike the lift: a pleasant but simple place where we got a double room overlooking the square. Across from us was the Egyptian Museum and not far beyond that the Nile, our view somewhat obscured by the tasteless Nile Hilton. We had arrived, but we were exhausted. Mike and I drew straws for the shower, had a brief bite of street food in the fading light and dived into bed. All night cars hooted. I hoped one of them wasn't a stolen Landy.

Over the next few days we went on a binge of sightseeing. I wandered, amazed, through countless beautiful but often unlabelled objects in the Egyptian Museum, including a room full of gold from the tomb of the black boy-Pharaoh Tutankhamun. In the Coptic quarter of Cairo we visited the church where Moses prayed before leading the Jews out of Egypt. By then the city was a thousand years old. We made our way through the endless warrens of Kahn al-Khalili Market where I sniffed my way to the purchase of some alluring perfumes, for which the city is famous.

Along the Nile Corniche were towering buildings, parks, tree-filled islands and arching bridges; but a few hundred metres away were mud-brick houses where camels and goats wandered and people haggled and traded as their ancestors had done for thousands of years. The place managed to combine a sense of rush with one of timelessness.

There was still something missing... Early one morning, while the city still slept, we headed out to pay our respects to the Sphinx. We drove up to the main gate, the pyramids of Cheops and Chephren glowing in the dawn light, but the tourist police wouldn't let us in that early. Mike remembered another entrance near the horse stables and we took off to find it.

As we motored round a cluster of tea shops the sight stopped us in our tracks. Right there, maybe a hundred metres away, was the Sphinx greeting the rising sun, backed by the pyramids. I need to explain something here. What stood before us has been so iconised, stylised and embedded in the imagery of popular culture that there was a strong possibility the real thing would not measure up to the hype. The Sphinx and the pyramids, so glorious and huge, did the opposite: they trashed all representations of themselves in the sheer exhibitionism of their construction. Pliny wrote that while man fears time, time fears the pyramids. You have to see them to fully understand what he means.

For me we had finally arrived. The trip was complete: we had succeeded in our curious quest. It was time to go home.

XIX There was no way we were driving back to Cape Town, so we'd decided to ship the vehicle back in a container and fly home. It took much of a day just getting permission for someone from the shipping company to drive it to Alexandria. We were running late for our plane and were in a fret as our lift edged through traffic towards the airport. We finally got there, hauled our luggage – far too much – out of the car and waved goodbye to the driver. To be heading south felt good.

When we presented our tickets an official pointed out we were at the wrong airport. The one we needed was three kilometres away. We grabbed a taxi, threw our bags onto the roof carrier and urged him to greater speed, hoping our bags would stay in place. We ran to the check-in counter and, breathing hard, handed over our tickets.

'Sorry sir,' said the official. 'You did not confirm these so they have been cancelled.' It was such a shock that I almost burst into tears. We created a creditable fuss. How could we confirm from the middle of the Sahara Desert? Fetch the manager! They did. He was consoling and set off with the tickets to see what he could do. We waited an agonising 20 minutes as the Tannoy announced it was time to board. The official returned and we held our breath.

'You are lucky, sirs.' He smiled. 'There were cancellations. You are on.' We sat in the plane – most of the way back to Cape Town – grinning like kids in a sweet shop.

XX So there it was: Cape to Cairo – 22 500 kilometres through eight countries, 16 border posts and every sort of terrain. There were those who would sigh when they heard of our trip and say it had always been their dream. Others thought us mad to have risked our necks in the Dark Continent. There were times, I will confess, swallowed up in the infinity of spaces of which I knew nothing and which knew nothing of me, that I took fright and was amazed to see myself there. But there were other times when I couldn't believe my luck.

Such travel is seldom what we anticipate. Some would argue that it must always be disappointing. But it is truer and more rewarding to suggest that it is *different*.